The Rothschilds

The Rothschilds

The Financial Rulers of Nations

BY

John Reeves

SPECIAL EDITION – Extended with 30 pages:
20 Add. Illustrations & Appendices

REFERENCE

History of International Finance

2020
L'Apache

THE ROTHSCHILDS

The Financial Rulers of Nations

By John Reeves

Special Edition – Extended with 30 pages

ISBN: 979-8612-3349-72

Cover by: K. Nolan

Edited and published by: L'Apache publishing

Sampson Low Marston Searle and Rivington (London) first published this book in 1887.

Cover Credits: [Front]—caricature of N.M. Rothschild inspired by "*A Pillar of the Exchange*" by W. Clarke (1856). [Back]—The house with the "red shield" {Roth Shild}, first house of the family, which is located in the Jewish suburb of Frankfort am Main, Germany.

This book is available on:

Amazon.com & Lulu.com

Fig. I: THE OLD HOUSE IN FRANKFORT.

PREFACE

SHOULD the following pages prove fortunate enough to be favourably received by the public, they will owe it entirely to their subject-matter. To this, and not to vigour of language or lucidity of style, must be attributed whatever interest they may possess. The Author makes no pretensions to the character of a practiced writer and feels that the subject is worthy of a more able and experienced hand; he therefore ventures to solicit the indulgence he so sorely needs for his literary short-comings, of which no one can feel more conscious than himself. On the other hand, he boldly and frankly claims for his work the merit of perfect and impartial truthfulness; and, in the words of Montaigne, he conscientiously asserts, with perhaps justifiable pride: "C'est icy un livre de bonne foy, lecteur."

TABLES OF THE BOOK

I. CONTENTS

Preface 7
1. About the Jews. 23
2. Mayer Amschel Rothschild. The Frankfort firm 39
3. The progress of the firm 65
4. Anselme Mayer Rothschild. The Frankort firm *(continued)*. ...99
5. Nathan Mayer Rothschild. The London firm. 121
6. Lionel de Rothscild. The london firm *(continued)*. 173
7. Baron Karl von Rothschild. The Naples firm 207
8. Baron Salomon von Rothschild. The Vienna firm. 224
9. Baron James de Rothschild. The Paris firm. 239
10. Rothschildiana 298

II. ILLUSTRATIONS

1. The old house in frankfort 2
2. The forbidden caricature 33
3. Mayer Amschel Rothschild 47
4. William IX, Prince of Hesse-Cassel. 53
5. Friedrich von Gentz 93
6. Anselm Mayer Rothshcild. 104
7. Nathan Mayer Rothschild. 142
8. Carlo Pozzo Di Borgo 149
9. Duke of Wellington 150
10. Nathan's caricature 167
11. Baron Lionel Rothschild 177
12. Lord Nathaniel Rothschild. 198
13. Carl Mayer von Rothschild 210
14. Adolphe Carl von Rothschild. 215

15. Baron Mayer Carl von Rothschild. 221
16. Baron Wilhem Carl von Rothschild. 222
17. Salomon Mayer von Rothschild. 228
18. Baron Anselm Salomon von Rothschild. 237
19. Ferdinand Anselm von Rothschild. 238
20. Jacques Laffitte 254
21. Casimir Perier 257
22. The King Louis-Philippe 268
23. Émile Pereire 273
24. Isaac Pereire 274
25. Baron James de Rothschild 280
26. The "Battle of Smala" 287
27. Baron Alphonse de Rothschild 291
28. The Château de Ferrières 292
29. Otto von Bismarck 301
30. Klemens von Metterich 303

III. APPENDICES

1. Table of currency conversion 319
2. The origine of the fortune of the rothschilds 321

TABLE OF CONTENTS

DETAILED CONTENTS:

Key themes of the ten chapters

Chapter I

PAGE 23. The value of a name — The phenomenal success of the Rothschilds and their poor beginnings — Their reputation for unstinted benevolence — Persecutions to which the Jews have been subjected — The hatred of them still rampant in some countries — The spirit of intolerance dying out in England — What the world owes the Jews — Universal pre-eminence accorded to the works of their great lawyers and prophets — Spinoza — Large number of Jews distinguished as musicians and composers, and likewise as dramatic and operatic artists — Eminence of the Jews as mathematicians and astronomers — The Jews in commerce and finance — The Jews as lawyers and as politicians — Charges brought against the Jews — Misleading impressions regarding them — Mayer Amschel Rothschild, "the honest Jew"— Unimpeachable lives and characters of the Rothschilds and other prominent Jewish families — The secret of Jewish success — Sir Thomas Gresham — Queen Elizabeth — Jewish pride of race.

CHAPTER II

PAGE 39. Mayer Amschel Rothschild — The city of Frankfort — The Judengasse — Condition of the Jews in Frankfort during the early part of the Middle Ages — First massacre of the Jews in 1241 — Galling restrictions imposed on them — The Judengasse burnt down in 1711; rebuilt and widened in 1717 — The House of the Red Shield — Amschel Moses Bauer — Birth of Mayer Amschel Rothschild in 1743 — He is at first intended for a rabbi — Abandons his theological studies and enters the service of a banking firm in Hanover — Returns to Frankfort, where he settles permanently — Marries Gudula Schnapper — Is known as "the honest Jew"— Is appointed Court Banker to the Landgrave of Hesse — The Landgrave's whole fortune entrusted to his keeping — Fanciful stories connected with this circumstance; the true account — Mayer Amschel Rothschild conveys specie to the Duke of Wellington in Spain — His death in 1812 — Heine's reminiscence of Gudula Rothschild.

CHAPTER III

PAGE 65. Respect entertained by the Jews for their parents — Mayer Amschel's five sons — The success achieved by the founder of the firm; to what greatly due — Archives of the Rothschild family a sealed book to the public at large — First period in the history of the firm — Mayer Amschel and the Danish Government — His philanthropy and benevolence — Second period in the history of the firm — Branch firms established — Nathan Mayer acknowledged as the business head of the family — The business in Government Funds — Stock Exchange speculations — Amount of the loans negotiated by the Rothschilds, between 1815 and 1830, for England, Russia, Austria, France, and Prussia — Principal loans issued by the Rothschilds — Honours and decorations showered on the latter — Third period in the history of the firm — A heavy blow dealt to the great banking-houses — New path struck out by the Rothschilds — Effect of political events on the fortunes of the Rothschilds — American War of Independence — The first French Revolution — Rise and fall of Napoleon — The French July Revolution — Immense landed estates possessed by the Rothschilds — Sugar manufactories — How the Rothschilds accumulated their wealth — The two causes specified by the Chevalier von Gentz — The " one power in Europe."

CHAPTER IV

PAGE 99. Anselm Mayer von Rothschild — Historical sketch of Frankfort — Character of Anselm Mayer — Account of him by a friend — His humour and shrewdness — Neat compliment paid by him to Thorwaldsen — Anselm Mayer at Ems — His great charity — His love of art and flowers — Immense amount of business transacted by him — Loans undertaken by him — His supremacy on the Frankfort Exchange — His two nephews, Baron William and Baron Carl von Rothschild, succeed him in the management of the Frankfort firm.

CHAPTER V

PAGE 121. The London firm established by Nathan Mayer Rothschild — Great Britain at the beginning of the present century — Its political condition — Power of the landed aristocracy — Mr. C. P. Villiers and the Corn Laws — Land held in England on conditions differing from those on which it is held abroad — Evils resulting from the National Debt — Devices employed by the earlier English sovereigns to raise money — Plans adopted for this purpose by Richard I, Henry III, Edward I, Edward III, Henry VII, Henry VIII, Charles I, Charles II, and James II respectively — William III and Louis

XIV — Principal objection to the financial innovation introduced by William III — Various expedients adopted by him to obtain supplies — State of society and of finance at this period — Affairs under Queen Anne — Growing influence of wealth — Marlborough — Infamous tone of parliamentary-morality — The great Hebrew capitalist and speculator ^ Medina — The Bank of England — Improvement of the national finances under William Pitt, in 1782 — The suspension of cash payments — Disastrous consequences of it — What first impelled Nathan Mayer Rothschild to visit England — His great talent for speculation — He speedily becomes the leading man on the Stock Exchange — Maintains a staff of agents and couriers to insure early intelligence of important events — Organizes a pigeon-post — News of Napoleon's return from Elba — Nathan Mayer Rothschild sets out for Belgium, and is present at the Battle of Waterloo — Immediately after the action he hurries from the field, rides to Brussels, and. thence proceeds to Ostend — His difficulty in procuring the means of crossing over to England — He reaches Dover — Without stopping to rest, he posts up to London — His appearance, seemingly broken in health and spirits, on the Stock Exchange next day, gives rise to the most gloomy apprehensions, which he might allay but does not — The Funds fall rapidly, but, when the truth is at last known, they go up again with a bound, and Nathan Mayer Rothschild pockets nearly a million sterling — He marries in 1806 — He may be considered the first to introduce foreign loans into England — Principal loans issued by him — He purchases the Almaden quicksilver mines in Spain — The Bank of England no match for him in finesse — He is, however, sometimes outwitted — His adventure with the stockbroker Lucas — His meanness towards the persons in his employ — His tactics on the Stock Exchange — His two maxims — His disregard of the courtesies and amenities of civilized life — Description of him by an anonymous writer — Nathan Mayer and the German Prince — Life of anxiety — His two mysterious visitors and the ledger — Nathan Mayer and Spohr — Nathan Mayer's death at Frankfort — His funeral.

CHAPTER VI

PAGE 173. Baron Lionel de Rothschild — Succeeds Nathan Mayer in the management of the London firm — His great financial talent; his prudence — His activity in connection with foreign loans — Awkward predicament — His political career — His deep interest in the welfare of his co-religionists — Efforts for the removal of Jewish disabilities — Sir David Salomons — Baron Lionel elected one of the members for the City of London — Lord John Russell's Bill — It is carried in the House of Commons but rejected by the Peers — Baron Lionel resigns his seat and is re-elected — Sir David Salomons returned as a member for Greenwich — Further progress and conclusion of the struggle — Baron Lionel a great sufferer from rheumatic gout — His irritable temper — His broad charity — His wife; her death — Marriage of his eldest daughter — Marriage of his youngest daughter; her death — His London mansion — His delight in pictures and flowers — His humour — His unexpected death — His two brothers — Character of Baron Mayer — Sir Lionel succeeded in the London firm by his three sous, Nathaniel, Leopold, and Alfred — Their respective characters and pursuits — Sir Nathaniel raised to the Peerage — Conduct of the firm towards Egypt — Scene in St Swithin's Lane — Probable future of the firm.

CHAPTER VII

PAGE 207. Baron Carl von Rothschild — The Naples firm — Change in the political circumstances of Italy — Social condition of that country — Finances of the Papal States — Indescribable peculation and fraud — French system of taxation introduced — Expenditure of the Duchy of Parma — Expenditure of the Grand Duchy of Tuscany and the Duchy of Lucca — Expenditure of Sardinia — Pecuniary difficulties of the kingdom of the Two Sicilies — A Bankers' Syndicate formed in Paris to oppose the Rothschilds — The result — Death of Baron Carl von Rothschild — He is succeeded by his son, Baron Adolf von Rothschild, who, however, soon retires from the management of the firm.

CHAPTER VIII

PAGE 224. Baron Salomon von Rothschild — The Vienna firm — Part played by the Jews in Austria — Their pecuniary assistance eagerly sought — They are subjected to a poll-tax, compelled to wear a distinguishing badge, and obliged to dwell in a particular quarter of the city — Peculations of a certain Hirschel Mayer — Collision between the Jews and the Vienna students — The Jews expelled from the Judenstadt, but ere long permitted to return — The Court-Factor, Samuel Oppenheimer — His house pillaged and his life endangered — Joseph Michael Arnstein, the first Jewish Baron — Austrian Funds at one time an exceedingly favourite investment — Sway exercised by Salomon von Rothschild over the finances of the Austrian empire — Baron Salomon's special stockbroker — An unofficial Stock Exchange — The quicksilver mines at Idria and at Almaden — Baron Salomon elected an Honorary Freeman of Vienna — Baron Salomon and the cabman — Loans issued by the Vienna Firm — Ferdinand, Nathan, and Salomon Albert von Rothschild.

CHAPTER IX

PAGE 239. Temporary character of the French Government since the First Revolution — Baron James de Rothschild — His boldness and sagacity in establishing his firm in Paris —

Financial condition of France at the period — The Russian campaign and Napoleon's retreat — The Restoration — Napoleon's return from Elba — French finances under Louis Philippe, under the Second Republic, and Second Empire — Enormous fortunes — Reason assigned for the stability enjoyed by the Paris firm — Baron James and the Polignac decrees — Ouvrard — The fall of M. Thiers brought about principally by the Rothschild firm — The Black Arts in the Middle Ages and Stock Exchange manœuvres at the present day — Lamentable want of principle on the part of speculators — Fabrication and circulation of false news — Prominent public men implicated in disreputable stock-jobbing transactions — Mr. Walsh, M.P.; Mr. Cochrane Johnstone, M.P.; Count de Guisne, French Ambassador at the Court of St. James's; the great Duke of Marlborough — Victory achieved by Baron James over the financial world in Paris — Corrupt state of French society during the reign of Louis Philippe — End of the Rothschild monopoly of French loans — Baron James the "Railway King" of France — Construction of the Northern Railway of France — Rivalry between Baron James and Émile Pereire — The Vienna Credit Bank founded by Baron James — Gigantic fraud perpetrated by Carpentier, Grellet, and others, on the Northern Railway of France — Mode of action adopted by them — Services rendered by Baron James to France recognized and rewarded — Slight put upon him by the Duchesse d'Angoulême — How he avenged it — His rough manners — His behaviour to Prince Paul of Württemberg — Baron James and the Deputy — The Baron and Jadin the painter — The Baron and the three peaches — The Baron and Horace Vernet — Baron James's great beneficence — His motives frequently misrepresented — Ungrateful return for his noble charity in 1847 — Absurd calumnies circulated against him in connection therewith — His subscription for the wounded and unemployed workmen in 1848 — His conduct towards Caussidière — His reported charity at others' expense — Heine's description of him — His death — Baron Alphonse de Rothschild — His remarkable business abilities — Payment of the French indemnities to Germany entrusted to him — His intense anxiety during the siege of Paris and the existence of the Commune.

CHAPTER X

PAGE 299. ROTHSCHILDIANA. Baron Anselm von Rothschild loses the ring given him by the Emperor of Austria — It is found by a poor girl — How Baron Anselm rewarded her — Anecdote narrated of him by Dr. Busch — Eugene Delacroix and Baron James de Rothschild — The latter as an artist's model — A kind action — How requited by Baron James — Baron James and the porcelain service — His decrepit visitor rejuvenescent — The Baron mystified — An excellent comedian — Baron Alphonse and the barometer — A millionaire without a sou — A porter becomes his surety for ten francs — Attempts to ruin the Rothschilds — Mr. James H. and his speculations — Is ultimately ruined — Georges Sand and Baron Rothschild — Georges Sand's autograph — An American in England — He goes to see the mansion then being built by Baron Lionel de Rothschild in Piccadilly — His interview with an old gentleman — How the Rothschilds made two fortunes — His interview with a younger gentleman — Who the old gentleman was, and who was the younger gentleman.

In Memory of
John Reeves

THE ROTHSCHILDS

The Financial Rulers of Nations

by

John Reeves

This new edition of the book is extended with an appendix and enriched with 15 illustrations

THE HOUSE OF ROTHSCHILDS.

CHAPTER I

ABOUT THE JEWS.

"WHAT'S in a name ?" asks Shakespeare. The answer, when the name is such as Rothschild, is not difficult. There is a volume of meaning in its mere sound. It is a name which conjures up in the imagination visions of untold wealth and unrivalled power, which appear so startling and amazing as to be more appropriate to romance than real life. It has become a household word synonymous with unbounded riches, and is as familiar to the ears of the struggling artizan as to those of the banker or trader. No name has, indeed, been so prominently before the public during the last sixty years or more, as that of this great financial firm. Its origin was so shrouded in humble obscurity, and the rapidity with which it sprang forward to prosperity and fame was alike so extraordinary and so remarkable, that the public gaze has been kept by a species of fascination upon the movements of the well-known financiers. From one corner of the world to the other, the success of the Rothschilds has been the subject of universal wonder and envy. When we recollect the poor beginnings of this eminent firm, and contrast them with the exalted position it now holds, there is good reason to be surprised. History does not record another instance of such unparalleled success, of such immense fortunes won in such a short time by sheer force of intellect rising superior to all adverse circumstances. The firm startled the world like the flash of a meteor, but the brilliance of its first successes was soon eclipsed by its subsequent achievements. The more one considers the marvellous manner in which it won its way to fame and fortune, and how it rose within the short space of ten or fifteen years' from the filthy confines of the Judengasse to take its station at the foot of a royal throne, the more incredible the story seems. But facts are stubborn things. There is no denying the fact that at the beginning of this century the Rothschild family was unknown beyond the limits of Frankfort; neither can it be gainsaid that before Napoleon's-downfall the firm had rendered immense service both to the Emperor and to the Allied Princes by its advice and its financial aid. Ere a quarter of a century had elapsed the firm which had commenced business in an unpretending shop in the Judengasse was courted and favoured by all the reigning families of Europe. From being dealers in old coins, the founder of the family and his sons rose by their skill and financial abilities to be the trusted and valued friends of the governments of every European nation. And well indeed might they be trusted, seeing that, in more than one instance, their aid was indispensable to ward off impending bankruptcy and disaster. Great, however, as is their fame as skilful financiers, the Rothschilds enjoy a reputation for liberal and unstinted benevolence which does them far greater honour.

The rise of the Rothschilds is the more remarkable seeing that they belong to an outcast and down-trodden race. No other race has experienced such persecution, nor passed through such trials as have the Jews. From time immemorial they have been loaded with scorn and contumely, they have been harassed and fettered by tyrannical laws and barbarous edicts, but they have always passed through their tribulations patiently and triumphantly. Their very name has been a term of reproach to them, and they have been the common butt for the sneers and ridicule of their Christian neighbours. It would be difficult to describe in a few words the intense hatred which the mere word: "Jew," roused in the breasts of Christians, but ample proofs of the bitter animosity between the believers in the old and the believers in the new dispensation are to be found in the writings of our poets and historians. "Thou dog of a Jew," was a term eloquent with savage hatred and unmeasured contempt. These feelings were formerly far more rampant than they are now, but even in these much vaunted days of liberalism and progress there is a very general inclination to cast the words of Shylock in the face of anyone who by his features or manners excites the slightest suspicion of a Jewish origin:

> "You call me misbeliever, cutthroat, dog,
> And spit upon my Jewish gabardine."

That the long-standing hatred of the Christian for the Jews is not extinguished, has been proved only too clearly of recent years. In Russia, Turkey, Poland, Hungary, and elsewhere, the Jews are still, in the eyes of the populace, an accursed race, to be despoiled and persecuted without mercy. Those who cannot compete with them in industry, thrifty habits, or intelligence, show a painful and deplorable eagerness to lend themselves to a propaganda of extermination started often by scheming tricksters, with the result that many innocent lives are sacrificed to the fury and ignorant passions of brutal mobs. Especially is it to be regretted that such lawless proceedings receive a powerful support in some countries from Court chaplains and others, who profess—but whose professions are belied by their deeds—to act up to a creed in which "charity that thinketh no evil" holds a distinguished place. Nothing surely can be more detrimental to true religion than the sanction given by men of education and influence to the perpetration of such barbarities. These continual outbreaks are a forcible proof that even in these enlightened days the spirit of persecution is but poorly concealed, and that a spark may at any moment set it ablaze, when the law would be powerless to control or restrain the excited passions of the multitude.

In England the spirit of intolerance is, we are thankful to say, fast dying out. It is our just pride and boast that our island is the land of liberty, the refuge to which the persecuted of other lands flock. No doubt there still is among Englishmen a prejudice against the Jews, but bitterness in the feeling is now less marked than pity. We no longer regard the language or nationality of those who live in our midst; it is the mental qualities and abilities that awaken our regard and esteem. Here in England we welcome men of every nation, whether Jew or Gentile; here all can and do live in friendly rivalry without any animosity being excited. The thrifty and industrious habits of the Jews, combined with their great intelligence, have long been recognized and acknowledged here in England, and any attempt to start a crusade against those who trusting to our generosity and good nature have settled in our midst, would at once meet with general and well-merited disapproval. In no other country do the Jews enjoy such liberty and privileges as in England. Abroad they live apart, despised and shunned by their so-called Christian neighbours, and harassed in their business and private life by restrictions and edicts originating in the envy inspired by their success. Here they live peacefully and quietly, enjoying the same privileges and opportunities as the rest of the community; no hindrances bar their way to attaining the highest civil or military honours in the land; they are looked upon as a worthy and estimable part of the nation. But whilst on the one hand they are rapidly abandoning their peculiar habits, and are assimilating themselves to our own mode of living, they still fondly cling to their ancient religious ceremonials and doctrines, and assert their claim to a history that dates back to the genesis of our race and reproduces the symbolism of their desert wanderings. Their ceremonies and memories flourish under the protection which is accorded to them in the same measure as to all the other numerous sects and communities that exist in our great' metropolis. No less honour or respect is accorded to the Jewish creed than to any other; they are all on an equal footing, and have to trust to their own efforts for support. While in religious matters we practically ignore the existence of the Jews, it cannot be denied that we, in common with all civilization, owe them a debt which we are very prone to forget, for it is certainly to them that we owe the very bases of our faith, and, were it not for the books of Moses, Christianity would lose one of its main supports, and much of its power.

From the Jews we have that short pithy code of morals embodied in the Ten Commandments, which are placed in the most prominent parts of our churches. The Jews have contributed to the ranks of poets, historians, philosophers, and musical composers a long succession of names that are the admiration of the whole world. In every department of science, art, or philosophy, we have representatives of the Jewish nation, who have by their labours and researches left an indelible impress upon the pages of history and helped to enlighten and ennoble the human race. It is from the Bible that many of our poets and writers have derived their greatest inspiration; the Bible is a storehouse full of the most noble, the grandest ideas, inspiring our writers to their greatest and most successful efforts. The Psalms of David, the Book of Job, and the teachings of Isaiah have never been surpassed, and still retain their sway over the hearts of millions. No higher homage to the intelligence and lofty genius of the Jewish writers could be paid than the universal pre-eminence accorded to the works of their great law-givers and prophets. The moral Law of Moses is virtually unaltered; the principles are still as sound and true as when first propounded, and it is only in the details by which their execution is effected that any change has been made. In the more ordinary and prosaic spheres of thought the superior intelligence of the Jews has been equally conspicuous. The doctrines of Spinoza lie at the root of the whole of that metaphysical philosophy which has had an immense influence upon the opinions and modes of thought of the whole civilized world, for he may undoubtedly be regarded as the founder of modern Rationalism. In music and the acted-drama the children of Israel are far ahead of all their rivals. The number of Jews who have distinguished themselves in these two branches of art is surprisingly large, and includes such famous masters as Meyerbeer, Mendelssohn, Rubinstein, Ernst, Moscheles, Benedict, whilst on the stage are to be found such brilliant performers as Grisi, Rachel, and Sarah Bernhardt. It would be altogether superfluous to specify those Jews who have distinguished themselves in literature, science, or philosophy; their name is legion. One thing is certain and unquestionable: to the Jews we owe our knowledge of the sciences of mathematics and astronomy. During the Middle Ages, in spite of the risk they ran and the suspicion they were likely to incur of being astrologers and necromancers, they were the only students of mathematics and astronomy, the mysteries of which they patiently and unceasingly laboured to solve. In these two branches they have from the most ancient times been preeminent for their surpassing knowledge, as these two subjects have always had a great attraction for minds in which the powers and habits of calculation are innate and conspicuous. The earliest professors of mathematics in our universities were Jews, and in Germany, notwithstanding the ill-feeling that exists between the Christian and Jewish communities, the bulk of the mathematical professors belong to the Jewish faith. In commerce and finance the reputation of the Jews for success and ability is remarkable and worldwide, whilst in politics we have but to mention such distinguished names as Gambetta and others, to prove that in whatever path the Jews enter their talents and indefatigable energy will invariably enable them to place themselves in the foremost rank. If any further proofs of the great intellectual powers of the Jews are required they will be found in the leaders of the legal profession. Few will be prepared to question the learning and acumen of such eminent lawyers and advocates as Lord Herschell, Sir George Jessel, Mr. Benjamin, and Mr. Cohen. Among the well-known politicians with a promising career opening out before them we must not overlook such men as Mr. Mocatta, Baron de Worms, and others.

Of the many charges brought against the Jews, rapacity was by far the most frequent. It was a charge that could be brought forward with very little support, any evidence in refutation of it being sure to find but scant credit in the minds of Christian judges imbued with the strong prejudice everywhere prevalent against the Jews. It was the universal belief that the Jew would always exact his pound of flesh from the poor victim in his clutches. No abatement or reduction was ever to be expected from the relentless, merciless Shylock. Doubtless there was some reason for these accusations, but it will be somewhat of a surprise to our readers to learn that it was to the possession of qualities considered unusual and unlooked-for in a Jew, honesty and integrity, that the founder of the Rothschild family owed his success. From our infancy we have been taught to regard Jews as above all things sordid, mean, and selfish, ever grasping and coveting the goods of others. No impression could be more misleading or mistaken. The wish was father to the thought, and ignorant and intolerant Christians seized upon usury as a weapon with which they could wreak their vengeance upon inoffensive Jews. Whether these charges of rapacity brought against the Jews were often unfounded, or whether the first Rothschild was a marvellous exception to the rest of his co-religionists, we will not argue; it is sufficient for us to know that Mayer Amschel Rothschild was well known in Frankfort for his justice and fairness, and that even his Christian neighbours agreed in calling him "the honest Jew." Why honesty should be so generally regarded as an exceptional trait in a Jew's character, we cannot say, but that such is the general opinion few will dare to deny. When we remember the frugal, abstemious habits of the Jews, and the careful economy by which they are distinguished, it should surely not appear surprising or incompatible if they were found to be not altogether wanting in honesty and love of fair dealing.

Fig. II: THE FORBIDDEN CARICATURE

"BLAUSCHILD" is a caricature of Mayer Amschel Rothschild. This artwork was considered as a moral outrage by the Court House of Vienna, Austria, which decided to burn the original of the infamous artwork in 1927. The Rothschilds of Vienna underwent a huge wave of resentment because of the numerous financial games they played against the interests of Austria as well as many other nations. "Rothschild": Red Shild; "Blauschild": Blue Shild.

The narrow prejudice that formerly existed against the Jews on the score of their grasping avarice is not so pronounced now, but still it cannot be said to have altogether ceased to exist. That public opinion should have become so much more lenient and favourable to the Jews is no doubt greatly owing to the respect and esteem that cannot be denied even by Christian rivals to the unimpeachable lives and characters of the Rothschilds, the Montefiores, and other prominent families. The history of such well-known firms has done much to remove the ill-feeling formerly so rife, and has gone far to prove that Jews when placed on an equal footing with their Christian fellow-citizens can and do trade with a fairness and justice not a whit inferior to those of their business rivals. But, while this prejudice is nearly extinct in England, it still burns with undiminished fury on the Continent. Even when its fury is apparently exhausted and smouldering away, Court chaplains and others, as already stated, abuse their position and fan its dying embers once more to a flame. There is no just cause for this violent outcry; it arises more from envy and jealousy than from any reasonable and well-founded grievance. In Germany of late years there has been a violent agitation or crusade against the Jews, in which all the charges formerly brought against them, such as that of sacrificing Christian children, have been revived, and have found belief among the ignorant classes. The only objection for which there is the least show of reason, is that the Jews everywhere supplant the Christians, and secure all the best and most lucrative appointments, whether in commerce or in the learned professions. But that the Jews do this is surely we think a great and convincing proof of their superior talents and abilities, for they would never receive such honour, in the face of the general ill-will, were it not for their surpassing and undeniable abilities. In making this the basis of an unwarrantable agitation to secure the expulsion of the Jews, the greatest want of reason and justice is displayed. The success of the agitation is rendered impossible by such conduct, which deprives the movement of the support of all thinking men, who cannot fail to see that jealousy and envy are the real causes which excite the animosity of their Christian neighbours in the nineteenth century. Their bitterest opponent never thinks of accusing the Jews of gaining their successes by foul or unfair means. The secret of their invariable success in life is that they not only have an innate and remarkable aptitude for business, but that they at the same time excel their Christian rivals in frugality and economy. The saying that "A penny saved is a penny gained," recommends itself strongly to their minds, and they fully appreciate the wisdom of Fielding's remark, that "Men do not become rich by what they get, but by what they keep." Now thrift is a quality which we have always heard described in terms of praise and approbation, so that to persecute the Jews simply because they are industrious and thrifty is certainly a novel, but hardly a commendable doctrine. Jealousy is however proverbially blind, and will seize on any pretext, however weak, as an excuse for its mad and unjustifiable proceedings. The Jews are thrifty, the Christians luxurious; consequently success must always rest more with the former than with the latter. The great cry now against the Jews is not so much that they are rapacious, as that they undersell or do business cheaper than others, and thus gradually get the bulk of whatever business there is into their hands.

But in these days of free trade, when competition is the soul of business, it would strike most persons on considering the matter that the greatest gainers must be the public at large. Christians are always at liberty to do business on the same terms as their Hebrew rivals, but they find themselves unable to maintain the struggle, for their luxurious habits are against them, and they see themselves practically handicapped out of the contest. The remedy however is in their own hands; let them adopt the thrifty, economical habits of their rivals, and they will soon cease to have any grievances on the score of underselling. Jews, we do not deny, like to make the best bargains they can, and are apt to be cute and sharp in their dealings, but in this they are by no means singular. Their Christian competitors, if we mistake not, are not so disinterested in their dealings as to be ready and willing to abandon a large profit for a smaller one. Sharp practices are common to both parties. The great Sir Thomas Gresham in many of his business transactions displayed great financial skill and a careful solicitude to secure an ample return for the accommodation he was pleased to place at the disposal of his clients. Had he been a Jew the large percentage of profits he made on many of his transactions would have called forth severe denunciation and many hard words. Our gracious lady, Queen Elizabeth, a perfect mistress of the art of diplomacy, but above all things a woman of the world, proved herself remarkably sharp in her money matters. She forced the loyal City companies to advance her large sums, and, finding she had more money than she required, very graciously returned the surplus, – but with the condition that she was to be paid interest on the amount so restored to its owners. Taken as a body, the Jews will be found as honest and open in their dealings as others, and in any case it is a matter of history that the Rothschild family is largely indebted for its present unexampled prosperity to the honesty of its founder. It cannot, however, be denied that his successors, in their anxiety to augment the fortune bequeathed them, did not hesitate to employ those expedients in common use on the Stock Exchange, which are not free from objection, but which they in common with other speculators were at perfect liberty to adopt. Playing their cards with greater skill than their opponents, the Rothschilds were invariably successful in their speculations, and it was only after their defeat that the losers began to doubt and question the morality of their rivals' manœuvres. Those who engage in such contests should count the risks beforehand, and should remember that the laugh is with him that wins.

We have now said enough to prove what great intellectual gifts the Jews as a race possess, and how well qualified they are to become successful in whatever walk of life they may enter. There is, however, one question which cannot fail to suggest itself: —How is it that with their acknowledged abilities, with their remarkable industry and thrift leading them to the acquisition of splendid fortunes and fame in their careers; —how is it that the Jews still remain an outcast and an alien race amongst the civilized nations of the earth ? The answer is short and simple, being contained in the few words — pride of race. Amidst all the sufferings and trials through which they have passed, despite the universal contumely and disdain heaped upon them, careless of and undismayed by the jeers and derision hurled at them, the Jews have clung steadfastly to the belief and conviction that they are the chosen people, that in the distant future their promised supremacy will be achieved and recognized.

> "A people still, whose common ties are gone,
> Who, mix'd with every race, are lost in none;

A part there are, whom, doubtless, man might trust,
Worthy as wealthy, pure, religious, just;
They who with patience, yet with rapture, look
On the strong promise of the Sacred Book."

This faith has made them hold themselves apart; they have neither adopted the religious teachings, yielded to the national spirit, nor mingled their lives with those among whom they live. They have no foothold in the countries in which they have settled, but are indeed strangers in the land. To be let alone and allowed to pursue the even tenor of their way is all they desire, but even this is a concession not readily granted them in many countries. Though for centuries they have had to endure the opprobrium and hatred of those in power, they have never tried to resent their wrongs, but have borne them with patient and silent resignation. An outcast race, they still maintain their proud reserve, and never solicit aid from any but coreligionists, which is certainly more than can be said of the Christian community whose benevolent institutions receive handsome and liberal support from Jewish philanthropists. The isolation in which they live not unnaturally gave rise to feelings of suspicion and distrust, which were intensified by the envy inspired by their enormous wealth and extraordinary success. The rough intellect that found itself unable to cope with the subtle Hebrew mind lent a ready belief to every wild rumour of sorcery and supernatural agency. The results have been seen in Poland, Hungary and elsewhere, where raids on Jewish households have been frequent, ending in many cases in cruelty, spoliation, and bloodshed.

In England a better feeling prevails; the barriers that separate the Jews from their neighbours are rapidly falling away, and the Jews are steadily amalgamating with their fellow citizens, as is proved by the ever increasing number of mixed marriages that are made. Besides this there is a feeling among Jews that England is their home, that here their nature and qualities are best appreciated, as it was here that they received the full benefits of citizenship.

CHAPTER II

MAYER AMSCHEL ROTHSCHILD.

THE FRANKFORT FIRM.

IT was in the Jewish quarter of Frankfort that the founder of the great financial firm first saw the light. Goethe, who also owned Frankfort as his birthplace, has left us a graphic description of the imperial city, which he states was composed of "town within town, fortress within fortress. «Not the least interesting portion of his description is that of the Jewish quarter, enclosed within the ramparts, but yet shut off from the rest of the city by heavy gates and high walls. It was a quarter frequented by few Christians. The houses, huddled close together, were packed from floor to roof with human beings living in a state of squalor and dirt baffling description, while the air was polluted with smells so vile and strong as to drive back all but those whose olfactory nerves had become deadened by long residence or familiarity with the noisome atmosphere. Goethe narrates how he would sometimes peep through the heavy gates and steal a glance at the strange scenes passing in that narrow lane, and goes on to describe what a shudder the sight caused him when he remembered the tales then current of the horrible cruelty and treachery of the Jews. At that time there was a general belief that human sacrifices were offered in the synagogues. Charges were often laid against the Jews of having kidnapped Christian children, who were never seen alive again. Through the midst of this home of the world's outcasts ran the Judengasse, a narrow, dirty lane, lined with dilapidated houses, crowded with dusky, repulsive looking Jews, who would wrangle, argue, and bargain with each other in tones so harsh and discordant that a stranger might well hesitate to venture among them. When, at last, Goethe did pass through the gates, and came into contact with them, their servile cunning, obsequious entreaties, and the filthy state of their persons, combined with the pestilential smells everywhere prevalent, so filled him with disgust that he determined never to visit them again. Years later he was led to considerably modify his opinion regarding these descendants of Israel, and he frankly acknowledged that on closer intimacy he found among them many men of quick intelligence and honourable principles, ready at all times to give him a hearty welcome. "Everywhere I went I was well received, pleasantly entertained, and invited to come again." He witnessed many of their ceremonies, visited their schools, and confessed to having been very fond of walking with the dark-eyed, merry-tongued Jewesses to the Fischerfelder on Sundays.

A writer in a recent number of the "Journal des Débats" gave the following interesting particulars respecting the Judengasse and its inmates:—

"No trace," said he, "will shortly be left of the houses in which Borne, the German writer, and Mayer Amschel Rothschild, the founder of his family's fortunes, first saw the light. Since 1872, only a single row of houses has been left, as one side of the street has been pulled down after the fall of two houses, when thirty-one persons were buried in the ruins. Looking at the Judengasse in its present aspect one is struck by the narrowness of the houses. They have three storeys facing the street, and the whole of the façade is studded with small windows. The gables are pointed, and access is gained to the houses by three or four steps. The doors open into a dark passage, at the other end of which is a worm-eaten wooden staircase, the boards of which bend as one puts one's foot upon them. The rooms are small and low-pitched. They are inhabited by a few of the poorest and most squalid families, Jew and Christian alike. The room upon the ground floor is used as a shop by dealers in old clothes, shoemakers and tinkers. Several of the wealthiest merchants in Germany at the present time may regard these hovels as the home of their ancestors, who are now replaced by the poor wretches just mentioned. There is little that is picturesque about the Judengasse, and those who have had their curiosity whetted by the descriptions in 'Baedeker' will see nothing comparable to what one comes across in Italian ghettos. More curious than the Judengasse is a tavern hard by, where the Jewish beggars meet at nightfall. This tavern, kept by a man named Levy, consists of one long room, the walls of which are painted yellow. Little drink is consumed in this room, but the customers take their meals there and play cards. Round a circular table a cosmopolitan company, consisting of Jews from Poland, where the caftan and the long curls are still worn, as well as from Paris and Berlin, may be seen conversing in low tones, and, upon the evening when the writer paid a visit to the place in the company of a detective, several women were there knitting, one of them being one of the handsomest persons he had ever seen, with magnificent eyes, a white skin, and jet black hair encircled by a kerchief of red wool.

"But, though the Judengasse is not picturesque, its disappearance removes a most interesting historical monument. These decrepit houses revive recollections of another age. The land on which they are built, with the exception of the site owned by the Rothschilds, and on which their house stands, belongs to the town of Frankfort. The Jews confined within their ghetto were not the owners of the soil, being merely tenants at the good will of the Council of the Free City. The Judengasse does not indeed date from earlier than the middle of the fifteenth century, and the walls of the quarter were destroyed by Kleber's army in 1796. During the first part of the Middle Ages the condition of the Jews was comparatively easy. They were the serfs of the Imperial Chamber, and the Emperor, in return for a fixed tribute, accorded them his protection, and was all the more interested in guarding them from ill-usage as he was anxious to preserve for himself the privilege of taxing them. There is no precise evidence as to when the Israelites came to settle in Frankfort, their presence, being officially referred to for the first time in 1240. The first massacre of the Jews took place in 1241, when 180 of them perished. A hundred years of comparative peace ensued, though their relations with the Christians gradually became more strained, their wealth and their mode of life and religion inflaming the superstition, the fanaticism, and the cupidity of the lower orders.

"The worst phase of persecution commenced in 1349, the year of the Black Plague. The country round Frankfort was scoured by bands of Flagellants, who went about declaring that the Jews ought to be put to death for having poisoned the wells. When the inhabitants seemed deaf to their appeals, the Flagellants set several houses on fire, and then spread through the streets exclaiming 'The Jews are burning your houses!' The stratagem succeeded, and there was a general massacre. In the same year the Emperor, Charles IV, had mortgaged his Jews to the town of Frankfort for a sum of about £80,000. This sum was never repaid, and the Jews came under the immediate jurisdiction of the Council. This rendered their position much worse, for the Emperor had allowed them to manage affairs much in their own way, and to choose their own judges. They preserved, nevertheless, a certain degree of autonomy, and for some time the only thing which distinguished them from the ordinary citizen was that they had no political rights. Their existence-was, however, precarious, and their fortunes often threatened. Thus in 1389 the Emperor Wenzel suppressed by one stroke of the pen the obligation to pay what was due to them, and now and again during a riot numbers of the account books in which they inscribed the sums owing to them were burnt. There was about this time a Jews' street at Frankfort, but it was not inhabited exclusively by Jews, for many of the best Christian families lived in it. Thus the Burgomaster resided there from 1364 to 1375. Still as their synagogue, their baths, and their assembly room for dancing were in this street, most of the Jews lived near it. But, as it was close to the cathedral, their enemies declared that their cries and blasphemies disturbed the Catholic worshippers. Public feeling became more and more hostile to them, and in 1425 they were prohibited, under a heavy penalty, from taking the name of burgher. The most cruel blow, however, was yet to come. Frederick III, in compliance with the prayer of the clergy, ordered the Jews to remove from the neighbourhood of the cathedral, and, though they offered to wall up the gate of the street leading to that edifice, their offer was refused. The Council selected a site outside the ancient walls of the town, and had houses built at the expense of the Jews. It is thus that the Council owns the ground on which the Judengasse stands. The gates of the ghetto, which were very strong and lined with iron, were kept closed every Sunday and saint's day, as also upon the days when the Emperor entered the city. The Jews were enjoined not to show themselves in public, nor to pass by any church. If business brought them to the Town Hall, they were not allowed to enter by the main door but by a small door from behind. The men were compelled to wear a yellow patch about the size of a crown piece upon their garments, and the women blue stripes to their veils. They were also enjoined to make room for other citizens on the pavement, and not to touch any of the articles in the market. They were not allowed to buy fish before a certain hour of the day, nor to hire Christians as servants. The Council consented to dispense with their wearing the distinguishing cap on payment of a fine of 250 florins, but they were compelled to have either a black or a grey hat. They were forbidden to lend money to minors or to women, to sell new clothes, or to lend upon clothes which were wet or stained with blood.

"These minute regulations, together with many more of a similar nature, were read out every year in the synagogue. The Jews, in short, must have paid very dearly for the privilege of living in Frankfort; the number of marriages between them was even limited, for there could be only a fixed number of houses, the different couples having to wait their turn. Strange Jews were not allowed in Frankfort, and yet that city must have offered them comparative security, for the Jewish community of Nuremberg sought refuge there in 1498. Protected by their walls, the Jews of Frankfort escaped pillage during the revolt of 1525, but the democratic revolution of 1614 drove them out of the city, and they did not return for two years. When order, however, was restored they came back, and, so as to make it quite clear that they were under the protection of the Empire, the Imperial coat of arms was displayed above the gate of their street. In 1711 the whole street was burnt down, but the Jews were so afraid of pillage that they would not open their doors, and many perished. The Judengasse was rebuilt in 1717 and made rather wider. While the work of reconstruction was progressing the Jews were allowed to lodge in the town, the poorest being accommodated in an empty hospital. There were two other fires in the Judengasse during the eighteenth century, and the shells from Kleber's guns in 1796 set fire to 150 houses. The wealthiest of the Israelites availed themselves of this opportunity to settle in the town, and they were not again molested. The gates were demolished in 1808, and many restrictions were removed. The Prince Primate granted the Jews, in 1811, equal civil and political rights with those enjoyed by the other inhabitants, but they lost these again in 1815, and did not recover them until 1853 and 1864. In 1811 there were 159 houses, inhabited by 2,214 persons, in the Judengasse, while at the present time the Jews number 14,000, or eleven per cent, of the whole population."

Here, then, in the Judengasse, in the house numbered 152, but better known as the House of the Red Shield (Rothschild) – afterwards adopted as a surname – lived Amschel Moses Rothschild, earning a livelihood as a dealer in curiosities and old coins. In the course of his business he was in the habit of travelling about the country, hawking his wares and keeping his eyes open in search of curiosities, and an anecdote is related of him tending to show on what a thread the destiny of the family at one time hung. In reproducing this anecdote, we wish it to be understood that we do not attach any value to it ourselves, our object only being to make the narrative as complete as possible. Many of the stories related of the Rothschilds are pure myths, for lively imaginations have placed a halo of romance about their history, as about that of every other person of notoriety, so that implicit credit cannot always be attached to the anecdotes told of the different members of the firm. The story in question is to the effect that Rothschild was one day walking along a country road, when he was overtaken by a brother pedlar in more flourishing circumstances than he himself, seeing that he had an ass to carry his wares. In the course of conversation, Rothschild was invited to relieve himself of his load by placing it on the ass's back: an offer he was glad to accept. On coming to a narrow ravine where the bridge across was formed by a single plank, Rothschild prudently removed his sack from the ass's back to his own shoulders, remarking as he did so:—"Accidents sometimes happen at places like this, and, as this sack contains all my fortune, it is well to be on the safe side." His comrade laughed at his fears, but Rothschild's prudence was fully justified by events, for no sooner had the ass, followed by his master, reached the middle of the bridge than the plank gave way, and both were precipitated down the chasm. Thus by a miracle Rothschild saved both his life and his money.

We have already mentioned that the number of Jews allowed to marry was limited, but Rothschild having gained permission availed himself of his privilege and took unto himself a wife, who, in 1743, gave birth to a son whom they named

Fig. III: MAYER AMSCHEL ROTHSCHILD
INTERNATIONAL BANKER – (1744–1812)

Founder of the M. A. Rothschild Bank in Frankfort

Mayer Amschel is the father of all Rothschild's family members and the first Rothschild to open a bank. He sent his five sons to establish banks in the leading European capital. After his death, Mayer continued to control the direction of the family by promoting intermarriages. In only few years and without stepping foot in the New World, the dynasty he founded dominated international finance. In 2005, he was honoured by Forbes as the seventh most influential businessperson of all time and the inventor of modern banking whom introduced "concepts such as diversification, rapid communication, confidentiality and high volume." (Source: businessindider.com)

Mayer Amschel. When the boy grew up and his parents had to decide as to his future in life, they resolved to have him educated with a view to his becoming a rabbi, or teacher in the synagogue. This resolution was not unnatural, seeing that several of the family, had been or were then celebrated for their knowledge of the Talmud and the doctrines of the Jewish faith. Dr Lewysohn states that in the Jewish cemetery at Worms is buried Rabbi Menachem Mendel Rothschild, who had been the chief rabbi to the congregation there. Isaac Rothschild was warden of the Frankfort synagogue, Solomon Rothschild was chief rabbi of Würzburg and Friedburg, and Boaz Rothschild was the author of a Hebrew work published at Fürth in 1766. Mayer Amschel, in 1755, lost his parents and was sent by his relatives to Fürth to complete his studies. Theology was, however, not to his taste. He had been born and bred in the midst of a community whose whole thought centred upon getting and accumulating money. He had early learnt to see in wealth the only true standard by which one could judge his fellow, and he not unnaturally shared the ambition that fired his comrades to acquire riches and a consequent name among his co-religionists. His instinct for business was too powerful to resist. Even while at college he had become well-known as a collector and dealer in old coins on a small scale, and in this way had made the acquaintance of several numismatists in the neighbourhood.

This is surprising when we remember that he could not have been much more than twelve years old at the time, but with Jews the talent for business is innate, and their natural shrewdness and skill in making bargains more than compensate them for their youth and inexperience. Notwithstanding the limited resources at his disposal, Mayer Amschel seems to have pursued his youthful speculations with considerable energy and—profit.

At length, rightly judging that he was better fitted for commercial than theological pursuits, he abandoned his studies altogether and returned to the Judengasse, where his abilities and shrewdness soon became known among his co-religionists. His reputation reaching the ears of some of the large firms, several offers of employment were made him, and not being one of *"those who are content to spend their lives trotting on a cabbage leaf"* as the proverb says, when a wider field of enterprise was thrown open to him, he accepted the offer of a banking firm named Oppenheim in Hanover. In their service he remained several years, gaining and maintaining a high character for steadiness and reliability, while his energy and abilities were recognized by his gradual promotion to the responsible post of co-manager. Frugal and economical in his habits, he was able to save a considerable portion of his salary, until he thought he possessed sufficient capital to make a start on his own account. He therefore left Oppenheim's service and set up in business for himself, dealing in old coins, bullion, and anything by which he thought he could make a profit. For some time it was a hard, uphill fight, and more than once the budding firm was in danger of collapse, but the untiring energy and honesty of its founder, triumphing over all difficulties, placed it on a sound basis and secured its future safety. Some years later he determined to transfer his business to his birthplace, where he settled for good, as in 1770 he married Gudula Schnapper, and lived in his father's house in the Judengasse. His business was at the outset of a very mixed description, ranging from coins and curiosities, to bullion, bills of exchange, etc., but as his speculations, distinguished by cautious boldness, were almost invariably successful, he was soon in a position to abandon the business of a dealer in works of art for that of a banker and financier. One of his earliest investments was to purchase the freehold of the house in the Judengasse, which has given birth to one of the greatest financial houses in the world. In all his business transactions he displayed remarkable honesty and integrity; so widely did he become known as the "honest Jew" that his reputation spread through the surrounding provinces, and was largely the means of securing him fresh business. A man of his character has never lacked friends, and Mayer Amschel found many persons ready and anxious to recommend him and gain him new clients. Oppenheim, his old employer, was especially zealous in promoting the success of his former employee, and never allowed an opportunity to slip of saying a word in his favour.

During his apprenticeship at Oppenheim's Mayer Amschel had more than once come into contact with Lieutenant-General Baron von Estorff, an intimate friend of William IX, Landgrave of Hesse, and had won his good opinion and esteem. When years later Baron Estorff, who, from his own knowledge and Oppenheim's accounts, was able to form an estimate of Rothschild's worth, had an opportunity of advancing his fortunes, he did not hesitate to recommend him to the Landgrave as a person well qualified to act as his financial agent. Seeing that the Landgrave had a private fortune of thirty-six million thalers, it was indeed a most lucrative post to obtain. Rothschild received a summons to wait upon the Landgrave. When he was ushered into the room, he discovered his Highness deep in a game of chess with Baron Estorff, who seemed to be getting the best of the struggle. Not caring to disturb the Landgrave's calculations, which absorbed his attention so entirely that he had not noticed his visitor's entrance, Rothschild stood by, a silent spectator of the game. At last the Landgrave, in his perplexity and despair, threw himself back in his chair, and in so doing caught sight of the banker. He at once inquired of his visitor:—

"Do you know anything of chess?" Rothschild's answer was to point to a particular piece, saying:—

"Would your Highness move this piece to that square?"

The move he suggested was adopted, and at once put a different complexion on matters. So far from the game being lost to the Landgrave, it slowly turned in his favour, and was eventually won by him. He then conversed with Rothschild on the subject of the latter's visit. He was so highly impressed by his visitor's intelligence and address that he told Baron Estorff, after the banker's departure, that he had "certainly recommended him no fool." The result of the interview was that Mayer Amschel Rothschild was appointed Court Banker to the Landgrave of Hesse.

In 1804, Rothschild contracted with the Danish government for the issue of a loan of four million thalers: a sign of his growing influence and prosperity. At that time all Europe was in arms against Napoleon, who defeated and overran kingdom after kingdom. In 1806, the Emperor sent a portion of his army to chastise Frankfort and Hesse-Cassel for the support they had given to the cause of the Allies. The truth was that the Landgrave, having a keen eye for business, had found he could largely augment his already handsome fortune by placing his troops at the-disposal of the Prussian and English governments, receiving in return large subsidies. This conduct reached the ears of the "child of fortune" who determined to administer a severe punishment to the Landgrave, by plundering and sacking Hesse-Cassel. The approach of the French becoming known, the Landgrave concluded that under the circumstances discretion was the better part of valour. He therefore made hasty preparations for flight. But, although he would by flight secure the safety of his person, he could not render his money safe, for that he was forced to leave behind. Consisting as it did largely of specie, its mere bulk was a hindrance to its removal, and yet to leave it where it was would be but making a present of it to the French. In his dilemma he recollected Rothschild, and, thinking the banker might be able to take charge of his money, he had it packed and sent to Frankfort.

"Mayer," said the Landgrave, "I have already had some experience of your honesty and integrity, and have now to put it to further proof. I wish to deposit with you my whole fortune; to your care I leave it, to be returned to me in more peaceful and happier times."

"Such a signal mark of your confidence and esteem flatters and honours me, your Highness; but do you not forget that the French will be here in a few days?"

"Do you think so?"

"And that in their train there always follows a band of lawless ruffians, who will fall upon us and plunder us without mercy. It will be a time of unrestrained pillage, as your Highness must know full well."

"Ah, well, Mayer, I leave my fortune to your care, and you will act as you think best. I ask no receipt from you, knowing that in your hands the money will be safe, if you can but keep the French from handling it."

Fig. IV: WILLIAM IX, PRINCE OF HESSE-CASSEL (1743–1821)

William IX, Landgrave of Hesse-Cassel (1785–1805), the Prince of Hesse-Cassel under the name of William I, was one of the richest man in the world at the early 19th century. He had an immense fortune and spent his life to increase his wealth, especially when he decided to enter into a formal partnership agreement with the Rothschilds. William IX was well-known for his legendary greed and for his great cupidity that led him to conduct various speculation operations.

Painting of Wilhelm von Hesse-Cassel (1853), by Anton Wilhelm Tischbein (1730–1804). Museum of Hanau, Fermany. Source: www.hanau.de/stadt/geschichte/

With these words the Landgrave left, paying no heed to Rothschild's protestations, on finding himself thus suddenly and unexpectedly saddled with the responsibility and anxiety attaching to the custody of so large a sum. Before the week passed all his prophecies were fulfilled. Frankfort was in the hands of the French, who gave themselves up to plunder and wanton destruction. Rothschild, being a man of well-known wealth, was one of the first visited, and had to endure calmly and unmoved the sight of his premises being sacked and stripped of everything of value. He had, however, good reason for his calmness. By thus quietly allowing the French to seize his own property, of no small value, he prevented a more thorough search of his premises being made, and so secured the safety of the Landgrave's money, which he had artfully concealed in wine casks in his cellars, or had buried in his garden.

This was the turning-point in Rothschild's career. It was the tide in his affairs, taken at the flood, and leading on to his future prosperity and fortune. Had the founder of the Rothschild family refused to undertake the trust confided to him, the course of European history might have been altered, and some of the most remarkable characters of the nineteenth century have remained unknown to fame. The trust was, however, faithfully kept, and Rothschild, after the French had once more left the city, started business afresh, and made such good use of the Landgrave's thalers that in a few years he was reputed to be richer than ever. He seems to have transmitted the whole of the money to his son Nathan, who was established in business in London. This son was already a well-known man in the English capital, where the astounding skill and-boldness of his speculations had taken the City by surprise. He thus referred to the fortune left in his father's hands:—"The Prince of Hesse-Cassel gave my father his money; there was no time to lose, so he (my father) sent it me, and I put it to such good use that the Prince made me a present of all his wine and linen."

A period of respite followed, during which most of the German rulers gave in, either willingly or from necessity, their allegiance to Napoleon. Being raised by the Emperor to the dignity of Elector of Hesse-Cassel, William IX was enabled to return from his exile. One of the first persons he visited was, not unnaturally, Rothschild. He was aware, from the papers and other sources, of the pillage of Frankfort, and knew that the house of the Jew-banker had not escaped a visit. It had been reported to him, with every show of truth, that Rothschild had been robbed of all he possessed, and was completely ruined. Not knowing anything of the stratagem by which his fortune had been saved, the Elector concluded that his thalers had gone to fill the pockets of the French soldiery; but he still resolved to visit his old agent, if merely to show that his regard and esteem for the latter had suffered no change.

> "Good day, Mayer, good day," said he, extending his hand; at last we have peace again, though rather dearly bought. "You see before you a poor devil of a prince as badly off as Job was."
>
> "You poor, my lord!"
>
> "Yes, to be sure, since those cursed thieves have run off with my thalers as well as yours. If it is not inconvenient to you, I should be glad to get some small advance from you against the indemnity that is to be made me."

"But your Highness has no need to borrow. The money your Highness entrusted to my keeping is safe and untouched."

"*Teufel!* cried the Prince; why did not the French plunder your premises?"

"Pardon me, and I will explain. The French stripped me of everything belonging to myself, but I was careful not to irritate them by any violent resistance, else they might have made a more careful search in my cellar, where your money was hidden."

"What! can it be…"

"Yes, my resignation was a ruse; they little dreamt how great a prize they missed."

"Is it possible!" exclaimed the Prince, almost dumb with surprise.

"For the last nine years, your Highness, I have taken the liberty of making use of your thalers to compensate myself for the loss of mine. All my speculations have been successful, and I can at this moment, without inconvenience, restore the whole sum to you, with interest at five per cent."

The Prince was deeply moved, and with difficulty could express his gratitude and his admiration of Rothschild's noble conduct.

"Friend Mayer," said he, "you are the most honest Jew I know; keep my money, and do what you think fit with it. I want no interest on it for the time it has been in your custody, and for the next twenty years I undertake to leave it with you, and to receive no interest on it above two per cent."

This is the account given by some writers who, dazzled by the immense riches and power of the Rothschilds, were unable to ascribe those riches and that power to ordinary business transactions, and so have gone out, out of their way to invent a romance for which they have no better authority than their imaginations. This story is derived from the *"Sprüchwörter der Deutschen"* and to show how little dependence can be placed upon its truthfulness, we need only mention that it is related about a "Moses" Rothschild of Frankfort, of whom no one has ever heard, as there was no Rothschild of that name living. Further, the Landgrave fled from Cassel at the first approach of the French, and could not have gone to Frankfort, as that city was already in the possession of the enemy. Neither could the money have been buried in the garden, as no gardens existed in the Judengasse, and the Jews were forbidden by law from owning any freehold property in any other part of the city. The true unvarnished story seems to have been the following:

Some writers maintain that Rothschild's connection with the Court of Hesse Cassel commenced during the lifetime of the Landgrave Frederick II, who died in 1785, leaving an immense fortune of fifty-six million thalers. This he had acquired by means of his poor subjects, whom, for handsome subsidies, he had placed at the disposal of the English Government. In 1775 he raised a levy of 12,800 Hessian troops, who were shipped off to quell the rising of the American colonists, and further detachments, amounting to about 4,000 more, were sent at intervals. For the services of these men he received from England twenty-two million thalers. On his death he was succeeded by his son, William IX, a warlike prince, who had seen some service under Frederick the Great.

He followed his father's plan, and increased, by large subsidies from the English Government, the vast fortune left him.

In 1787 he was paid six hundred thousand thalers for the services of 12,000 men, and in 1794 he furnished the English with 4,000 more, who were employed in Spain against France. When the French invaded Germany the petty German princes were unable to offer any opposition to their advance; they all fled before the soldiers of the Republic. The Landgrave in the first place went to his brother in Schleswig, but afterwards, in 1808, proceeded to Prague, where he met with a some-what unpleasant surprise in the shape of an Imperial decree which stated that *"the House of Hesse Cassel has for some years past sold its subjects to the English crown, and by that means has amassed a large fortune. This detestable avarice has brought about its own punishment, as the house has ceased to reign."* When the treaty of Tilsit was concluded Hesse Cassel was incorporated with the Kingdom of Westphalia.

Whether M. A. Rothschild was appointed Court Jew by Frederick II, as some assert, or first became connected with the Court owing to some dealings he had with William IX, an ardent lover of old and rare coins, and whether his honesty and integrity had won the Landgrave's favour, is shrouded in doubt. It is certain, however, that when William IX became Landgrave M. A. Rothschild was the "Court Jew," and managed all the Landgrave's financial affairs. The bulk of the Landgrave's fortune, there is every reason to suppose, was invested in the English Funds, as being the only safe and reliable investment, and it was Rothschild's duty to collect the dividends as they became due by drawing upon the firm of

Van Notten in London, in whose hands the stocks were deposited. The commission he charged for this business must of itself have amounted to a large sum. That the Landgrave was satisfied with the way in which Rothschild managed his affairs may be inferred from the fact that he gave Rothschild's third son, Nathan, when he established himself in London, full power to deal with his stocks as he deemed best, and transferred to him all the business which the Van Notten firm had formerly conducted. His confidence must have been great, as Nathan Rothschild was allowed perfect liberty of action, and could sell out and re-invest the stocks confided to him as he pleased. When William IX fled from Cassel, his first great care was to provide for the safe custody of his money, and this we know M. A. Rothschild undertook to do. What was the exact sum entrusted to him on this occasion we cannot say with any certainty, though it is stated by some writers to have amounted to two million thalers. Now, instead of hiding or burying the money, as some have asserted, it would surely be more characteristic of such a shrewd man of business as Rothschild to have transmitted this sum to London to be disposed of as Nathan Rothschild thought fit. To conceal so large an amount from the French would be next to impossible, and, besides, it would have been madness for M. A. Rothschild to have kept the money himself, when its safety could have been secured by sending it to London; and that he did send it we have his son's word. The romantic version, therefore, seems to have very little truth in it, with the exception of the main point that the fortune of the Landgrave was the original cause of the subsequent success of the Rothschilds. The commission gained by the London and Frankfort houses every year for managing the Landgrave's affairs must have been considerable, and would of itself have formed a sufficiently strong base for the many successful speculations which the Rothschilds entered into in the money market. Under these circumstances, they may not have speculated for their own benefit with the Landgrave's money at all, and were therefore able to restore it to its owner whenever he thought fit to claim it back.

During the war in Spain the Duke of Wellington experienced great annoyance and embarrassment from the failure of the specie supplies, and the English Government were unable to assist him in his difficulty, as they could induce no bankers to assume the responsibility of conveying the money to Spain. At this juncture M. A. Rothschild stepped forward and offered to undertake the task for a pretty heavy commission. His offer was accepted, fortune smiled on his enterprise, and the money reached the Duke safely. This was a most profitable piece of business, as Rothschild is said to have cleared annually for eight years a sum of about £150,000. The success of this operation, and the punctuality which distinguished its execution, induced the Government to entrust the Rothschilds with the payment of the enormous subsidies to the various Continental princes, and this, again, still further increased the growing reputation and influence of the firm.

Thus it was that the Rothschilds made their first millions, and few can say they have gained their fortunes in an equally honourable and praiseworthy manner. When once the first million had been made, it was a comparatively easy task to add others. Water always flows to the sea, or, in other words, money makes money. But streams in their progress to the ocean become discoloured by the muddy waters of affluent streams, and so with the Rothschilds' millions. The first were gained by the fairest of means, but some of those that succeeded were undoubtedly won by recourse to those expedients and artifices, common on the Stock Exchange, which are open to serious moral objections.

Mayer Amschel Rothschild died on the 13th September, 1812, in his sixty-seventh year. Just before his decease he summoned his five sons to his bedside, and with his last breath, after giving them his blessing, enjoined them to remain faithful to the Law of Moses, to remain united until the end, and to undertake nothing without having first consulted their mother. "Observe these three points and you will soon be rich among the richest, and the world will belong to you"—a prediction that has been fulfilled to the letter.

He left five sons, Anselm Mayer, Salomon, Nathan, James, and Carl, who soon after his death established a pentarchy, Anselm retaining command of the original house in Frankfort, whilst the others founded new branches in Vienna, London, Paris, and Naples respectively. By so doing they wonderfully increased the reputation and influence of the firm, and gradually gained that control over the different money markets which enabled them to augment their fortunes with such astounding certainty and rapidity.

Although Mayer Rothschild is known to history merely as an eminent financier, money-making did not monopolize his time or thoughts. With all his engagements, he still managed to find leisure and opportunities for administering relief from his well-lined purse to his suffering fellow-mortals, and many tales are told of his benevolence and charity. He would often stop a poor, starving creature in the street, to place a coin in his hand and hurry away to prevent his face being recognized. He moreover exerted his influence to obtain an extension of the civil and political rights of the Jews, and the abolition of the tyrannical restrictions from which they suffered.

His wife Gudula survived him many years, dying in 1849, at the ripe old age of ninety-six. Notwithstanding its dismal and filthy surroundings, the old house in the Judengasse was her home to the last. No entreaty or attempt at persuasion could induce her to abandon the house so intimately associated with the growth and success of the great firm, whose very name was derived from the sign by which the house had been distinguished from its

Superstitious scruples and a love of the old place combined to prevent her forsaking it.

In her eyes it had some mysterious connection with the prosperity and greatness of the family. Here then she lived on, distinguished by the simplicity of her habits, until the thread of life was snapped and her remains were carried to the grave.

"The mother of the Rothschilds, the Hecuba of the European Croesus family" wrote an eye-witness during her lifetime, "must be almost a centenarian, but so vigorous and active is she still, that she manages to visit the theatre nearly every night. There she sits in her box, with a fan in her hand to shield her eyes from the dazzle of the lights, with an old Jewish hood, adorned with flowers, upon her head, no hair visible, dressed in coloured silks, with the most costly lace about her neck and breast. Of her sons, Anselm is most like her. She lives in the Judengasse still, in the same house as when she, at that time the wife of a needy shopkeeper, brought her children into the world. This old musty house, in the dampest and most unhealthy street in the city, she has never been willing to abandon."

"Here I have seen" said she, "my sons grow rich and powerful, and, as I have not become conceited in my old age, I will leave them their good fortune, which would certainly forsake them, were I from pride to abandon my humble dwelling." Owing to the narrowness of the street, no vehicle could approach her house, and her son's carriage could come only as far as the entrance of the Gasse when she returned from the theatre, so that she was always carried home from the carriage.

Heine, in his work, "Ueber Börne," gives us a pleasant description of a walk he took through the Judengasse, together with an interesting reminiscence of the first Rothschild and his wife:—"In this small house lives the worthy dame, the Letitzia, who has given birth to so many Napoleons of finance; the, great parent of all loans, who in spite of the world-wide rule of her kingly sons, will never consent to leave her little, but fondly cherished palace in the Judengasse, and to-day, owing to the great festivities, her windows are adorned with white hangings. How pleasantly the lamps shine which she lit with her own hands on the 18th October of the Jews, which has been celebrated now for more than two thousand years in remembrance of the day when Judas Maccabæus, with his equally brave and heroic brothers, set his country free, as did Frederick William in our day. The tears spring to her eyes as the good old dame looks at the lamps, for they bring back to her the memory of Mayer Amschel, her dearly loved husband, and of her children—then young children—who would plant the lamps in the ground, and with childish glee jump over and round them. Old Rothschild, the founder of the reigning dynasty, was a noble soul, goodness and kind-heartedness itself; a benevolent face with a pointed little beard; on his head a three-cornered hat, and his dress quiet and sober, if not poor. Thus would he go about in Frankfort, and frequently surrounded, as if holding a levée, by a crowd of poor people, to whom he would either give alms or address a kind word. If a row of beggars was met in the street, with cheerful and pleased countenances, one might be sure that Rothschild was in the habit of passing down that way."

CHAPTER III

THE PROGRESS OF THE FIRM

THE dying injunctions of Mayer Amschel to his five sons were faithfully observed with the filial obedience so characteristic of the Jews. The Jews, with all their faults—and Jews are no more faultless than the rest of mankind—still display many qualities which deserve our praise and admiration. The importance and value they have always attached to reverence and respect towards their elders, and especially towards their parents, are too well known to require demonstration, and certainly few nations excel them in this respect. No doubt the habits of the Jews encourage the development of such qualities as filial obedience and reverence of old age. With their proud reserve, which holds them aloof from their Christian neighbours, they are necessarily forced to foster the pleasures and comforts of their own domestic circles and to knit the family bonds more firmly together. In Jewish families the wish of the father has far more weight, and is far more highly respected than in Christian families. That the last wishes of Mayer Amschel should have been scrupulously fulfilled, need excite no surprise, for, even if filial obedience had not led his sons to live in unity together, their natural shrewdness would have at once pointed out to them the advantages which would follow from their combined action. But, be the motives what they may, it is a matter of history that the five sons, after their father's death, started business in five of the European capitals, each brother managing his own, but always acting on important occasions in concert with the others. The result of this union of aims and action was that they all rose simultaneously to fame and fortune, rising, too, with a rapidity which appears incredible. There is one drawback to this principle of combined action for their general benefit—the impossibility of writing a lucid and accurate description of the career of each of the brothers, owing to the impossibility of ascertaining what part each played in the many gigantic operations undertaken and carried out conjointly by all. The business of the Rothschilds since 1812 has been so immense, and the bonds linking the different members of the family together so interwoven, that to unravel them appears well-nigh hopeless. The best course for us to pursue under these circumstances is to give in the first place a clear and concise account of the family, and then to deal with the career of each individual member. By the adoption of this plan we hope to avoid confusing the reader by frequent reference to other portions of the narrative.

The success achieved by the founder of the firm was no doubt greatly due to the disturbed state of the financial and political world. Had he fallen on more peaceful times, it may well be questioned whether he would have met with the success he did. In more senses than one we may regard Mayer Amschel as a child of fortune equally with his illustrious contemporary Napoleon. The period from his starting in business to his death in 1812 was a period rife with wars and rumours of war—a period eminently favourable to such a shrewd and daring speculator as he was. It is in such disturbed times, when the prices fluctuate greatly, yielding to the influence of any and every rumour, that speculators reap their richest harvest. Peace, which means prosperity to the country at large, is their dread and abhorrence. Times could hardly have been more auspicious for Mayer Amschel. Trade was then almost annihilated on the Continent, and confidence and credit were at such a low ebb that Rothschild could obtain for his advances pretty well whatever interest he chose to demand. Favoured by fortune and circumstances, and aided as it was by the remarkable faculty he displayed of forecasting the future, his progress was rapid. We are forced to write in these general terms of the founder of the firm, as little but tradition remains to afford us information either as to his business or private life. To the public the archives of the family which could throw so much light upon the history of this century are a profound secret, a sealed book, kept hidden from profane eyes. What a mass of interesting information must the pages of those archives contain! and yet no stranger has been allowed to inspect and make known their contents. No encouragement is offered by the family to any who may desire to obtain information respecting the early history of the members of the firm; indeed, such inquiries, however laudable may be their object, are regarded as intrusive, if not impertinent, and an evasive answer is all that is usually received. The reticence of the family can be easily understood; but still it is to be regretted that some relaxation of this hard and fast rule cannot be made, seeing that the family, owing to the exalted position and relations it holds towards all the States of Europe, has long since ceased to retain its private character. The movements of the Rothschilds are carefully watched, and are as important to the public as those of any

Minister. It is said that one enthusiastic inquirer was informed that "they much regretted that no information could be given him on the subject of the business of the founder of the firm, as no record of his loans and other financial operations had been kept, neither could they furnish a photograph, as he had never sat for his portrait; and, in conclusion, that it was impossible to name all the members of the family, as a full pedigree did not exist."

In the previous pages we have narrated how Mayer Amschel started in business as a dealer in coins and bullion, and how, as his reputation for honesty became known, he was able to extend his sphere of action by dealing in bills of exchange, merchandise, etc. We have described how he became known to and appreciated by the Landgrave of Hesse, through whose influence he gained a large number of wealthy and princely clients, and how his fame and credit were still further augmented in 1801 by his being appointed Court Jew in succession to Feidel David. In this way he laid the foundation of the substantial fortune he bequeathed his five sons. In 1804 Mayer Amschel found that he had prospered so well in his undertakings that he was in a position to lend his assistance to the Government of Denmark, whose finances were not then in a flourishing condition. This transaction was followed by several of a similar nature, Denmark being overtaken by a series of undeserved and unforeseen calamities which quite crippled her for the time. The greatest and most hurtful shock' she received was when the English fleet appeared in the Sound without any previous declaration of war, and demanded the surrender of the Danish fleet. This demand being refused, General Cathcart landed some 30,000 men a few miles above Copenhagen, and then bombarded the town for three successive days. The result of these vigorous measures was that General Pyrmann was induced to comply with the English terms and surrender the Danish fleet. In the ensuing year war with Sweden followed, and still further crippled the financial resources of the Government, which was compelled to impose fresh burdens on the already heavily-taxed and impoverished country. Besides issuing an enormous amount of paper money, the Government was compelled in their extremity to apply to the Rothschilds for assistance, an application which, as we have said, met with a favourable response. Between 1804 and 1812 the loans issued by M. A. Rothschild on behalf of Denmark amounted to no less than 10,000,000 thalers; a large sum for any one firm to be responsible for at that time, when money was dearer than it is now. This large business proved, no doubt, very lucrative to the contractor, and gave a turn to the business of the firm which it has since retained. After 1812 the miscellaneous business was gradually abandoned, Government operations taking its place. It is not certain whether the last Danish loan was issued during the lifetime of Mayer Amschel or not; that, however, is a trifling matter. Having established the firm on a solid basis, Mayer Amschel during the last years of his life left the management to a great extent in the hands of his sons, and devoted himself to work more congenial to his better nature. His philanthropy and benevolence were unbounded, and endeared him to the memory of his fellow-citizens. The esteem in which he was held was proved by his being nominated by the Grand Duke a member of the Wahlcollegium, when Frankfort was made the capital of the new Grand Duchy. It was to the Grand Duke that the Jews of Frankfort were indebted for the grant of the full enjoyment of political and municipal rights which had hitherto been withheld. With the death of Mayer Amschel in 1812 the first period in the history of the firm closed—a period small and insignificant in results when compared with those that followed, but still considerable if compared with the results achieved by any other banking firm.

The second period in the firm's history dates from 1812 to 1826. On the death of their father, four sons out of the five started each a business of his own, in Paris, Vienna, Naples, and London respectively. The branch in London had, however, existed some time previously, having been founded by Nathan Mayer Rothschild, who saw that Frankfort was too small to afford scope for the operations of himself and his brothers. With his characteristic decision, he resolved to repair to England and win his way to fortune by his own unaided efforts. In subsequent pages we shall detail the business he conducted, and will content ourselves by stating here that the financial ability he displayed was so marvellous that he gained an unprecedented success in the country of his adoption. He contributed largely to the prosperity of the parent firm in Frankfort by inducing the English Government to entrust his father with the payment of its subsidies to its foreign allies. That this was a profitable business may be inferred from the fact that in one year the subsidies amounted to no less than £11,000,000, which must have left a handsome commission in the coffers of the firm. On the death of Mayer Amschel, an exception was made to the rule always since observed by the firm, that the eldest member should be regarded as its head and ruling spirit. The brothers, fully cognizant of his superior intellectual capacity, willingly acknowledged Nathan Mayer as the most fit to direct all their most important transactions. That they acted wisely in doing so, results have proved, as their business began from the year 1812 to assume cosmopolitan proportions, and to pervade all parts of the world. Its operations were of a most gigantic nature, whilst the success it achieved was correspondingly rapid. Its success was indeed so remarkable that the only explanation of it seems to be in the extraordinary vicissitudes and excitement through which many of the European States passed during that period, and of which the Rothschilds took advantage. From 1812 the firm quitted the old conventional paths and struck out a new line of business, which it has made peculiarly its own. Its fortunes and its resources had then grown so large that the old banking operations were no longer worthy of its attention. Government business, such as issuing State loans and the emission of Government funds, proved more congenial, and no doubt more profitable, so that we find the firm between 1812 and 1830 engaged in the transaction of a series of vast operations, which raised it to a position of power no other firm has ever attained. Its influence was so all-powerful that it was a saying, no war could be undertaken without the assistance of the Rothschilds, since the control exercised by them on the money markets was such that they could effectually withhold or procure the requisite funds.

The inauguration of this new business opened up a new field of industry, if we may so call it, which possessed such attractions in the shape of facilities for making and losing money, that it soon became popular. Every year the business in Government funds increased in value and importance, for the advantages the funds possessed were so many and so great that merchants and persons of every rank and station hastened to invest in them. By the purchase of Government securities the buyer knows he holds the best security for his money, since the credit and solvency of the country are pledged to him, and, as it is of the greatest public importance to preserve these uninjured, so his security is practically safe from destruction. No other way of investing money with equal safety exists, for in private enterprises, in which the security may be goods or landed property, the whole capital may suddenly be lost by fraud, fire, or other accidental causes. Then, again, an investor can rely with "certainty on regularly receiving a fixed interest on his capital, whereas, were he to invest his money otherwise, the interest would be dependent on contingencies beyond his control. Another advantage, and a very great one, is that anyone can purchase what amount of Government stock he pleases, and in this way make use of all the money he can command. He is not limited to a round sum, as would be the case if he lent his capital on mortgage, which might demand either a larger or smaller amount than that at his disposal for the time being, but in Government stock he can invest the amount down to the last shilling. Most Government stocks are negotiable in all the leading European markets, so that their popularity may be due in no small measure to their portable and saleable qualities. It is scarcely to be wondered at that the demand for these stocks was for ever increasing, and that the business done in them be-came in a few years of the greatest importance. In addition to the intrinsic value of the stocks, an additional value was derived from the speculation which took place in them. By the exercise of a certain amount of shrewdness, and aided by good fortune in the choice of the moment for buying or selling, it was possible to make hitherto unheard-of gains. This possibility naturally caused a general desire to share in such easily-earned profits, and in this way speculation went on increasing. In the course of time, when the public appetite for investing was no longer appeased by Government funds, stocks and shares of every description were issued and snatched up with avidity. Year after year speculation grew, and gradually degenerated into one vast system of gambling. No objection can be raised to legitimate purchases or sales of stocks, but since the bulk of Stock Exchange business has been based on speculation there can be no doubt that the effects are far from beneficial. When it is possible to make enormous and fabulous gains, with comparatively no exertion, by operations on the Stock Exchange, it would be surprising if many business men were not found to quit the old paths in which their fathers made their fortunes by steady persevering industry, to enter upon one surrounded with such rosy allurements, where failure appears Out of the question. The commerce of a country must be affected by this endless speculation, as the amount of capital sunk in keeping stocks up at fictitious prices must at times be immense. To make matters worse, everything imaginable is done to encourage this speculation. The disclosures recently made in connection with the managers of several of the London banks prove with what ease unscrupulous persons might without means embark in speculations amounting to hundreds of thousands of pounds. How largely chance enters into Stock Exchange operations is shown by the custom of buying or selling stocks for delivery at some future day. A man may perhaps sell an amount of stock now at a certain price to be delivered to the purchaser say a month hence, in which case he trusts to Providence to be able to buy the same amount of stock himself at a lower price before the time expires, and so clear a profit without having really risked any money. Should he buy, then the opposite principle guides his action. As a proof to what extent gambling of this kind is carried, we may mention that in the corn market crops are frequently sold before the seed has even been planted. The facilities offered are so great that speculators enter into operations out of all proportion to their means, for, being anxious to make as large a profit as they can, they are forced to engage in transactions on a gigantic scale. Should their calculations turn out wrong, or the fickle goddess not be amiable, the result is that ruin stares them in the face. But they seldom yield without making a violent effort to turn the tables in their favour. This they try to do in one of two ways: they either plunge deeper into the speculation, trusting by this plan to obtain a control of the market, or they resort to the fabrication of false news, hoping that the effect produced will be such as to once more make prices favourable to their operations. Rumours, lying, and every possible artifice are adopted by those who speculate on the Exchange, and it is certainly not beneficial to public morality that those should frequently succeed best who prove themselves the greatest adepts in this species of manœuvring. These few explanatory remarks, though perhaps out of place, will enable the reader to understand how practicable it is to acquire rapidly by speculation an enormous fortune, which in the ordinary course of business could be gained only after a life of persevering activity and industry.

The greater part of the Government loans which press so heavily upon the leading European States have been issued through the agency of the great financial and banking houses, at whose head stands the family of Rothschild. Being to a certain extent the originators of this description of business, and possessing such influence on the different European markets, in all of which they had branches or correspondents, it was only natural that the five brothers should manage to secure the goodwill and patronage of the various Governments. We have seen that they issued a series of loans for Denmark between 1804 and 1812, but it was not till tranquillity was restored to Europe in 1815 that the firm was called upon to show the great things of which it was capable. With that year the brothers began a period, lasting for fifteen years, during which they were incessantly engaged in the issue of Government loans. Unvarying success followed them in all their undertakings, and the firm rose to a position of such power and repute in the political and commercial world that they were the dictators of Europe. To give the reader an idea of their power, we may mention that Ferdinand I of Italy was compelled to accept the condition named by them as the only means of obtaining their aid—the recall and reinstallation in office as Finance Minister of their friend the Chevalier de Medici. And this is no exceptional case; other Governments in their extremity have been forced to agree to the terms dictated by the great financial house. We do not intend to follow and analyse each individual step the Rothschilds made on their road to fame and fortune, but will content ourselves with giving a summary of the leading operations undertaken by them in the course of the second period of their history. According to the Chevalier von Gentz, the annual business of the firm during the twelve years preceding 1826 amounted to no less than eleven or twelve hundred thousand thalers, mostly loans, but partly subsidies. This period was undoubtedly the most prosperous, and at the same time most brilliant, through which the firm has passed. The explanation of this extraordinary activity is easy. The long struggle in which all the European States had been engaged for a quarter of a century, either as the friends or the enemies of Napoleon, had drained the State treasuries of their supplies, whilst the countries were impoverished by the excessive war contributions levied to meet the expenses incidental to the prosecution of the campaigns. When the efforts of the Allies to forcibly shake off the heavy yoke of the Emperor were rewarded with success, and Napoleon placed in a position where he was powerless to threaten the peace of Europe, it was possible to form an estimate of the enormous sacrifices and expense the struggle had cost. Every State, without exception, found itself burdened with debts which seemed to crush its energies and to defy any attempt that might be made to remove them. However, all this was set once more in order and prosperity restored between the years 1815 and 1830; thanks chiefly to the assistance lent by the Rothschilds. According to a careful estimate, the loans negotiated by them during this period for the five great European States, England, Russia, Austria, France, and Prussia, amounted to very nearly one thousand million thalers. Hitherto we have spoken in very general terms of the business of the firm, but it is almost impossible for the reader to form a just conception of the magnitude of the firm's operations without some details being given. We shall therefore proceed to describe a few of the principal loans brought out under the auspices of the Rothschilds.

One of the earliest loans contracted for by the Rothschilds was that issued in 1818 for the benefit of the Prussian Government. This loan, better known as the English loan, was for £5,000,000 sterling. The terms on which it was issued were far from favourable to the Government, and gave a good idea of the low state of credit prevailing at the time. The Government guaranteed interest on the loan at the rate of 5 per cent. They found, however, that they were utterly unable to obtain a better price than 70 per cent, on the first half. The other half was issued, in two portions, at the price of 72½ and 75 respectively, but the whole amount was not applied for. That everything was done to gain the favour of the public is clear, as provision was made to pay off 3 per cent, of the loan in the first year, 2½ per cent, in the second, 2 in the third, 1½ in the fourth, and 1 per cent, in the fifth. In 1830 the remainder of the amount was converted into a Four per Cent., to redeem which a sinking fund of 1 per cent, and the interest accruing from bonds drawn after 1835 were set aside. In 1822 a second English loan of three and a half million at 5 per cent, was concluded, and was followed in 1830 by the third Prussian-English loan at 4 per cent., of which mention was made above.

Austria found herself compelled, like Prussia, to issue several loans, partly through the agency of the Rothschilds, and partly through them and other banking firms. The first loan was the lottery loan of 1820 for 20,800,000 guldens, contracted for by S. M. von Rothschild, in conjunction with David Parisch. The second followed in 1821, and was for 37½ million guldens, in shares of 250 guldens, bearing 5 per cent, interest. In 1834 Austria negotiated a third loan for 25 million guldens at 4 per cent, in shares of 500 guldens, with the firms of Rothschild, Arnstein, Eskeles, Sina, and Geymüller and Co. The same firms issued a fourth loan in 1839, amounting to 30 million guldens, in bonds of 250 guldens each.

Russia in 1822 raised a loan of 3½ million sterling through the Rothschilds, and in 1847 France followed suit with a loan of 250 million francs, issued at 75. In 1834 a Greek loan of 66 million francs was issued at 94 per cent., whilst in 1831 Belgium floated one for 50 million francs. The operations of the firm were not confined to Europe, as on several occasions the Empire of Brazil sought its assistance—to the extent of £3,200,000 in 1824, and £800,000 in 1829.

In addition to these Government loans, others were issued in large numbers on behalf of the different German principalities. It was thus the Grand Duchy of Hesse obtained in 1825 6½ million guldens, and 2,375,000 guldens in 1834. The Duchy of Nassau in 1837 placed a loan of 2,600,000 guldens.

Besides these the following loans were issued at different periods. In 1821, for the kingdom of Naples, 16 million ducats, 20 million in 1822, and £2,500,000 sterling in 1824. The Papal States, 16 million francs in 1831, followed by 2,160,000 francs in 1845. Hesse-Homburg, 1¾ million guldens, 1829; Hohenzollern-Hechingen, 260,000 guldens in 1829; Sachsen-Coburg-Gotha, 3½ million guldens; the Duchy of Lucca, 1,050,000 guldens in 1840, and 1,120,000 in 1843. Baden, in 1840, 1845, 1848, 1849, and 1850, issued loans for 5, 14, 2½, 1½, and 1½ million guldens respectively. Hanover in 1847 had a loan of 3,600,000 thalers; Bavaria, in 1848, 22 million guldens; Hesse, four loans from 1848 to 1851, amounting to 6½ million guldens; and Nassau, 1,200,000 guldens in 1849.

The above list is far from complete, but it will suffice, we think, to convey some impression of the vast proportions and unlimited extent of the business transacted by the Rothschilds since the commencement of their remarkable career. During this second period the reputation and influence of the firm may be said to have reached its zenith. Honours and decorations were showered by grateful Governments upon their benefactors, who were everywhere treated with a deferential consideration a monarch might well envy. In 1815 they were nominated private financial advisers to the Elector of Hesse, and in 1818 appointed members of the aulic commercial council of Prussia. In 1815 the Emperor Francis of Austria conferred upon them a hereditary title of nobility, and in 1822 raised them to the rank of barons. In addition to this the brother in London was appointed at first Consul and then Consul-General for Austria, an honour which his brother likewise enjoyed in Paris. In 1823, Baron James of Paris received the cross of Chevalier of the Legion of Honour, and was afterwards created a Commander of that order. Sir Anthony de Rothschild received his baronetage in 1846, and the title has now descended to Sir Nathaniel de Rothschild (Lord Rothschild), the present head of the London firm.

The third period of the firm's history dates from 1830 to the present time. During the latter part of the second period there occurred in the financial and commercial world that memorable crisis, even now recollected by many as if it were but of yesterday, so terrible was the panic it created. Owing to the abundance of money in the years immediately preceding, some difficulty was experienced in investing capital in good paying undertakings, and by degrees a speculative mania, which reached its climax in 1825, took possession of the public. A collapse ensued, and in 1826 its effects began to be felt, as one by one firms and banks of hitherto undoubted credit and solvability failed.

The ruin and distress caused by these failures were widespread, the whole country being more or less affected; and, as is usual in such cases, the evil was felt most by persons who had been led away by the plausibility and specious promises of designing rogues. So great was the blow given to credit, that many firms were brought to the verge of ruin owing to the support of the banks being suddenly withheld?

The Bank of England even came in for a share of suspicion, or at least the confidence of its customers was so shaken that a run upon its coffers took place, and threatened at one time to make it close its doors. That this was prevented was, as is well known, largely due to the loyal support rendered the bank by Nathan Mayer Rothschild. Scarcely had credit recovered from this shock, and commerce once more regained its prosperity, than an unexpected blow was struck, and again shook the financial world to its very foundations. In 1830 the French Revolution of July took everyone by surprise, and brought about a period of great uncertainty and anxiety. On this occasion, as in 1826, the Rothschilds rendered great and inestimable services to the public by aiding, with their immense means and credit, many houses threatened with ruin through no fault of their own. There can be no doubt that this bold and public-spirited course of action went far to restore confidence, whilst it certainly added greatly to the repute and honour of the firm. For the next eighteen years after this subversion of things in France, matters remained undisturbed under Louis Philippe, the head and founder of the new dynasty, and Europe enjoyed a period of unbroken repose. And never did the star of the Rothschilds shine with such unrivalled brilliance as during these eighteen years, when their advice was sought for by those in power.

But at the expiration of that time events occurred with equal suddenness, and as little anticipated as those of 1830, which have had a prejudicial effect on the business of the great financial firm. During the period of undisturbed tranquillity through which France passed after the Restoration, time was found to attend to the introduction of much-needed reforms in the Government and Constitution. Necessarily the finances were the first subject to come under review, and in 1848, after a great deal of debating, a reform was made in the system by which the Government had been wont to raise what money it required to borrow, and the hitherto all potent influence of the Rothschilds received a blow from which it has never since recovered. From the beginning of this century the credit of the European Governments had risen steadily.

In the early part of the century it was impossible for them to obtain even at 6 per cent, the money they required, whereas in 1848 no Government would have experienced any difficulty in borrowing what sum they pleased at 4 per cent. After the revolution of 1848 the French Government felt convinced they could obtain the money required by the State on easier terms than those previously accepted; they were confident they could procure first hand, without the intervention of any banker, the funds of which they stood in need; they addressed themselves frankly and directly to the people, and the people fully justified the faith reposed in their liberality by placing at the disposal of the Government sums frequently ten times the amount demanded.

The quite unexpected success that attended the Government's action has had an immense bearing on the mode in which State finances have since been conducted, and has proved highly beneficial to the State itself, as well as to individual persons. Since that time the immense preliminary profits, in the way of commission, which always went into the banker's pockets, have been abolished, and, whilst the business is conducted far more economically, the intervention of bankers and others is done away with, and the State and its subjects brought into closer contact. The result of the new measures was that all the great banking firms who had been accustomed to undertake loan business for the Government were unable to secure for themselves any advantages not enjoyed by every private person, by every citizen; the old connections with the Government were severed, and thenceforth financiers, banking houses, and citizens were equal. The gilt having been so roughly taken off the gingerbread, the great houses were forced to seek the profits they had been wont to make out of Government business in enterprises of another description. Gradually we find commercial undertakings engaging the attention of the leading capitalists and bankers.

The new arrangements of the Government were a severe blow to the Rothschilds, who had issued for many years the majority of the loans needed by the different States. From that time forward, from that "mad year 1848," so detrimental to their interests, the great firm have pursued an entirely new path. They have, for instance, aided in the formation and establishment of every description of industrial enterprises, in railways, mining, and such-like companies, but more especially in banking and credit institutions, all of which formed admirable foundations for speculation. It cannot be denied that the immense and preponderating influence possessed by the Rothschilds up till that time, began to wane when they lost the business which had been regarded as peculiarly their own, and could no longer sway the money market by their nod as of old. They were forced to put themselves on a level with many other great banking and financial firms.

In writing thus it must be distinctly understood that we do not mean to say that the pecuniary resources of the firm were in the least affected by the change; their financial position was as strong as ever, but naturally their having been for so long the trusted and favoured agents of the Government had lent their name a certain pomp and splendour which disappeared when the Government determined to act in future without their aid. Backed up as the Rothschilds are by the enormous wealth of the whole family, and the immense credit attached to their name, they are able still to make large profits in their enterprises, as they are able to wait until a favourable moment occurs for securing the success of their operations. Nothing proves more strongly the energy and vigour of the firm and their capability of still engaging single-handed in colossal enterprises, than the assistance they have of late years lent the English Government. In 1876, as is well known, they advanced the sum of four million pounds sterling to the British Government, to enable the latter to complete the purchase of Suez Canal shares from the Khedive, and in 1884 they once more responded to an appeal for pecuniary aid, by lending the Egyptian Government a sum amounting to one million sterling. Though perhaps more sedate in its movements than in its earlier years, the great firm shows no sign of decay or weakening of its powers.

The first, and head establishment of the firm, was that founded by Mayer Amschel Rothschild in Frankfort-on-the-Main. It was the only one till 1798, when a second establishment was formed in London, to be followed, in 1812, by that in Paris. These two establishments belong to the first period of the firm's history. In the second period falls the creation of the other great houses, namely, that of the Vienna house, about 1816, and that of the house in Naples, in 1820. At the head of these five houses were the five sons of Mayer Amschel.

The eldest, Anselm, directed the affairs of the Frankfort house until his death on the 3rd December, 1855; the third brother, Nathan, guided the fortunes of the London firm until 1836, in which year he died. James de Rothschild, the youngest of the five sons, presided over the destinies of the Paris house; he outlived all his brothers by some ten or twelve years, dying on the 15th November, 1868. Salomon von Rothschild of Vienna, died on the 27th July, 1855, and Carl Mayer de Rothschild, the head of the Naples firm, on the 10th March of the same year. The Naples firm has since ceased to exist, but at the head of the remaining four firms are the descendants of the five brothers. In addition to these great establishments managed by members of the family, there are, in every great capital, agents and representatives who watch vigilantly over its interests, and execute the orders given them.

The political events of this century have had so important a bearing on the fortunes of the Rothschilds that we may be allowed to give a brief summary of the leading incidents which have been so instrumental in promoting the success of the millionaire family. In the first period of the firm's history there occurred a succession of remarkable events which threatened the welfare of many European States. The first to attract attention was the outbreak of the War of Independence in America, a war which terminated so disastrously for the honour of England. But, disastrous as was the end of this outbreak to England, it was not to be compared with the evil and ruinous consequences the first French Revolution entailed upon France. Yet, harmful as these episodes were to the countries concerned, they were far from being so prejudicial to the interests of individual persons. To the Rothschilds nothing could have occurred more propitiously than the outbreak of the American revolt, and that of the French Revolution, as the two enabled them by their intimate relations with the Landgrave to lay the foundation of the immense wealth they have since acquired.

To this same period belongs the gradual rise of Napoleon, and his elevation to the throne of France, followed at length by his overthrow and abdication, but not until he had forced all Europe to acknowledge and tremble beneath his despotic sway. As Napoleon's star sank and disappeared, that of the Rothschilds rose and increased in brilliance. When Napoleon was finally crushed at Waterloo, his star vanished forever, whilst that of the Rothschilds seemed to grow every day in power and to dwarf all others. The Rothschilds belong to no one nationality, they are cosmopolitan, and, whilst on the one hand they provided supplies for the armies of Napoleon, on the other, they raised loans for his foes, who used the funds thus obtained in defraying the cost of their campaigns against him; they belonged to no party, they were ready to grow rich at the expense of friends and foes alike. The fall of Napoleon was the rise of Rothschild. By means of couriers and expresses who brought the great firm news of Napoleon's defeat long before the world generally was in possession of the joyful intelligence, the Rothschilds were able to purchase on a gigantic scale, so that when the news became known and the funds in response to the public joy rose with a bound, the gains accruing from the transactions were unprecedentedly large.

From that time forward the house occupied a prominent position in the political world; it was regarded as a power whose opinions must be consulted before any great financial operation was undertaken. From that time forward the co-operation of the firm was sought by all the leading States whenever a loan was required, and to receive such assistance was regarded by the recipients very much as a favour not granted at random. With the French July Revolution the firm entered upon its third period, a period during which the influence and position of the several houses attained a height which would have vastly surprised the old banker, Mayer Amschel. History does not record another instance of any one private firm holding so prominent a position, or exercising such a powerful control over the destinies of nations, as is furnished by the Rothschild family. It is almost impossible to describe their influence upon the history of the last fifty years, for the effect of their actions and advice upon the policies of the different Cabinets is not easily seen, owing to the unobtrusive and undemonstrative way in which they always bore themselves in public affairs. They never held any official Cabinet rank, consequently their opinions were seldom publicly ventilated; but, notwithstanding this, they always enjoyed the full confidence of the different Governments who were forced on more than one occasion to seek the counsel of the powerful financiers.

No firm or family has ever figured so prominently in history, and yet no family has been so uniformly quiet and unassuming in its demeanour. It never tries to force the public to adopt its opinions, but is content to bring the weight of its influence to bear privately, in a manner which cannot fail to secure careful consideration to whatever plans or suggestions it may think fit to propose. In France it is well known that

Baron James was one of the most trusted and esteemed counsellors of the Bourbons and of the Emperor Napoleon, and it is the same in England, Germany, and Austria. The late Baron Lionel de Rothschild was for many years a Member of Parliament, and sat on many of the Committees, where his opinions always commanded respect and attention. Nothing demonstrated so clearly the immense power exercised by the firm as the guarantee given by Baron Lionel at the conclusion of the Franco-German War to the German Government to maintain the stability of the foreign exchanges—a guarantee which greatly facilitated the payment of the indemnity.

The Rothschilds are not content to allow their influence to rest merely on the possession of boundless wealth; they seek to extend and increase it still further by becoming owners of land on a large scale—a course by which their interests and those of the nation are more closely linked together. In England, France, Germany, and Austria they possess immense estates, and there can be no doubt that the fact of their possessing such an important stake in the continued prosperity of the different countries, leads the public to attach greater weight to their opinions, and greater importance to their proceedings, than would otherwise be the case. One of the largest estates belonging to the family was that acquired by the purchase, in 1844, of the manors of Schillersdorf, Oderberg, and Hultschin, in Ober-Schlesien, near the Austrian frontiers. Schillersdorf was at one time in the hands of the Jesuits, and afterwards passed into those of the von Eichendorff family. This extensive property, which included a number of villages, was at first laid out for agricultural purposes by its new owner, and supplied the beetroot and turnips for the sugar manufactories which were erected on it. Owing to lower taxes and State subsidies, the manufacture of sugar could be carried on much more profitably in Austria than in the Zollverein, and the profits were still further increased by a little artifice which cheated the Government out of part of the duty. A large proportion of the sugar manufactured was for Russian consumption, and, as the manufactory was close to the frontier, the beetroots were brought across in a dried state, as produce for which the duty was a mere trifle. The weight being considerably reduced by this means, a large saving was effected in the duty. The profits derived from the estate were, however, not large enough to please its owner, and it was afterwards split up amongst a number of tenants. In France the Rothschilds have several very large estates and vineyards. Baron Alphonse's chateau at Ferrieres is famed for the brilliant hunting parties that frequently assemble there, and has been the scene of more than one historic meeting. During the siege of Paris it was chosen as the headquarters of Prince Frederick William of Prussia and Prince Bismarck. It was there that Ferry went to negotiate for an armistice, and that the terms of the capitulation were finally arranged. In England the Rothschilds are amongst the largest landowners, and own between them a large part of Buckinghamshire and Hertfordshire, in which counties there is quite a cluster of their estates. Sir Nathaniel de Rothschild owns a fine property at Tring; Mr. Leopold de Rothschild has an estate at Ascott, near Leighton Buzzard; Mr. Alfred de Rothschild, one at Alton; Lady Anthony de Rothschild, one at Aston Clinton; Baron Ferdinand, from Vienna, one at Waddesden. In addition to these country estates, they each have a palatial town residence, where the most brilliant receptions and most sumptuous dinners are given. There is still to be mentioned the grand old Gunnersbury House, with its magnificent grounds, where the late Baron Lionel de Rothschild used to reside.

"How has the house of Rothschild amassed such untold wealth?" is a question one is continually striving to answer, but to answer it fully and completely would necessitate our examining and analysing all the manipulations and undertakings of the great firm from its commencement. It is indeed remarkable that this one firm should have so speculated as not only to have enriched and strengthened itself, but to have risen steadily to a position exalted far above all rivals. The ways and means employed by its members were open to all, and all were at liberty to make what use they pleased of them 5 but the Rothschilds were ever masters in the art of speculation, and soon outstripped all competitors, and left them far in the rear. Their speculations were at once simple and clear.

These masters of finance first laid down the lines of the speculation, and fixed the aim and object of their efforts clearly in their minds, keeping their whole attention fixed on the main points, and never troubling themselves about the details. The manifold and apparently often contradictory manœuvres effected by the firm were always dictated by an unswerving regard to the object they had in view. Nothing, indeed, was simpler than the mode in which they won their enormous profits. For instance, they issued a loan at a certain price—already, perhaps, 2 or 3 per cent, above the contract price. This of itself was a handsome profit to start with, and one which can seldom be secured now, when nearly all first-class loans are brought out on commission. Competition was less keen then, whilst joint-stock banks and kindred institutions were in their infancy. But the public had confidence in the loan, the Stock Exchange was in its favour, and it at once rose to a good premium on its issue price.

An ordinary speculator would perhaps have been content with profits such as these, but not so the Rothschilds. They still further multiplied their gains by selling, buying, and re-selling continuously the same stocks, until the profits reached, in many cases, an almost incredible figure. Through operations calculated to bring about a fall or a rise, as the case might be, in the prices of particular stocks, the Rothschilds went on unceasingly amassing their millions, and these operations, by the violent fluctuations they produced, formed the basis on which the fortunes of the firm were laid. In order to render these great speculative operations successful, every means at their command was employed. Every method that could be devised was resorted to; every Stock Exchange manœuvre and artifice called into requisition; every sort of rumour and false news promulgated; and money in large and small sums sacrificed to secure the success of their schemes. This, then, was how the earlier Rothschilds amassed their millions, which the present representatives strive to keep and augment steadily and cautiously, without grasping at the handsome, old-fashioned profits of by-gone days.

The greatest gains are made during times of great excitement, when war is imminent, or when a political crisis paralyzes trade and fills the public with anxiety and doubt. To obtain early and previous warning of such weighty occurrences is of the most vital importance to speculators, because, possessed of such information, they are often enabled to steal a march on their rivals and turn their knowledge to profitable account. To gain a start of a few minutes is of immense consequence, making a difference of perhaps thousands of pounds, and, certainly, in this sense, time is unquestionably money, for the fortune or ruin of many on the Stock Exchange is decided in a few moments. Knowing this, it has always been the first care of the Rothschilds to secure the earliest information possible of all such weighty events, more particularly of those in the sphere of politics, and it is especially their interest to discover and favour persons who, owing to their position in official or business circles, are likely to receive the earliest news of occurrences of that description.

In addition to their agents and informants in political and official circles, they had in every great capital throughout the world representatives whose duty it was to hunt up and report all that was going on of a nature likely to affect the money market directly or indirectly. The excellence of their system of obtaining early information of passing events has been proved on many occasions, and they have been the first to furnish the Governments with details of more than one occurrence long before the reports reached them through official and privileged channels. The expresses and couriers of the Rothschilds tore along at break-neck speed, as if on a matter of life and death, whilst the Government couriers were content with journeying by comparatively short and easy stages. The news of Napoleon's defeat at Waterloo was, as already stated, known to the Rothschilds several days before the public learned the joyful tidings, and Lord Aberdeen was indebted to them for the first information regarding the outbreak of the French July Revolution. Then, again, the position they held with respect to the Continental railways was greatly in their favour. They were the "Hudsons" of the Continent; all the leading lines were of their creation, and at their disposal. This gave them an immense advantage, and it was nothing unusual when important news reached them to dispatch a special locomotive with a courier to communicate the news as speedily as possible to their other houses. After the invention of the telegraph the capabilities and advantages of the new means of communication were readily appreciated by them, and most extensively employed to promote the success of their operations. It is indeed scarcely surprising, when the odds were so much in their favour, that their career should have been an almost unbroken success. It happened, of course, at times that their anticipations were disappointed, that their information proved incorrect, and that their calculations were upset; but such an occurrence was rare and exceptional.

The success of the Rothschild family is ascribed by the Chevalier von Gentz, an intimate personal friend of Baron Salomon von Rothschild, of Vienna, and consequently well qualified to form an opinion, to two causes, which he specifies in the following terms:—"The question how the house of Rothschild has been able to undertake and carry through in so short a time all that it has really accomplished has exercised the brains of many a business and political head. Perhaps, however, the answer is not so difficult as it is generally thought to be. He who, without waiting upon chance, has sufficient sense to perceive that the issue of all great transactions depends not alone on the choice and use of a favourable moment, but also, and even more, on the rigid adherence to once-recognized fundamental principles, will readily acknowledge that there were two principles especially, of which this firm never lost sight, and to which, combined with prudent management and profitable conjunctures, it is certainly indebted for the greatest share of its present prosperity.

Fig. V: CHEVALIER FRIEDRICH VON GENTZ
(1764–1832)
GERMAN POLITICIAN, DIPLOMAT & PHILOSOPH

Source: Hans Wahl, Anton Kippenberg: Goethe und seine Welt. Insel-Verlag, Leipzig 1932 S. 162.

"The first of these principles was that which led the five brothers to conduct all their businesses in a long and unbroken unanimity of aims and interests. This was the injunction left them by their father on his death-bed, and, if a lucky star has stood over them, they have ever remained firm in their resolve never to prove forgetful of that injunction. Since their father's death, every proposition, no matter from what quarter it came, has been the subject of their united consideration and discussion. Every operation, even if of only comparative importance, was carried out on a concerted plan, and with the united efforts of all, and all were equal participators in the profits. Though their places of abode have for some years been far apart, even this circumstance failed to destroy the close understanding which exists between the brothers, but rather worked to their advantage, since each, being more thoroughly informed of the state of affairs in the different capitals, was able to prepare and manage so much more effectively the businesses that were to be undertaken by the firm as a body." In this view the writer is backed by the author of "Society in London," who is evidently intimately acquainted with the family, and well qualified to express an opinion. "The family genius of the Rothschilds," says he, "shows itself equally in the understanding they maintain amongst themselves and the relations they establish with all those who can be useful to them. It is only natural that a house divided, as the Rothschilds are, into branches, each branch being a separate dynasty, should have its own little jealousies. There could be no more solid monument to their shrewdness and sagacity than that they should not suffer these jealousies to hold them apart at critical moments when union is strength. Nor do they choose their friends and agents outside themselves with less discrimination, or treat them with less of wise generosity and forbearance. They know exactly whom to select for their purposes, and, once having made their choice, they are loyal to it. Many men are indebted to the Rothschilds for their fortune. No one who has once placed his trust in them, and whom they have found it worth their while to trust, can reproach them with having deserted him."

"The other principle," continues von Gentz, "which demands notice, is that which guided them never to strive after extravagant profits in any of their undertakings, but to set limits to their operations, and to render themselves independent, as far as human foresight and wisdom could do so, of the freaks of chance. In the maxim *Servare modum, finemque tenere*, lies one of the great secrets of their strength. There can be no doubt that with the means at their command they could, in this or that operation, have raised their profits to a much higher figure. Even if, however, the safety of their undertakings would not have suffered thereby, they would in the long run have gained less than by extending their forces to a larger number of businesses, ever requiring renewal under all kinds of circumstances. To fail in their undertakings was out of the question, for they staked not merely their wealth and their credit, but also the confidence with which the fairness of their demands, the punctuality of their payments, the clearness and simplicity of their plans, together with the clever way in which those plans were carried out, had inspired the various Governments and all the great business firms. What others sought to gain by so-called decisive strokes, which lead to victory on the field of business as on the field of battle, but which also often lead to great reverses, the Rothschilds have won by the happy use of the best principles of commercial strategy; not through boldness, but by prudence and perseverance.

"The personal and moral characters of the five brothers have contributed in no small measure to the success of their enterprises. If he is powerful enough it is not difficult for a man to secure a numerous following on his side, but in the present instance the voices of all parties unite, and the Rothschilds are, as the phrase goes, respected by great and small, not merely on account of their wealth, but for qualities of heart and soul not invariably associated with riches and power. To be always extending their sphere of kindness, to withhold their hand from none in distress, to advance readily to the assistance of all who solicited their aid, no matter to what class they might belong, and ever to bestow their most substantial favour in the kindest and most feeling manner,—these were the ways by which the Rothschilds won the real and well-merited popularity that is theirs, as many thousands of witnesses and whole families will testify. And this beneficence springs from their innate good-nature and humane disposition, and not from calculation. Moreover, they have been so fortunate as not to have raised up a host of enemies along with their host of friends, which is rarely the case with persons who have risen suddenly to wealth and celebrity. It may be truly said that they have disarmed envy itself, and rendered harmless the tongue of slander."

"There is but one power in Europe," said the French writer Weill, "and that is Rothschild. His satellites are a dozen other banking firms; his soldiers, his squires, all respectable men of business and merchants; and his Sword is speculation. Rothschild is a consequence that was bound to appear; and, if it had not been a Rothschild, it would have been someone else. He is, however, by no means an accidental consequence, but a primary consequence, called into existence by the principles which have guided the European States since 1813. Rothschild had need of the States to become a Rothschild, while the States on their side required Rothschild. Now, however, he no longer needs the State, but the State still has want of him."

CHAPTER IV

ANSELM MAYER von ROTHSCHILD.

THE FRANKFORT FIRM *(continued)*.

WHAT the considerations were which guided Mayer Amschel Rothschild when he turned his back upon Hanover to select Frankfort as the place for starting in business on his own account, and for laying the foundations of a fortune which was to eventually attain such colossal proportions, are of course unknown to us, but we may reasonably suppose that his choice was influenced by early associations.

Frankfort was his birthplace, and it may be to this circumstance that it is indebted for the immense benefits it derived from the subsequent career of the great family within its walls. There can be no doubt that to the Rothschilds the city of Frankfort owes not only its present importance, but much of its commercial prosperity. In settling in his native town and in starting business there, Mayer Amschel increased the chances in his favour, as he was intimately acquainted with the neighbourhood and the opportunities of making money that were likely to present themselves. But, whatever may have been his motives for returning to and settling in Frankfort, we know that he did, in or about 1770, set up there in a humble way of business as a dealer in old coins, etc., with a capital derived from his savings, and that his industry and honesty were such as to enable him to extend his sphere of action by dealing in works of art, old gold and silver, and, in course of time, to add to these pursuits bullion and bill-broking. Gradually, as he strengthened his position, his business assumed more the nature of an ordinary banking business, which continued to raise the name and repute of the founder as a skilful and fair-dealing financier, in whom every confidence could be safely reposed. Little could Mayer Amschel have anticipated that the humble shop was destined to ultimately grow into one of the largest and most renowned banking firms of the world, and that his sons would in after years come to exercise such an unbounded sway that the peace of nations would depend upon their nod; that the powerful control they exercised on the European money markets would enable them to pose as the arbiters of peace and war, since they could at their pleasure withhold or furnish the pecuniary means required to carry on a campaign. But this, incredible as it may seem, was what their vast influence, combined with their enormous wealth and unlimited credit, enabled them to do, for no firms existed strong enough to oppose them for any length of time, or rash enough to take up a business which the Rothschilds had refused. To reach this exalted position Mayer Amschel and his sons required the cooperation of the States, but, when once he had climbed over their backs and reached the height of his ambition, he was independent of all aid and could act with the greatest freedom, whilst the States remained in a suppliant attitude at his feet.

The house of Rothschild when at the summit of its might was the ruling power in Europe, for all the political powers were willing to acknowledge the sway of the great financial despot, and, like obedient vassals, to pay their tribute without a murmur.

Frankfort, the birthplace of this great firm, derives its name from a fort built by the Romans on the banks of the Main, to guard the frontiers and to resist the incursions of the Goths, on the opposite bank, who, though daring enough in hand-to-hand contests, shrank from attacking an enemy hidden in a fort surrounded by high ramparts and deep ditches. By what Roman general Frankfort was built is not, we believe, known, but during the reign of Charlemagne the place acquired additional importance from the palace constructed there by that great warrior, who brought quite a colony in his train. The Römer, or town-hall, is probably part of this palace, which was erected on the same plans as that at Aix-la-Chapelle. The natural advantages which Frankfort possessed, from its favourable situation on the banks of the navigable Main, and the fruitfulness of the neighbourhood, were all conducive from an early date to the growth of its trade. The whole of the commerce of Germany was at that time of the smallest, and Frankfort was but a poor place, with an inconsiderable traffic, until the bright thought struck Charlemagne of uniting the Main with the Donau by a canal, thus enabling merchandise to be brought from Constantinople and the East directly into the heart of Germany. In order to attract thither people from other parts of Germany, and foreigners from other countries, he instituted yearly markets which afterwards gave rise to the famous fairs. In the midst of endless feuds between rapacious neighbours and riving knights, and in spite of the disturbed times, Frankfort continued to grow in prosperity and importance, which were still further favoured and fostered by several laws, passed with a view to providing escorts and protection to all visitors and traders—for the emperors saw and recognized of what vast moment trade was to the public welfare. Warehouses, granaries, and shops were built in large numbers, and Frederick II showed how greatly he appreciated the advantages of trade by granting the city a charter for its autumn fair, a privilege still further extended by Ludovic II, who contributed largely to the prosperity and consequence of Frankfort by the many diets he held there. There are numerous proofs existing to show that the power and influence of Frankfort during the Middle Ages was considerable. Cologne and Strasburg were its only business rivals. These three towns were by far the greatest centres of trade in that part of Germany. In wealth Frank-fort was inferior to few, whilst its dignity cannot have been small when it took precedence of stately Nuremberg at the coronation of Maximilian I The Golden Bulls of the Pope declared that the Roman elections should always be held in Frankfort, and this cannot have failed to favour the fortunes of the city, necessitating as it did splendid pageants and sumptuous banquets which made money flow freely into the pockets of the worthy citizens. In the course of time patents and privileges of all kinds tending to foster and encourage trade were conferred upon the city, and in 1510 the right of coining money was conceded to it by the emperor.

The powerful Hanseatic League had broken down, and the fetters which it had kept on commercial activity in Germany were removed. Frankfort was immediately sensible of the beneficial effects of the change, as Nuremberg began to send thither part of its manufactures, Augsburg its cloth and silk goods, and Ulm its linen and cotton goods. Even Aix-la-Chapelle and Dortmund entered into business relations with their young rival, who soon outstripped them in the race for first place, and continued to grow in consideration and wealth. The discovery of America was turned to profitable account, as the merchants and traders of Frankfort were among the first who endeavoured to extend their business relations to the New World. Trade in Frankfort during the early part of the seventeenth century had been severely affected by the war, but towards the latter part it began to make rapid progress towards recovery, owing, no doubt, in a great measure to the famous fairs which attracted men of business from all parts of Europe. The rapid revival of its trade was still further promoted by the disappearance of the Hanseatic League, which had till then enjoyed a monopoly of the English cloth trade. This, however, now passed out of the hands of its traders, as a direct market was found for English goods in Frankfort. The wine trade was equally flourishing, for Rhenish wines were highly esteemed in all parts of Europe. At this period a new branch of industry was started and rapidly extended by the enterprising traders—the trade in books. In a comparatively short time, owing to the extensive printing works which were erected, the book trade of Frankfort assumed enormous proportions. The great autumn fair soon came to be recognized as the lagest book fair on the Continent, for it was the rendezvous of booksellers and dealers from all parts of Europe. The concourse of persons attracted by the fair is said to have numbered as many as 400,000, so that the advantages derived from these monster gatherings must have been of the utmost value to the prosperity of the city. The rapid rise of Frankfort had been watched with bitter jealousy by many of its older rivals, who tried to injure and destroy its trade by all means at their command. How intense was the animosity they cherished against

Fig. VI: ANSELM MAYER ROTHSCHILD
(1808–1879)
INTERNATIONAL BANKER
HEAD OF THE BRANCH OF FRANCFORT

Painting by Moritz Daniel Oppenheim (died 1882), National Portrait Gallery: NPG 3838.

their younger rival is seen from the fact that Nuremberg carried its hatred and envy so far as to forbid its citizens under pain of death from attending the Frankfort fairs. Frankfort, however, shrank from no sacrifice and spared no exertion to secure the safety of its trade. In all its leagues with its neighbours the main condition of its co-operation was the support and protection to be given to the fairs. Everything was done to insure the safety of visitors and their goods, escorts even being provided for that purpose. These famous fairs have evoked the wonder and surprise of many writers, who have borne testimony to their importance by the lavish praise they have bestowed upon them. "The Frankfort fair," said one, "is the chief of the yearly markets of the world," whilst another concisely described it as "the world in a nutshell; or the magazine of the Germans." To the fairs Frankfort is indebted for its first newspaper, the "Messrelationen," which was in existence for some two hundred years. The fairs likewise called into prominence a branch of business, namely, bills of exchange, which has tended greatly to facilitate and develop commercial transactions all over the world. Instead of the inconvenient and cumbrous method of settling every transaction by a money payment, recourse was had to the far more convenient and reasonable plan of paying by the medium of bills of exchange. If some such plan as this had not been adopted the trade of Frankfort could never have gone on increasing as it has done. When dealings had to be settled by a payment in money, they were necessarily on a very restricted scale owing to the immense weight of the coin, to say nothing of the risks that a person would run who was in the habit of carrying about with him large sums in cash. With bills of exchange the risk is greatly reduced, whilst the advantages they offer in transferability and portability are such as to need no demonstration. The fairs, as we have said, brought a vast business to Frankfort, which was moreover a sort of half-way house for the rest of Germany, a large portion of the imports and exports passing through the hands of its merchants. Being then the centre of trade, and doing an immense business in bills of exchange, the Frankfort prices came to be watched and studied with as much care as those of other great commercial centres such as Rotterdam or Antwerp. The importance of the Frankfort Exchange after the Rothschilds had founded their extensive business was vastly increased owing to the intimate connections and vast influence possessed by the firm in the other large cities of Europe. In every large town they have either branches of their own, or active agents who are ever seeking to promote their interests, and ever faithfully reporting to them all that occurs in financial or commercial circles. This goes far to explain the problem how they have been able to amass their immense fortune so rapidly, for it must not be forgotten that the members of the family, while carrying on their respective businesses independently of each other, on all momentous occasions unite their forces for the common benefit, and temporarily concentrate all their thoughts and energies on achieving the success of the operations in hand. It is hardly strange, therefore, to find that the wheel of fortune, when the family bring their collective wealth and influence to bear in this fashion upon it, should yield to their persuasive efforts and take the direction they desire.

On the death of Mayer Amschel, the founder of the firm, the management of the affairs of the Frankfort house naturally passed into the hands of his eldest son, Anselm Mayer, who retained it until his death, which took place on the 6th December, 1855. Anselm Mayer was above all things a man of business, in which his inmost soul seemed concentrated. These words sum up his whole character. But, able and clever as he was, the individuality of his third brother Nathan, the head of the London house, was even more striking in regard to business matters, for he distinguished himself from his elder brother by his unrivalled financial skill and daring, by his greater shrewdness, and by his intuitive power of forecasting the course of either the money market or of politics, all of which gifts he turned to the utmost profit. In a word, Nathan Mayer was a greater financier, a greater speculator and manipulator, and, although self-taught, of more solid and useful acquirements. To the house this was, however, of secondary importance, seeing that the more weighty operations were planned and carried out by all the brothers in concert, whilst the times in which they lived were so eminently favourable to the success of their enterprises that to them they are as much indebted for the sudden growth of their immense wealth and power as to their own abilities and energies. It is here, indeed, that we must seek the explanation of the problem how they have been able in so short a time to extend and develop their business so amazingly. Circumstances, or, in other words, luck was on their side. Not that they trusted blindly to their luck, for they contributed in no small measure to their success by the prudent caution which marked all their dealings, and by the observance of maxims which had been carefully learnt and as carefully practised by all members of the family, and of these maxims the most important was: to seize upon the right moment in all political or commercial crises and turn it to profitable account.

We cannot pretend at this distance of time to be capable of giving a faithful and lifelike description of Anselm Mayer von Rothschild, the head of the Frankfort firm. We prefer, therefore, to reproduce the words of a writer who was for many years on the most intimate terms with him, and whose account may consequently be regarded as privileged and deserving credit:—

"Anselm Mayer is the oldest of the European Nabobs, with thoroughly eastern features and all the old Jewish customs and practices. He wears his hat down on the back of his head, which is covered with snow-white hair, and his coat, usually unbuttoned, hangs negligently down from his shoulders. He has an open and frank countenance, on which rests an air of assumed vivacity, whenever he thinks he is observed. His hands are usually in his trouser pockets playing with money. He invariably goes on foot, and to every beggar who accosts him he gives a coin of more or less value. His beneficence is very great—indeed, the poor Jewish families in Frankfort are mostly dependent on his bounty. It was he who contributed the greater part of the funds for the erection of the new Jewish hospital. When the weather is unusually severe, or when, for instance, a poor family is burnt out, he is particularly liberal in his charity. Should a hard frost or a prolonged drought sot in, a large crowd is sure to be seen collected before the doors of his town residence in the Fahrgasse. His house in the above-named street is an ill-looking building from the outside, and no stranger, as he passed, would guess that it was the abode of one of the richest merchants in the world. Anselm Mayer sits in his office in the midst of his clerks like a Padischah; below him are his secretaries, and around him may be seen a crowd of brokers, for ever coming and going. With a few words he dismisses each, for like a true business genius he knows at once what answer to give to every question, and what decision to arrive at on any business that may be laid before him for consideration. No one in the universe, when Anselm Mayer's yes or no has once been pronounced, would venture to renew the discussion. To speak to him privately on a matter of business is well-nigh impossible; everything in his office is done openly as in a law court. He observes and keeps the office hours as scrupulously as any of his clerks, and has indeed less opportunities for recreation than they have, seeing that even in the theatre he is likely to be disturbed and called away by the arrival of one of his couriers. For the same reason he is often forced to rise from bed in the night, to peruse the news and despatches just brought by an express, so that he can, in case of need, forward them on without delay to his brothers in Paris, Vienna, or London. To facilitate this business he has had an office erected adjoining his bedroom. He has many orders and titles, but usually he wears only the Hessian ribbon. The diplomatists resident in Frankfort, and those who may make a transitory visit there, vie in doing the great financier honour, and the most splendid banquets are given on each side. At these entertainments Anselm Mayer sits in true penance, as he never touches any viands or dishes that have not been cleansed or prepared in the Jewish fashion. This strict and unaffected observance of the religious injunctions of his faith is greatly to his honour; he is indeed regarded as the most religious Jew in Frankfort."

All writers agree in describing Anselm Mayer as a man of great shrewdness of judgment, with a thorough knowledge of mankind. By a sort of intuition he was able to form a pretty correct opinion of the character and motives of the men with whom he came in contact. No matter what cloak they might use to conceal their real object, he saw through their hypocrisy almost before they had said a word. He seldom erred in his judgment, and was remarkably quick in detecting the vanity or self-conceit of those who addressed him. True and able men were always appreciated by him at their just value: he would always deal with them at par. A man who showed himself quiet but efficient in the discharge of his duties was sure to be noticed and favoured. In his conversation Anselm Mayer was somewhat confidential, though he always allowed a certain reserve to be visible which effectually prevented the display of any want of respect towards himself. He was a man of some humour, and is remembered for the many sly and witty sayings which figured in his conversation, and with which he was in the habit of administering keen rebukes, or speaking unpalatable truths, calculated, if uttered in a stronger and plainer form, to have given offence. The many anecdotes related of him all display more or less the humour and shrewdness for which he was remarkable, and are often conspicuous for their brevity. He knew also how to clothe his sallies in befitting language. When Thorwaldsen passed through Germany he was received with enthusiastic welcomes everywhere, and innumerable banquets were given in his honour. At one of these gatherings Rothschild was introduced to the sculptor, and made the neat remark: "You look so handsome, Chevalier, that one is forced to believe you created yourself." Thorwaldsen after-wards acknowledged that he had never been paid a more novel or more flattering compliment.

Fond of wit and humour as he was, Anselm Mayer could recognize and reward wit in others, even if the sally was directed against himself. On one occasion a man wrote to him, simply saying, "Herr Baron, send me a thousand guldens—and forget me." The brevity and essentially witty character of the demand at once struck Anselm Mayer, who, in forwarding the sum demanded, replied: "I send you one thousand guldens—and have forgotten you."

When Baron Anselm Mayer went in 1832 to spend a few months of the summer at Ems, he took up his quarters in a private house on the Römerberg. At the same house there was also staying Baron von E——, a dashing Prussian Uhlan officer, with whom Baron Anselm soon became exceedingly friendly. One evening they went for a stroll in the direction of the Four Towers, and in the midst of a spirited conversation Rothschild came to a sudden halt. Taking advantage of this, an ill-clad man stole noiselessly up behind the famous banker and cleverly opened his pocket. Baron von E——, who had noticed the suspicious movement, naturally concluded that theft was the man's object; but to his surprise he noticed that the man quietly slipped a letter into the pocket and disappeared. Scarcely had Baron Rothschild resumed his walk ere the inconvenience arising from the recent contribution made itself felt. He put his hand into his pocket to discover the reason, and at once exclaimed, "Ah, I know now." It was evident that the mere touch had explained the mystery. The walk was continued along the road to Coblentz, and when they at last turned to retrace their steps dusk was already setting in. Suddenly from behind a tree a ragged fellow sprang forward and placed himself directly in Baron Anselm's path. The Baron's companion was about to strike the fellow, when he noticed the latter had neither pistol nor stiletto in his hand, but simply a begging-letter, which he sought in this violent fashion to force on Anselm Mayer. The latter betrayed not the slightest surprise or alarm, and it was evident he was by no means unaccustomed to this novel way of delivering begging-letters.

One very warm summer's day, when Baron Anselm was entertaining some friends at dinner, a window directly opposite his seat happened to be unclosed. Through the aperture thus left there presently came flying, during the dessert, a packet, so well-aimed that it fell right upon the Baron's plate. The guests were not unnaturally astonished, but Anselm Mayer quietly felt in his pocket, took out a gold piece and put it in the cover of the still unopened letter, which he returned with the same celerity and by the same way it had come. This novel and unique mode of bestowing charity was highly appreciated by his guests. Rothschild, however, was not satisfied; he could not feel easy until he knew what had become of the letter and its contents. Apologizing, therefore, to the company, he asked permission to rise a moment. He then advanced to the open window, leant out and returned, evidently satisfied and happy, saying, half audibly, "*placirt.*" It is interesting to notice how solicitous the wealthy financier was, from force of habit, to know whether even such a trifle as that which he had just given away, had been well bestowed.

Baron Anselm Mayer was proud and aristocratic in his manners only to the extent that the consciousness of his personal importance and influence was allowed to be visible; but still without any arrogance. He related, not unwillingly, the small beginnings and struggles of his firm, his walks to the office, the Friday evenings spent in the old house in the Judengasse, where white bread and roasted nuts were his fare. He referred with sovereign contempt to the conceit and arrogance of certain upstarts. He did not mix himself up with politics, and invariably spoke with considerate forbearance of the different Governments, though his partiality for Austria was always unmistakably manifest. He bestowed enormous sums in almsgiving, and, when they remembered the many calls upon his purse, and the immense amount actually distributed by him every year among the poor and the suffering, many persons, whose petitions soliciting aid for themselves or for others failed to meet with the response anticipated, have come to think more favourably of the seeming coldness they had experienced. It is impossible to estimate or describe the wonderful good effected by means of Baron Anselm's beneficence. But how great it was and how profoundly appreciated, is evidenced by the thousands of applications for relief which were annually submitted to his consideration. When he died the poor lost one of their most liberal, and at the same time most unostentatious benefactors.

He had been brought up in the midst of a family struggling hard to earn a living; his youth was passed in continued and incessant toil, so it is but natural that he was not able to boast of a very high or classical education. In later years he tried, not without success, to improve his knowledge of languages and history, and to strengthen his bodily powers, but, ever conscious of his shortcomings, he would turn away offended if any sycophant flattered him on his horsemanship or any other accomplishment. French and English he spoke very indifferently: indeed, it was only the interests of his business and perhaps a little vanity that led him ever to converse in these languages, which he spoke even worse than he did his native German. Towards ladies he always displayed a very engaging address, a lively gallantry, which he retained to the last. His love of art showed itself most strongly in his taste for coins and old metal-work; but still on paintings he was often heard to say a shrewd word of criticism. Above all things, however, he loved his garden; it was his delight to revel among his beautiful flowers, of which he never grew weary.

His position as a resident in Frankfort differed in no way from that of any other member of the Jewish community. Great as were his wealth and influence, they did not enable him to share the civil and political rights enjoyed by every Christian living in the city. For a brief period the Jews were permitted by the Prince Primate in 1812 to rank on an equal footing with their Christian neighbours, but in 1815 they were deprived of these privileges, which were not restored to them till 1853 and 1864. Whilst at one time the founder of the house of Rothschild was a member of the Elective Assembly, his son, equally with the poorest Jew in Frankfort, was debarred from taking any active part in the management of civic affairs, for he lacked the first qualification—the freedom of the city, without which none could hold office. Although siding with the strictly orthodox party of the Talmudic Judaism, Anselm Mayer did not allow any difference of opinion to disturb his sympathies with his co-religionists, and he is known to have frequently contributed largely to the erection of synagogues where the teaching would be wholly opposed to that which he favoured. At his death he left a fortune estimated as amounting to from fifty to sixty million guldens, which he willed to one of his nephews. To the Jewish community he bequeathed a handsome legacy of 1,200,000 guldens, and several others proportionately large for the benefit of the poor, who, he was fond of saying as he walked through the streets, were his "courtiers" He also left strict orders in his will for the maintenance and preservation of the old house in the Judengasse. Strict Jew as was the head of the Frankfort house, opposed as he was to every innovation in the doctrine and ritual of the synagogues, and exact as he was in his observance of the Sabbath, he nevertheless did not hesitate to trade and make money on feast days. Thus, on one occasion when he was in Aix-la-Chapelle taking part in the Congress there, a sum of money amounting to 160,000 thalers fell due to him on a Saturday. At the proper hour he presented himself at the office and demanded his money. On his attention being called to the day, he pointedly answered: "It is not every day one has to receive 160,000 thalers." He then carefully counted and pocketed the money.

The extent of the business transacted by the parent firm in Frankfort was something immense. It not only embraced the majority of the German states and principalities, but included in its clientele a large proportion of the nobility and aristocracy, especially those of South Germany, whose pecuniary resources were so embarrassed as to render the assistance of a financial house necessary and unavoidable. The number of accounts of the Frankfort house probably far exceeded that of any one of the other houses in London, Paris, or Vienna. To prove how liberal the Rothschilds were to the German princes, and to show what profitable customers the latter must have been, we give a list of those who were forced to apply to the firm for aid. Against the name of each we place the total amount of the loans, as far as can be ascertained, which he obtained:—

	Guldens
Isenburg-Birstein	1,100,000
Löwenstein-Wertheim	1,250,000
Sayn-Wittgenstein-Berleburg	300,000
Waldburg-Zeil	172,000
Graf Sandor v. Szlavnicza	670,000
Ritter von Riese	250,000
	Guldens
Isenburg-Wächtersbach	294,000
Solma-Licli	300,000
Lowenstein-Rosenberg	350,000
Prince Victor zu Isenburg	140,000
Count Viczay	700,000
Count Szapary	300,000
Count Leiningen-Westerberg	80,000
Count von Niczky	340,000
Count von Hunyady	500,000
Count von Szechenyi	1,800,000
Count Henkel v. Donnersmark	1,125,000
Count von Froberg	100,000
Prince von Galantha Esterhazy	6,400,000
Freiherr von Greifenklau	130,000
Prince Schwarzenberg	5,000,000
Prince Waldburg-Wolfegg	800,000
Prince Waldsee	350,000
Count K. von Wartemberg	2,070,000
	Total Guldens 16,021,000

This list is far from complete; still, even as it is, it gives some idea of the large business done by the firm with its private clients.

In conclusion, we may say a few words respecting the sovereignty of Baron Anselm Mayer over the Frankfort Bourse, and of the complete subordination of that institution to his will. Before the advent of the Rothschilds, Frankfort could claim no precedence over the other great trading cities of Germany; it had a large commerce, and large operations were carried on in foreign bills, but still its quotations were not so important or so influential as to cause them to be closely watched and studied. All this, however, is now altered: the movements of the Frankfort Exchange have through the magnitude of the transactions carried out by the house of Rothschild acquired an importance which makes itself felt on the markets of other leading financial centres. Paris, Frankfort, Vienna, and London are in such close communication and connection through the houses established there by the Rothschilds, that no great movement can take place in one of them without creating a marked impression in the rest.

In Frankfort the control and sway possessed by the parent house were more marked and manifest, perhaps, than was the case with its branches elsewhere. Loud and frequent complaints were made by other banking and financial firms of the prejudicial effects on business caused by the entire dependence of the Frankfort Bourse on the will of Anselm Mayer, who could at his pleasure raise or depress prices to the discomfiture of all who might happen to oppose him.

The public prints were for ever complaining of and animadverting upon the pressure of the great firm on the energies and spirits of the Bourse. Their complaints were always worded in the same unvaried strain, so that they became quite monotonous in their repetition. For instance, the remark that "money was more abundant, and might become still more so, were it not for the knowledge that the Rothschilds are so completely masters of the situation, and have the market under complete control," was a stock expression with the Frankfort editors. This pressure could not fail to prove injurious to many smaller houses, but complaints availed not; business was free to all, and speculation unhindered. The Rothschilds were at liberty to conduct their operations on whatever lines they pleased, without asking permission of any. The same freedom of action belonged to all, whether great or small. Might on the Stock Exchange means right, and if weaker speculators were made to pay heavily for the opposition, however slight, they offered to the rule of the colossal firm, they had but themselves to blame for their folly and loss.

Foreign loans became the perquisites, if we may so call them, of the Rothschilds, who were ever on the alert to secure them before a rival had any chance to step in. On one occasion another firm was bold enough to undertake a Belgian loan, on its own sole responsibility behind Rothschild's back, but was quickly made to repent of its temerity, as Rothschild put his forces in motion and bore down upon it with such resistless force that the rival house was soon glad to give in its submission and tender an apology for its presumption.

But, on the other hand, it is totally undeniable that, at different times, in circumstances of great financial pressure and during commercial crises, Rothschild rendered immense services by means of his unbounded wealth and credit to many houses, who, but for the support thus liberally provided, would have been forced to suspend payment. Not that we wish it to be supposed that Rothschild made such sacrifices from purely unselfish motives, for, however unfavourable they might appear, he usually managed to turn the circumstances of the case to profitable account. For instance, in 1832, a well-known banking establishment in Paris had accepted without adequate security a large number of bills drawn by a bank in North America, whose credit at that time was decidedly low. The suspension at an early date of the bank in Paris, was discussed and anticipated. Rothschild himself had a great many of these doubtful acceptances in his portfolio.

What did he do?

He voluntarily placed the sum of forty million thalers at the disposal of the bank, whose failure was averted, if only for a moment, as the public, seeing the apparent confidence of Baron Anselm in its solvability, not unnaturally concluded he had good reasons for his liberality and that the rumours to the contrary were ill founded.

The Paris house was saved, whilst the transaction proved very remunerative to Rothschild himself, as he had remitted this sum not in specie, or bills on other firms, but in bills, which he had bought dirt cheap, upon the bank itself.

"In this way," wrote a German journalist of Baron Anselm Mayer, "he has made himself king of finance, and his kingdom is no poetical creation but a reality. His vassals are the other banking firms and financial institutions, whom he can destroy, if he so pleases, when he no longer needs them, or support and strengthen as long as they are useful and necessary for his purposes."

Since the death of Anselm Mayer, the business of the Frankfort firm has been managed by his nephews, Baron William and Baron C. von Rothschild, who have faithfully observed the traditional policy of the family in all their financial operations. The wealth of the two brothers continues steadily to augment, thanks to the prudence and caution which mark all their undertakings. Baron Carl is a great patron of the arts, and has a collection of pictures and sculptures such as is possessed by only very few. Baron William is a most strict Jew, and rigidly observes the fasts and feasts of the Jewish calendar.[1]

[1] The death of Baron Carl, which took place quite recently, leaves his brother the sole head of the Frankfort house. Baron Carl's magnificent collection of art treasures will become the property of Lord Rothschild.

CHAPTER V

NATHAN MAYER ROTHSCHILD.

THE LONDON FIRM.

THE first step towards extending the business of the original house in Frankfort was taken in 1798 by Nathan Mayer, the third and most remarkable of all Mayer Amschel's sons, who in that year started for England with the object of creating a business of his own. To Nathan Mayer may be ascribed much of the subsequent prosperity of the family, as, by his splendid financial abilities and untiring energy, he contributed far more than any of his brothers towards raising the firm to the brilliant position it has held for the last fifty years. He it was who, by his vast schemes and far-reaching speculations, gave the firm its cosmopolitan character, whilst the great services which he, in common with his brothers, rendered to all the Governments of Europe in turn, gained for his family a reputation and a consideration such as no other firm has ever enjoyed. In an earlier part of our narrative we stated that, previous to 1798, all the business of the Frankfort house with England was transacted through the firm of Van Notten in London, who acted as the attorneys of the Elector of Hesse in receiving the latter's subsidies from the British Government, and collecting his dividends. When Nathan Mayer had established himself in London, these powers were transferred to him, and so great was the confidence reposed by the Elector in his integrity and shrewdness, that he was allowed carte-blanche as to the disposal of the moneys he received. He was left perfectly free and unfettered in dealing with the Elector's funds and stocks; he could buy or sell at his own discretion. The choice of London from all the European capitals, as promising the best opening for a branch business, affords a convincing proof of the natural shrewdness of the man. Before many years had elapsed, the splendid success he achieved forced the whole world to acknowledge the soundness of his judgment. His name, by that time, had become familiar to all the leading European statesmen, whilst the business conducted by him in London far exceeded, in the vastness of its proportions, that of any of his brothers. This, after all, was but natural, seeing that London, with its gigantic commerce, its unceasing activity, was the pivot round which the trade of the whole world revolved.

That a man of Nathan Mayer's temperament, whose chief delight was in vast and complicated operations, should have taken advantage of the opportunities which London afforded for embarking in enormous undertakings might have been safely anticipated. He could hardly have selected a spot more suited to his plans. A born speculator, he found himself in the midst of an incessant whirlpool of gambling and speculation, from which none but one possessing, as he did, a cool head and a shrewd intellect, could have emerged with flying colours. Whether intuition or instinct dictated his choice, or whether it was due to mature consideration, we do not pretend to say, but the results accruing from his selection must have far surpassed his most sanguine anticipations, as his family, through his influence and skilful management, became the supreme rulers of the money markets of the world, and gained the monopoly and control of all important financial enterprises.

At the beginning of the present century, Great Britain was hardly a pleasing picture to look upon, as, owing to false principles of government, to the ignorant and blind cultivation of our home trade, and the neglect of our foreign trade and manufacturing industries, it had the appearance of a State driven to the most opposite and contradictory extremes. Priding itself on the possession of the freest constitution in Europe, England yet concealed the greatest tyranny; possessing unbounded riches, it yet allowed the poor peasantry in Ireland to die of hunger, whilst the privation and distress prevalent among the labouring classes generally were so great and indescribable as to threaten to end in riot and rebellion. The hardships endured by the poorer classes in many parts of the country were still further aggravated by the disgraceful condition of our political system. Morality was at a discount; bribery and intrigue were the order of the day. It was a time when the thoughts of all were turned to their own advancement and to the complete forgetfulness of the sufferings of others. Before the Reform Bill of Lord Grey, corruption was so wide spread that the independence of the Crown and that of the constituencies were threatened by the machinations of unscrupulous politicians. The majority of the votes were in the hands of a limited few, eager and ready to advance their own interests at the expense of the nation at large. The Reform Bill in a great measure remedied the evil, which, however, was by no means annihilated. Corruption sought fresh pastures on which to flourish, and other malpractices ere long came into fashion. Apparently the democratic element had been admitted into the constitution, but we may fairly question whether the power of the landed aristocracy was in any way injured. The limited few still controlled the votes of the majority. Formerly the landed aristocracy ruled the elections, as they were able to influence their tenants, and so secure the return of particular candidates; but much of this power now passed into the hands of the moneyed aristocracy, the large capitalists, who, besides enjoying, this addition to their political might, are the principal ruling force in the financial and commercial world. The great landed aristocracy still exercises an important influence in the political world, but the few noble families who previously possessed the monopoly of the boroughs have now to share their power with their rivals, the landed capitalists. The repeal of the Corn Laws was, as D'lsraeli truly said, the abolition of the landed aristocracy by the moneyed aristocracy, of the nobility by the *bourgeoisie*, of pedigree by money.

The agitation preceding the repeal of the Corn Laws was instrumental in expunging from the political creed an article then generally accepted, which had caused much of the distress among the labouring classes, and had largely contributed to the stagnation of the home industries. Politicians up to that time had been unanimous in asserting that the true remedy for the prevailing distress, and the only reliable source of prosperity was to be looked for in agriculture, with a powerful landed aristocracy at its head. It was, they declared, a quixotic idea to suppose that the prosperity of the country could be permanently benefited by cultivating and extending our foreign trade and our manufacturing industries. The first to recognize the absurdity of this belief, and to point out the evils which would inevitably follow from such a mistaken policy, was Mr. C. P. Villiers, the pioneer in the Corn Law crusade. "My charge against the Corn Laws," said he in one of his speeches, "is, that they limit and endanger our foreign trade, and that all such laws proceed upon a policy directly the reverse of that which is recommended by the present circumstances and condition of the country. And my charge against the legislature is, that this policy has been pursued in this country since the close of the last war, now twenty-three years ago, though each year has proved the folly of it by the injury it has entailed, and is now inflicting upon the country So that, proceeding at home upon the monstrous fallacy that agriculture was the source of all our greatness, and abroad stipulating nothing for our foreign commerce, we were doing everything in our power to cripple our manufactures. Now, if all this had been the error of a particular Government, or the folly of a party that had ceased to exist, it would, I know, be idle to refer to it, the time to remedy the evil being now past; but it is our misfortune that it is the policy of the present hour. The policy of that day—that the home trade is the best trade, and that we ought to create customers by Act of Parliament for that trade, and be as little dependent as possible upon foreign trade, is the ground on which the Corn Laws are defended today. "The support and protection accorded by the legislature to the landed aristocracy in England were not enjoyed by the noble orders abroad. The conditions on which land was held on the Continent had undergone extensive modifications, and the nobility had by degrees, owing to the Revolution or modern legislation, lost the direct ownership of the land, with its attendant seigneurial rights and privileges. The tendency abroad has been to split up the land into small holdings, a course which rendered the disappearance of large proprietors inevitable. In England the contrary is the case; the tendency is towards consolidation in the hands of a few large proprietors. It could hardly be otherwise. The main principle in the English law of land tenure is, that the owner must either cultivate his land to the best advantage himself, or else lease it to those who will do so. This was hard upon small proprietors, who were called upon not only to cultivate the land but to contribute towards its improvement, and this a series of bad seasons would render impossible. The consequence was, that they were compelled to sell their land to the large landowners. In this way the small landed proprietors disappeared, and gave place to the thrifty tenant farmer. Whether it is right or wrong that the land should thus be concentrated in the hands of a limited few, is a question which has agitated the minds of many, and which we, for our part, do not feel called upon to decide. There can, however, be no doubt that, since it has been generally acknowledged that the prosperity and greatness of the country are dependent upon a flourishing foreign trade, the tendency has been to abandon agriculture for manufacturing pursuits, and to leave the cultivation of the soil to those whose wealth renders them independent of the profits or losses attending their labours.

Injurious as were the effects produced by this mistaken policy of fostering the home trade and neglecting the foreign, there can be no question that the country has also suffered severely from the evils resulting from the creation of the National Debt. To the increased taxation and the widespread corruption it engendered, may be ascribed much of the want and privation the poorer classes of the community have had to encounter. However much we may deplore the existence of the National Debt—or national nuisance, as some would call it—we must confess that William III had no other plan left by which he could procure the money he regret events from little causes spring, and it is to the necessities of earlier monarchs rather than to William that we must trace the origin of the system of State borrowing embodied in the National Debt. When our earlier rulers found themselves short of funds, they were accustomed to apply to their faithful subjects for aid, and, as they were not always couched in the gentlest terms, or made with that courtesy which so befits kings, the applications were sure to attract gold to the royal exchequer. In the pursuit of cherished schemes of ambition or revenge, monarchs would recklessly embark on enterprises the cost of which their loyal subjects were afterwards forced to liquidate. Richard I, in his eagerness to visit the Holy Land, stopped short of no device to procure the funds necessary for his object. He extorted money from his subjects, he farmed the revenues, mortgaged the customs, and even threatened to sell London rather than abandon his crusade. His successors imitated and improved upon his system of extortion. Henry III seized the merchandise of his subjects, and managed to borrow a large sum under the tempting offer of high interest, but, with a forgetfulness characteristic of the times, neither capital nor interest was ever paid. Under the pretence that he was about to start on a crusade, Edward I seized the plate and money of the monasteries, but, once secure in the possession of the spoil, declined to go. Edward III imposed heavy taxes, created monopolies, raised forced loans, and availed himself of every possible means to wring money from his unfortunate subjects. As time rolled on, each succeeding monarch strove apparently to rival and outdo his predecessor in unscrupulous exaction. Edward IV enjoyed the reputation of being the handsomest tax-gatherer in the kingdom. When on one occasion he kissed a buxom widow to show his appreciation of the readiness with which she yielded to his demands, it is said that she at once doubled her contribution in the expectation of being again favoured by the royal lips; but kingly gratitude did not go so far. Henry VII was guided by logic in his extortion. He forced frugal people to contribute largely, on the .ground that they must have saved money by their economy. Henry VIII, owing to his extravagant habits, was continually replenishing his exchequer from the pockets of his subjects; nor was he by -any means particular as to the methods by which the supplies were obtained. He seized upon the accumulated property of the monastic orders, and raised a loan of ten per cent, on all property from £20 to £300, increasing the percentage on sums above the latter amount. By courtesy the money thus raised was termed a loan, but, when years later he refused to pay the capital or to acknowledge his debt, the transaction was known by a harsher name. Elizabeth displayed a great deal of cuteness in her financial operations: she would borrow large sums of her devoted subjects, and, if at any time she had a balance lying idle, would graciously deign to lend it back again to her faithful citizens at a high rate of interest. The Stuarts were not behind their predecessors in recklessness or extravagance, while in extortion they went to extremes of which no one had ever dreamt. Charles I found to his cost that he had no sovereign right to-the property of his subjects, and paid a heavy penalty for rashly endeavouring to force them to yield to his exactions. His failure, however, did not deter Charles II from similar practices, and the Merry Monarch fairly excelled all his rivals in barefaced thieving, for that is the only term applicable to his action in closing the Exchequer and appropriating to his own use the money deposited there. James II would have liked to imitate his brother, but the offences which the nation overlooked in the graceful, rollicking Charles, were not to be excused or tolerated in one so universally hated and suspected as his successor. The Stuarts seem to have laboured under the impression that they had a sovereign right to whatever of their subjects' property they might fancy, and regarded all those who declined to accede to their oppressive demands as disloyal subjects and traitors. The result of this difference of opinion is too well known to need description here. William III, on his accession, created, willingly or unwillingly, the National Debt, and by so doing acknowledged the indebtedness of the Crown to the public for the money placed at its disposal. Whatever faults he may have had—and he was by no means faultless— William III at least deserves all credit for having laid down the principle which has ever since been maintained, that the faith of the State must be preserved inviolate towards its creditors.

The creation of the National Debt has been severely criticized and disapproved by later generations, wiser in their time than their ancestors.

We must, however, in justice to William III, remember that he had no option in the matter; it was a case of Hobson's choice. Had he been able to devise a better plan of obtaining the money he required to carry on the war with France, he would, we feel sure, have adopted it, but as no other method suggested itself he was forced to avail himself of the National Debt. To crush his life-long rival, Louis, was a mission which William felt called upon to perform, and which nothing would induce him to abandon. From his earliest years he had learnt to hate the name of France, and his life had been passed in one long struggle to humble the French monarch and frustrate his ambitious schemes. He, who at the head of the small but resolute Dutch Republic had defied single-handed the power of the two strongest nations in Europe; who had seen his countrymen tear down the dykes and canal banks to let loose the waters they confined rather than behold their fatherland desecrated by the presence of the conquering invader, was hardly the man to relinquish the struggle when his hands were strengthened by the resources and energies of England. Time had not effaced from William's memory the recollection of the wrongs and affronts his country had suffered, so that, on his accession to the English crown, he renewed hostilities with even greater zeal and determination than before. Louis on his side, being as anxious to crush William as William was to crush him, did not relax his efforts, but exerted all his strength, brought into play all the arts of diplomacy and intrigue to attain his cherished object. When he remembered how both Charles II and James II had been in his pay, how completely successive English ministers had been his tools, it must have galled him to find his hated rival placed on a throne which gave him such greater powers of defiance. Deep as his hatred of William had been formerly, it became deeper and bitterer as he noticed the resolute front and undisguised contempt displayed towards France by his foe after he landed in England. The rage and annoyance, the bitter disappointment and chagrin felt by Louis, were well known, for he made no attempt to conceal them. He sheltered the dethroned James, surrounded him with a mock Court, and did all in his power to irritate the Court of St James's. The contest was maintained by William with a certain amount of personal pride, but, however ardently he may have desired to see France humbled, it was even more important to the interests and welfare of England and of Europe that the ambitious designs and tyrannical projects of Louis should be checked by the strong hand. In addition to his own military genius and undaunted courage, William III called into requisition the strength and riches of the British Empire. The creation of the National Debt was, under the circumstances, fully justified. "Had he employed," remarks Mr. Francis, "the arbitrary mode of levying supplies of the earlier monarchs; had he made forced loans, and never repaid them j had he seized upon public money and wrung the purses of public men, the country might as well have been governed by a James as a William, and would in all probability have recalled from exile the unfortunate house of Stuart. The evils of William's reign were in the facts that his power was not sufficiently established to borrow on equitable terms; that the bribery, abuses, and corruption of men in high places increased with their position; and, above all, that instead of paying his debts by terminable annuities he made them interminable."

In spite of the great difficulties he experienced in obtaining supplies, William would never abandon the contest, which continued more or less languidly for a number of years, until both parties were thoroughly exhausted by it. At length Namur was forced to capitulate, and the long-desired suspension of hostilities came. The power of France in Spain was shaken; its coasts were assailed, and Louis, having lost his great captain, was glad to resume his overtures for peace. The peace of Ryswick terminated this memorable struggle, which had cost Europe 480 million of money and 800,000 men. No great achievement was recorded of this protracted war, nor was the peace it produced of long duration. Its earlier history, like that of most English wars, was not remarkable for its successes. The unanimity so essential to great deeds was at that time an impossibility, owing to the divided state of political parties. Had greater patriotism and less self-interest and advancement been displayed by the House of Commons, William might have been able to bring the war to a successful issue years before.

The principal objection to William's financial innovation was, as we have already observed, that he borrowed on irredeemable annuities. Had he borrowed on annuities terminable at a certain date, the operation would have been very little dearer, whilst, instead of saddling posterity with a heavy burden, the pressure would have decreased year by year, until the debt finally disappeared. Credit, moreover, would have improved as time went on, and the discontent have lessened. Whatever blame may be attached to William, still stronger must be the blame attached to the advisers of succeeding monarchs, who although perfectly well acquainted with the objections to the raising of money on irredeemable annuities still continued the practice. It was predicted by Sir Robert Walpole that the country would be ruined when the debt amounted to 100 million. If such was his sincere belief, he is much to be censured for steadily omitting to take steps to avert the calamity. It is needless to say that the debt has long since exceeded Sir Robert's limit, and yet the country is still far from being bankrupt.

In 1696, while the gold was being recoined, exchequer bills in amounts of £5 and £10 were introduced. These were found of great convenience in business, for, being issued on the credit of the Government, they were regarded as equal to gold, and passed freely from hand to hand under the confident knowledge that they would be paid off at par. The Treasury was authorized to contract with capitalists for the supply of cash, and, although these bills were for a short time at a discount, they soon stood at a premium. At first they bore no interest, but, when they were re-issued, interest was paid on them. They have always continued to be a favourite source of supply with succeeding ministries, and when it is found inconvenient to pay them off they are liquidated, with the consent of Parliament, by being added to the fixed debt of the country.

It is amusing and instructive to note the variety of expedients William was compelled to employ to obtain his supplies. At one time it was a mild remonstrance, at another a haughty menace, and often a reproach that he had risked his life for an ungrateful country. Heavy as was the cost of maintaining the war with France, the money spent with that object was as nothing compared with the enormous sums expended in buying members of the Lower House. Corruption was rampant throughout society; every man of influence had his price. Some were bribed with contracts, some with portions of loans, while others received titles, commissions, or places. So low had public credit fallen and so high were the demands of members and the premium on money that of 5 million voted for the war only 2½ million reached the exchequer. Mr. Francis, to whom we are indebted for much of the matter in this chapter, describes very faithfully the state of the finances and of society at that time: "Long annuities and short annuities, lottery, tickets and unredeemable debts, made their frequent appearance, and the duties, which principally date from this period, were most pernicious. The hearth tax was nearly as obnoxious as the poll-tax. The custom and excise duties were doubled. The hawker and the hackney-coach driver, companies and corporations, land and labour, came under supervision. Births, burials, and bachelors were added to the list, and whether a wife lost a husband or whether a widow gained one, the effect was alike. Beer and ale, wine and vinegar, coal and culm, all contributed to the impoverished State; and although some, who looked back with regret, occasionally indulged their spleen, the general tone of Parliament was submissive. Still there were times when the truth was spoken, and truths like the following were unpleasant:—"We have provided," said Sir Charles Sedley, for the army, we have provided for the navy, and now we must provide for the list. Truly, Mr. Speaker, tis a sad reflection that some men should wallow in wealth and places, while others pay away in taxes the fourth part of their revenue. The courtiers and great officers feel not the terms, while the country gentleman is shot through and through. His Majesty sees nothing but coaches and great tables, and therefore cannot imagine the want and misery of the rest of his subjects. He is encompassed by a company of crafty old courtiers?" The corrupt transactions which tended so much to increase the National Debt are very remarkable. The assembled Commons declared in a solemn vote: "it is notorious that many million are unaccounted for; "Mr Hungerford was expelled from the Lower House for accepting a bribe of £21, and the Duke of Leeds impeached for taking one of 5,500 guineas. The price of a Speaker—Sir John Trevor—was £1,050, and the Secretary to the Treasury was sent to the Tower on suspicion of similar practices. Money receivers lodged large sums of public money with the goldsmiths at the current interest. Others lent the Exchequer its own cash in other persons' names, and, out of 46 million raised in fifteen years, 25 million were unaccounted for. The commissioners of hackney coaches were accessible, and peculation in the army was discovered by the chance petition of the dwellers in a country town. By this it appeared that the inhabitants of Royston in Hertfordshire had large claims made upon them for money by colonels, captains, and cornets, in addition to the food and lodging which were their due. A few independent members took up the question; the public supported them; and at this juncture a book was delivered at the lobby of the house, which asserted that the public embezzlement was as enormous as it was infamous, and that the writer was prepared to make disclosures which would astonish the world. The offer was accepted; a searching inquiry was instituted, and defalcations were discovered, so great, that all wonder ceased at the in-crease of the National Debt, and at the decrease of the national glory. The abuses in clothing the army were plain and palpable. The agents habitually detained the money due to the soldiers and used it for their own advantage, or compelled the troops to pay so large a discount that they were in the utmost distress. The subaltern officers were not better off. Colonel Hastings—afterwards cashiered for the offence—obliged them to buy their raiment of him. If they hesitated he threatened; if they refused he confined them. In 1693, an inquiry was ordered into the application of the secret service money, when severe and deserved animadversion was passed upon those through whom it circulated. The power possessed by Government under such abuses may be imagined. They were sure of the votes of those who had places and pensions, and they were sure also of the votes of that large class of expectants which always haunts a profuse ministry; and thus the courtiers," as the ministerial party was long designated, could baffle any bills, laugh at all grievances, stifle any accounts, and raise any amount of money.

Under Queen Anne intrigue and corruption still permeated the political world. Money had learnt its innate power, and day by day its influence upon the politics of the nation grew more marked and unmistakable. Through the interest and pressure of the State creditors, the moneyed classes, a law was passed enacting that for the future no one should be eligible to represent a borough in Parliament unless he had an income of £300 a year, or £600 a year in the case of a county member. The power exercised by money waxed every day more prejudicial to the true interests of the country, and the greater that power grew the more baneful became its effects upon the morals of the nation. Bribery was universal. An eager scrambling after wealth disgraced the whole of society, and noble names of all ranks and parties were tarnished by an utter disregard for the laws of common honesty. Everywhere the cry resounded:—

> "Get money, money still,
> And then let virtue follow if she will."

Marlborough, it is well known, did not scruple to satisfy the cravings of his avarice at the expense of the soldiers to whom his successes were due. His victories were but a source of gain to him; the blood of his gallant veterans, a trifle unworthy of consideration if it interfered with his plans. Somerset, Newcastle, and other ministers lent the State money on terms settled by themselves.

The Funds were diverted from their legitimate purposes and employed in buying the votes of the Lower House. When the

Tories came into office no less than 30 million sterling were found to be unaccounted for in the budget. The scandal connected with this discovery was not diminished when the investigations afterwards instituted proved abortive. The whole tone of parliamentary morality was infamous, and the financial condition of the country was proportionately unsatisfactory and alarming. The National Debt is in a measure answerable for much of the corruption that prevailed, and there is undoubtedly much truth in the arguments which have been urged against this method of raising the money required by the State in emergencies. The objections are directed, not so much against the debt itself as, against the evils it has brought in its train. Speculation was promoted and encouraged by its creation, which, from a business point of view, has certainly been of little benefit to the mercantile world. Seeing fortunes quickly and easily won by speculations in the Funds, merchants were seduced from their own legitimate pursuits. In 1697 the debt amounted to 20 million, and it was found to be such a convenient agent, with such elastic qualities, that its proportions were for ever on the increase. The deficit in that year was no less than 5 million. This state of things was turned to account by speculators, who set afloat rumours of every description to disparage the Government. Capital was made out of the distresses of the Ministry, the interest on the debt was declared to be uncertain, and the public credit was depreciated by any and every means. The Funds in consequence attracted an amount of attention and acquired an importance which have but increased with the progress of time. The great Hebrew capitalist and speculator Medina aroused the envy of many by the large fortune he amassed in a comparatively short period.

Eager to imitate and rival his success, English merchants began to dabble and speculate in the Funds, and the Royal Exchange soon became—as Change Alley was later—the rendezvous where men of all creeds and nationalities met to tempt the fickle goddess, and enrich themselves by this privileged mode of gambling. Jews and Gentiles, Quakers and Ministers, rogues and hypocrites, all mingled in the fray. On that common ground all prejudices and enmities were sunk and forgotten. A greed for money swayed the hearts and minds of these worshippers of Mammon. The speculation fever spread with surprising rapidity; each day saw the crowd grow in proportion. If business in the Funds slackened, other sources of speculation were discovered: bargains in annuities, lottery tickets, tontines, exchequer bills were made briskly, and bubble companies were promoted with almost the same facilities as in the nineteenth century. "The poor English nation," said one writer, "run a madding after new inventions, whims, and projects, and this unhappy ingredient my countrymen have in their temper; they are violent and prosecute their projects eagerly."

William III created the National Debt, but the foundation stone was indirectly laid by Charles II when, in 1672, he appropriated to his own use half a million of money deposited by merchants and goldsmiths in the exchequer. Charles, however, repudiated all claims made upon him for the restoration of the money thus taken, and to William belongs the merit of having first acknowledged the indebtedness of the State to its creditors. Not only did he own his liability for sums he himself borrowed, but he added to them the amount misappropriated by his predecessor. The condition on which he negotiated his first loan was that those who advanced him money should receive stock representing double the value of their contributions.

Forty firms expressed their readiness to assist him on these lucrative terms, and in this way he raised half a million sterling towards carrying on the war with France. By making so liberal an offer he gained two immense advantages: he not only obtained the money he required, but he secured the support of the great body of English merchants, who, having placed their capital at his disposal, were naturally interested in the maintenance of his rule. At the same time he won the gratitude of the nobility, who on previous occasions had always been called upon to prove their loyalty by large sacrifices. In 1694, being again in want of funds, William announced that he wished to raise £1,200,000, and that he was willing to grant those merchants who first subscribed this sum, a charter in their joint capacity under the title of the Bank of England. By this charter they were allowed to carry on a general banking business, and were given certain privileges in buying and selling bills of exchange, bullion, and other commodities. The money was soon subscribed, and in this way the first public debt was handed down to posterity. At William's-death it amounted to 16 million, but so rapidly did it accumulate that it was 54 million when his successor died. The increase is partly accounted for by the cost of Marlborough's war, but by far the greater portion was due to the prevailing bribery and corruption.

In 1782 William Pitt first entered the Ministry, holding the office of Chancellor of the Exchequer, and the following year found him, as Prime Minister, at the head of the affairs of the country. To improve the finances was the task which before aught else claimed his attention. This was a problem worthy of his great genius, and the results of his remarkable skill and untiring energy were manifest before many years had passed. The revenue increased rapidly. In 1783 it amounted to but 10 million sterling, but by 1800 it had risen to 26 million, while in 1810 it was no less than 62 million. By Pitt's skilful plans the national finances which, under Lord North's administration, had been allowed to fall into a deplorable condition, were once more re-established, and public credit restored. The most convincing proof of the soundness of Pitt's financial policy is that his measures have been the basis of all subsequent legislation affecting the revenue and expenditure of the country. He likewise instituted a scheme for the reduction of the National Debt. The result of the various steps taken by him was so favourable that Consols, which in 1784 stood at 54, already reached 76 in 1786, and by 1792 had risen to 96, or a rise of 42 per cent, in eight years.

No event in the financial history of England has had such important results immediately and remotely as the suspension of cash payments during the reign of George III. In 1797 the English banks found themselves deeply embarrassed, mainly in consequence of the demands of the Government, who borrowed million every year for the war, and for the support by subsidies of half the Continental Powers. All cash payments were forbidden, the consequence being that Bank notes fell at once to a discount. The £1 note became worth only 17 *s*. or 18 *s*. The House of Commons at length voted that the value must be restored to par; but the mere vote was insufficient to stop the depreciation. At length, under Lord Liverpool's Ministry, cash payments were resumed, and all who had contracted debts during the depreciation found themselves compelled to pay in cash, by which they lost heavily. Bankruptcy and ruin were the inevitable results. Having given this hasty and imperfect sketch of the finances of the country up to the beginning of this century, we will proceed to narrate the career of Nathan Mayer Rothschild, the founder of the firm in London.

The London firm was the first branch of the Frankfort business, and was, as we have said, started at the commencement of this century by Nathan Mayer Rothschild, the third son of old Mayer Amschel, of the Judengasse. The immediate cause of his repairing to England was a dispute with one of the great cotton manufacturers from Lancashire, who treated Nathan Mayer, himself a rough, unpolished man, in an arrogant, overbearing fashion, which was keenly resented. At that time the Continent, Germany and Austria especially, was entirely dependent on England for its supplies of cotton goods, and the English manufacturers, secure as they thought in their monopoly, abused their position and treated their foreign customers in a very cavalier fashion. In their opinion it was quite a favour on their part to dispose of their wares at all. The Frankfort house did a large business in cotton goods, and it was the behaviour of one of the manufacturers who visited the firm that caused Nathan Mayer to adopt the sudden resolve to go to England.

We cannot do better than repeat his own version, as published in Sir Thomas Fowell Buxton's Biography, of his first experiences and successes in England. In one of his letters Sir Thomas says:—

"We dined yesterday at Ham House, to meet the Rothschilds, and very amusing it was. He (Rothschild) told us his life and adventures. He was the third son of a banker at Frankfort. 'There was not,' he said, 'room for us all in that

Fig. VII: NATHAN MAYER ROTHSCHILD
(1777–1836)
INTERNATIONAL BANKER & FINANCER
CO-FOUNDER & HEAD OF THE LONDON BRANCH

Portrait of N. M. Rothschild (1853) by Moritz Daniel Oppenheim (1800–1882), Rothschild Collection.

city. I dealt in English goods. One great trader came there who had the market all to himself; he was quite the great man, and did us a favour if he sold us goods. Somehow I offended him and he refused to show me his patterns. This was on a Tuesday. I said to my father: 'I will go to England' I could speak nothing but German. On the Thursday I started. The nearer I got to England the cheaper the goods were. As soon as I got to Manchester I laid out all my money, things were so cheap, and I made a good profit. I soon found out there were three profits—the raw material, the dyeing, and the manufacturing. I said to the manufacturer, 'I will supply you with material and dye, and you supply me manufactured goods.' So I got three profits instead of one, and I could sell goods cheaper than anybody.

In a short time I made my £20,000 into £60,000. My success all turned on one maxim. I said, 'I can do what another man can, and so I am a match for the man with the patterns and for all the rest of them.'"

Nothing could demonstrate more clearly Nathan Rothschild's profound confidence in his own powers, and his resolute character, than this simple narrative. So rapid was his success in Manchester, that before many years had passed he found even that was too limited a sphere for the mind which could grapple with three profits. He accordingly at the beginning of this century established himself in London, where he was afterwards destined to make such a name. Previous to his arrival in London, the business of the parent house in Frankfort had passed through the hands of the banking firm of Van Notten, but Nathan Mayer at once assumed the control and management of the firm's interests in England. In the concluding portion of his letter, Sir T. F. Buxton writes:—

"I forgot to say that soon after Rothschild came to England Bonaparte invaded Germany. 'The Prince of Hesse Cassel,' said Rothschild, 'gave my father his money; there was no time to be lost: he sent it to me. I had £600,000 arrive unexpectedly by post; and I put it to such good use that the Prince made me a present of all his wine and linen. '"

The immense profits realized by these early transactions, Nathan Rothschild soon found means to multiply. It was a period when a man gifted with his remarkable shrewdness and business capacities was bound to succeed. However great his folly may have seemed at the time when Napoleon's forces were trampling all Europe beneath their feet, Nathan Mayer learnt to form a favourable idea of the immense strength and resources of England, and his calculations as to the ultimate issue of the struggle were all in favour of his adopted country. Acting on his convictions, he on one occasion purchased a large amount of bills of the Duke of Wellington at a heavy discount, but knowing that the credit and faith of the country were pledged to their payment he felt he had made a good bargain. To quote his own words once more:—

"When I settled in London, the East India Company had £800,000 worth in gold to sell. I went to the sale, and bought it all. I knew the Duke of Wellington must have it. I had bought a great many of his bills at a discount. The Government sent for me and said they must have it. When they had got it, they did not know how to get it to Portugal. I undertook all that, and I sent it through France, and that was the best business I ever did."

Nathan Mayer was generally termed a merchant, but, although his commercial transactions were large and important, the scene of his greatest and most profitable triumphs was the Stock Exchange. At a time when the prices of the Funds and all securities were subject to violent fluctuations, the temptations to a great capitalist, with the speculative instinct so strongly developed as in Nathan Mayer, were irresistible. Though a mere stripling among the grey heads of the money market, his almost preternatural sagacity in the art of money making brought him at once into prominence, and he became the leading man on the Stock Exchange, none of the members of which could boast, like him, of having "multiplied their capital 2,500 times in the course of five years." He had now a field opened out to him for the display of his remarkable powers, and his immense speculations in the Funds, by which he realized large profits, proved him to be gifted with a wonderful intuitive foresight as to the course of events, combined with great fertility of resource, and unrivalled boldness. The introduction which his first business with the Government had secured him to the Ministers, was invaluable in his after career, as it enabled him to procure from privileged sources early information of all that passed in the political world likely to affect the money market. Every piece of early information was worth thousands to him on the Stock Exchange, the pulse of which none knew better how to feel than he. But he was ere long dissatisfied even with the privileges secured to him by his connection with the Government, and he originated a system of intelligence by which news was conveyed to him long before the arrival of the Government couriers and messengers. He had his own staff of active agents and couriers, whose duty it was to follow in the wake of armies or attend at the different

Courts to collect and transmit to him regularly, without regard to expense, reports of all that transpired. He organized a system of pigeon post, by which news was conveyed to him from the Continent rapidly and at short intervals. He was known to have spent immense sums on his pigeons, and was ever ready to pay liberally for birds possessing great strength and swiftness. The superiority of his intelligence over that of the Government was proved on several occasions. He was the first to inform Lord Aberdeen of the Paris July revolution, as he had been to announce the defeat of Napoleon at Waterloo. In connection with Waterloo an interesting little romance has been written upon the immense sum Nathan Mayer gained by his early knowledge of the victory of the Allies, which his financial strategy enabled him to use to the fullest advantage on the Stock Exchange.

Many of his large speculations had been based on the presumed success of the English arms, and he was perhaps congratulating himself on his shrewd foresight and the soundness of his calculations when the sudden and treacherous return of Napoleon from Elba shattered at once his golden dreams and renewed all his previous anxiety and fears. No man, indeed, had greater cause to tremble at the reappearance of the mighty despot than had Nathan Mayer; when the fruits of his victory seemed almost within his grasp, they were at a blow removed, and he was left surrounded with doubts and contingencies. In the midst of its rejoicings the whole of Europe was startled with alarm and dismay. That the deposed Emperor should ever return to harass and devastate Europe, had never occurred to men's minds; it was a possibility of which no one had ever thought. The public alarm was only increased as the news of the glad welcome Napoleon received on his way to Paris became known. So upset was Nathan Mayer by the news, and so intense became his anxiety to learn how matters progressed and were likely to end, that it would not allow him to rest satisfied with the speed of his couriers, but drove him to go himself to the Continent to watch the course of events with his own eyes. He accordingly proceeded to Belgium and followed close in the wake of the English army. When at length the Duke took up his position at Waterloo, and quietly awaited the French forces, Nathan Mayer felt that the critical moment on which hung the fortunes, not of Europe alone, but of the Rothschilds also, had arrived. He had such an immense stake dependent upon the issue, that his feverish anxiety would not allow him to remain in the background. He proceeded to the battle-field and took up a position commanding a view of both armies. We can imagine how eagerly he scanned the field, and noted the disposition and strength of the opposing forces. Those under the command of the Iron Duke must, we should fancy, have struck him as being outmatched and standing but a poor chance with the French army, which included the famous and hitherto invincible "Old Guard." Turning to the distinguished personages around him, among whom were to be seen Count Pozzo di Borgo, Baron Vincent, General Alava, Baron Muffling, and others of equal note, Nathan Mayer questioned eagerly and wistfully all who cared to give him a hearing. The answers he received were discouraging and but increased his fears, for all were too well aware that the struggle between two such remarkable commanders would be long and stubborn. Though hoping for victory, none felt confident enough to predict such a result. The battle began. A dense smoke, from the furious cannonade, soon enveloped the whole field in a cloud; but Nathan Mayer's straining eyes were able from time to time to see the fierce charges of the French cavalry, by which the safety of the English lines was more than once imperilled. Cold steel, however, conquered, and the assailants recoiled before the bristling hedge of bayonets. And so the battle grew and waxed fiercer as the day progressed. On the opposite hill of Rossomme, Napoleon was seated with a map outstretched before him, and from there he issued the orders for a last and desperate charge, on which all his hopes of victory were placed. The Old Guard, with the gallant Ney at their head, rushed forward to retrieve the fortunes of the day; but in vain. They had met their masters. They were driven back by the British bayonets, and were soon to be seen making their way from the battle-field in the greatest confusion and disorder.

With a ringing cheer that told which side had won, the English forces rushed after their foes, whilst Nathan Mayer, his anxiety allayed and his spirits restored, spurred his horse back towards Brussels. It was dusk as he quitted the field, and his solitary ride in the darkness must have been intensely exciting to his already highly taxed brain. It was a ride he cannot readily have forgotten. Having reached Brussels, he procured, after some difficulty, a carriage to convey him without delay, and at all speed, to Ostend, where he arrived, travel-stained and weary, on the morning of the 19th June. Tired as he was, he would not stay to rest. In spite of the tempestuous sea, and the threatening weather, he wished to make his way across the Channel, but even the fishermen shrank from the attempt.

Fig. VIII: COUNT CARLO A. POZZO DI BORGO
CORSICAN POLITICIAN & RUSSIAN DIPLOMAT
(1764-1842)

Portrait of C. A. Pozzo Di Borgo (1835), by Karl Bryullov (1799–1852) – Radishchev Art Museum, Russia

Fig. IX: ARTHUR WELLESLEY
1st DUKE OF WELLINGTON
(1769–1852)

Portrait of Arthur Wellesley (1804), 1st Duke of Wellington painted while he was serving in India. He is depicted in his Major-General's uniform. Painting by Robert Home (1752–1834). National Portrait Gallery: NPG 1471

In vain he offered bribes of five hundred, six hundred, eight hundred francs to the poor fellows; they would not venture. It was not until the offer reached two thousand francs that one of them consented to brave the tempest, and endeavour to take Nathan Mayer across to England, on condition that the money was paid to his wife before starting.

They set sail, and before they had gone far the threatening weather changed for the better, whilst a favourable breeze sprang up and considerably accelerated their passage. In the evening they sighted Dover and shortly after Nathan Mayer dragged his weary limbs ashore. Even here he would not rest, but, after procuring the swiftest post-horses to be had, resumed his journey to London. The next day he was to be seen leaning against his well-known pillar on the Stock Exchange, apparently broken in health and spirits, and looking as if he had been overwhelmed and crushed by some direful calamity. The greatest gloom and despondency had for days prevailed in the City, and as men looked at Rothschild, and then significantly at each other, they seemed to come unanimously to the conclusion that their hopes had been blasted, and that the worst was yet to be known. Had not Rothschild travelled post-haste from the Continent, and were not his agents already selling out? The Stock Exchange, generally so full of life and noise, was unusually silent; speculators moved about in a listless, aimless way, now and then stopping to discuss in low whispers the cause of the great financier's sales. The gloom and despondency was not lessened when a rumour became current that Rothschild had told a friend in confidence that Blucher with his 117,000 Prussians had been defeated on the 16th and 17th June at Ligny, and that Wellington could not hope with his handful of soldiers to arrest the progress of Napoleon's victorious and far larger forces. The evil news spread through the City like wildfire. The Funds dropped rapidly, and the greatest uneasiness and despondency prevailed. The change was so violent and so sudden. It seemed as if it were but yesterday that Europe had been exulting over the discomfiture of Bonaparte and the restoration of peace. The public thanksgiving, the grand reviews, the public rejoicing, the fireworks, had hardly yet finished, and now,—the whole was in vain,—the scourge of Europe was loose again. And so the day closed, with not a ray of hope to brighten the all-pervading gloom. But the next afternoon a sudden, wild reaction set in. It was everywhere reported, with sparkling eyes and heightened colour in men's cheeks that Wellington was victorious, and the French defeated. Nathan Mayer had himself been the first to announce the good news with undisguised delight and satisfaction to his friends on the Stock Exchange. When the glad tidings received official confirmation some hours later the public joy knew no limits. The Funds rose again at a bound. Many pitied Rothschild for the enormous losses he had, as they thought, suffered; they little suspected that, while his known agents had been selling openly, his unknown agents had bought up secretly every piece of scrip they could secure. Far from losing, he had by his manipulations pocketed nearly a million sterling.

In 1806 Nathan Mayer Rothschild married a daughter of Levi Barnet Cohen, one of the wealthiest Jews at that time living in London. After accepting Rothschild as his daughter's suitor, Cohen had some doubts as to the extent of his future son-in-law's riches. A man who speculated so boldly and so largely was not unlikely to be speculating with other persons' money, so Cohen prudently asked for some proof of his reputed wealth. This Rothschild declined to give, saying that as far as wealth and good character went, Mr. Cohen could not do better than give him all his daughters in marriage.

The name of Rothschild became familiar to the English public mainly through its connection with loans issued for various Governments. This loan business was perhaps the most profitable of all the many enterprises on which the firm embarked, as, to begin with, there was the certainty of a handsome commission; whilst the endless Stock Exchange speculations to which the loans gave rise were a fruitful source of gain to Nathan Mayer. He may fairly be said to have been the first to introduce foreign loans into England, and to have made them popular as investments. Foreign stocks had, of course, been largely held by English capitalists for years, but they had never enjoyed public favour, owing to the interest and dividends being payable abroad. Rothschild, however, arranged that they should in future be paid in London, at fixed rates in sterling money, an arrangement which contributed largely to the success of the loans brought out under his auspices. It speaks well, indeed, for his prudence and caution, that, although the loans issued through other firms were often repudiated and the interest stopped, none that he took up were ever known to suffer from the bankruptcy of the Governments for whom they had been issued. Rather than allow his loans to acquire a bad name through the inability of the contracting State, owing to temporary difficulties, to provide the funds necessary for the payment of the interest, he was known to have advanced his own money for that purpose, trusting to his influence and power to secure its due return. However unfavourable an opinion people may entertain of some foreign loans, it is quite certain that they cannot point to any loan issued by the Rothschilds that has come to a bad end. The first occasion on which he assisted the English Government was in 1819, when he undertook the loan of £12,000,000. This operation was unsuccessful, as the loan fell to a discount; but Rothschild had cleverly shifted the burden on to other shoulders. The list given below, which is by no means complete, will show how varied his loan operations were, and will enable the reader to form an idea of the immense profits attending this line of business. On one single loan he made a profit of £150,000, with which he purchased the well-known Gunnersbury House and grounds. This historical mansion was formerly the residence of Princess Amelia, the aunt of George III, and on her death the house and grounds passed into the hands of a Mr. Copland and ultimately became, as we have said, the property of Nathan Mayer Rothschild.

The principal loans issued by Nathan Mayer were the following:—

1818	Prussian	5%	£5,000,000
1822	Prussian	5%	£3,500,000
1822	Russian	"	3,500,000
1823	Austrian	"	2,500,000
1824	Neapolitan	"	2,500,000
1825	Brazilian	"	2,000,000
1829	Brazilian	"	800,000
1832	Belgian	"	2,000,000
		Total	£21,800,000

The majority of these loans were remarkably successful; but at times the sunshine was broken. On more than one occasion Nathan Mayer sustained such heavy losses that the stability of any other firm but his would have been endangered. He is estimated to have lost not less than half a million by Lord Bexley's scheme for funding Exchequer bills in a Three and a half per cent, stock. In 1823, at the time of the French invasion of Spain, he was threatened with severe losses through the French loan, but fortunately for him he saw his danger in time, and managed to distribute the loss among others less alert.

He would often decline proposals for loans without troubling himself about the terms, if the country soliciting his assistance was under the least suspicion, or subject to internal disorganization. With Spain, or the South American states which had formerly acknowledged the Spanish flag, he would never have anything to do. He always cautiously steered clear of every doubtful or unsafe business. During the great speculation fever of 1824 and 1825 he kept studiously aloof, and warned others to follow his example. It is true that, during this time, he established the Alliance Marine Insurance Company, but the history of the causes which led to its formation would seem to show that its establishment had no connection with the speculation then prevailing. When the numerous bubble companies which had been floated burst in rapid succession, and the inevitable panic occurred, Rothschild greatly relieved the market by his readiness to purchase at a fair price any amount of stock that might be tendered him. Brokers in many instances preferred accepting his offers to realizing their stock on the market. Nothing demonstrated more clearly the power and stability of the firm during this trying period, when the Bank of England had nearly to close its doors, than the unstinted and fearless manner in which it advanced funds to the Bank to enable the latter to meet its calls.

In 1831 Nathan Mayer did what he regarded as a very clever stroke of business. Mercury, as is well known, is a valuable article, indispensable in many trades, as well as in the dispensing-room. It is a powerful medicine, and is also largely used to separate gold and silver from the earthy impurities with which they combine. Most of the quicksilver found in Europe was derived either from the mines at Idria, in Austria, or from those at Almaden, in Spain. The latter mines had at the time of which we are writing been allowed to fall into disuse, but their richness was well known, even the Greeks and Romans having realized immense profits from the rich deposits there. Spain in her difficulties thought of her once famous mines, and willingly mortgaged them to Rothschild as security for the due payment of the interest on the loan he had undertaken. The immediate result of this agreement took the public quite by surprise: the value of Almaden quicksilver was doubled. Under these circumstances, they naturally turned to the Idria mines for their supplies, but only to find that the price there likewise had been doubled. Rothschild had managed to get the Idria mines also under his control, and by so doing had secured the monopoly of mercury. "This clever stroke of business—as profitable as it was clever—had one notable consequence for the sick and suffering of all nations. Mercurial preparations, largely employed in medicine, are at the present moment no more manufactured from the pure metal as obtained from the mines, but from the refuse of other articles containing quicksilver, such as the foil of old mirrors and looking-glasses." This piece of stratagem brought down upon Nathan Mayer a shower of abuse and condemnation from the press.

On another occasion he forced even that venerable institution, the Bank of England, in spite of its prestige and its Government support, to confess that it was no match for the finesse of the great financier. Rothschild particularly required an amount of bullion to promote the success of an operation he had in hand. This bullion the directors willingly lent him on condition that it should be returned by a certain day. On that day Rothschild appeared at the Bank to fulfil his engagement. When asked if he intended to return the bullion, his reply was to produce a bundle of notes for the amount. He was reminded of the terms of the agreement, the directors pointing out that to oblige him they had touched their reserve, and that they now urgently required the bullion. "Very well, gentlemen," he is reported to have said, "return me my notes; I dare say your cashier will honour them with gold from your vaults, and then I can return you bullion?'

This story is so characteristic of the man, that its authenticity seems undeniable, but the same cannot be said of the following anecdote, which is evidently due to the fertile brain of some imaginative writer. The very minuteness of detail and the dramatic completeness of the narrative are enough to make one suspicious of its genuineness.

The elements of improbability are too prominent and manifest to fail to strike the reader. The story runs that the Bank mortally offended Nathan Mayer, by refusing to discount a bill drawn upon him for a large amount by his brother Anselm of Frankfort. The Bank had haughtily replied that they "discounted only their own bills, and not those of private persons." But they had to deal with one stronger even than the Bank. "Private persons!" exclaimed Rothschild, when the fact was reported to him; "private persons! I will make these gentlemen feel what sort of private persons we are!" Three weeks afterwards, Nathan Mayer, who had employed the interval in collecting all the bank-notes he could procure in England and on the Continent, presented himself at the Bank as soon as it was opened. He drew from his pocket-book a £5-note, and the clerk naturally counted out five sovereigns, at the same time looking with great astonishment at Rothschild. It seemed strange that he should trouble himself for such a trifle. He, however, examined the coins carefully one by one, and put them in a little canvas bag; then drawing out another note, a third, a fourth, a tenth, a hundredth, he kept demanding change for his notes, never placing the money in his bag without first scrupulously examining the pieces. In some cases he would try them in the balance, "as," he observed, "the law gave him the right to do." The first pocket-book being emptied, and the first bag filled, he passed them to his clerk, and received a second supply of notes, thus continuing to drain the Bank of its gold till the doors were closed. He had spent seven hours in changing £21,000. But as he had nine of his employés engaged in the same manner, it resulted that the Bank had lost £210,000 from its reserve of gold. Moreover, Nathan Mayer had kept the tellers so occupied that no other persons could change a single note. Everything that bears the stamp of eccentricity always pleases the English public, and in this instance the pique of the great millionaire caused endless amusement. The directors, however, laughed less, when they saw him reappear next day at the opening of the Bank, accompanied by his nine allies they laughed no longer when they heard the financial despot say, with ironical simplicity: "These gentlemen refuse to take my bills; I have sworn not to keep theirs. I will merely warn them that I hold notes enough to keep them occupied for two months." For two months! eleven millions of gold drawn from the Bank. The Bank grew alarmed; something had to be done. The next morning a notice appeared that in future Rothschild's bills would be taken as readily as their own.

Shrewd and 'cute as Nathan Mayer proved himself to be, the laugh was not always on his side. He at times met with rivals whose cunning and strategy were too much even for his subtle calculations. A leading banker once lent him a million and a half against the security of Consols, which were then quoted at 84. The terms on which the money was advanced were clear and simple; the banker was to have the option of buying the Consols at 70, should the price recede to 74. Rothschild felt satisfied with his bargain, for the possibility of Consols dropping 10 per cent, appeared to him a very remote contingency. The banker, however, had acted on an idea which subsequently fully justified his course of procedure. He at once began unloading Rothschild's Consols on the market, following this up by a similar amount in his own possession. The market grew alarmed at the gigantic sales; uneasiness and doubt followed; the Funds dropped rapidly, and other circumstances occurring to help the depression, the fatal price of 74 was at length reached. The Christian had outmatched the Jew.

When he lived at Stamford Hill, Nathan Mayer had as an opposite neighbour a wealthy stockbroker named Lucas, who, on-returning home late one evening, noticed Rothschild's carriage standing ready at the gate. Thinking something must be in the wind, Lucas directed his coachman to drive round to the stable and not unharness the horses, but to wait till he sent for him. Concealing himself, he presently saw Rothschild and two companions enter the carriage, the driver being ordered to drive "to the City." Hastily summoning his own carriage, the stockbroker started in pursuit, and saw them alight at New Court. A few minutes later he followed, and, reeling past the housekeeper in an apparently hopelessly drunken state, forced his way, in spite of all opposition, to the financier's private room, where he fell prostrate on the floor. Nathan and his friends were not unnaturally startled by the sudden inrush of their unwelcome and uninvited visitor. They raised him, bathed his face with cold water, but without any benefit, the only result-being a convulsive trembling and shrinking.

They were at a loss what to do with Lucas, but, noticing that he seemed at length to settle into a heavy slumber, determined to let him remain where he had fallen. Time was precious; they had important matters to discuss, so they covered the reveller with a rug, and proceeded with their business. Important news had been received from Spain, and the result of the consultation was to order certain brokers to commence at once buying up cautiously a particular stock. This settled, Rothschild and his companions separated. After they had gone, Lucas began slowly to recover, and although still uncertain and shaky on his legs, and suffering from a dreadful headache, as he said, he insisted, in spite of the housekeeper's remonstrances, upon going home. On reaching the street he went at once to his office, where he made arrangements for buying up all the stock he could procure. Rothschild was dreadfully upset by this trick, and used always to refer to it as the "base, dishonest, and nefarious stratagem" of Lucas.

In addition to his loan business and speculations, Rothschild embarked in many commercial enterprises, for he was ready to support any undertaking which appeared to him at once sound and likely to prove lucrative. By his immense bill transactions he must have won hundreds of thousands of pounds. A writer in "The Gentleman's Magazine," shortly after Rothschild's death, said: "He never hesitated for a moment in fixing the rate, either as a drawer or as a taker, on any part of the world; and his memory was so retentive that, not-withstanding the immense transactions on which he entered every foreign post-day, and though he never took note of them, he could, on his return home, with perfect exactness, dictate the whole to his clerks." Nothing was too gigantic for his grasp; nothing too minute to escape his notice. His mind was as capable of contracting a loan for millions, as of calculating the lowest salary on which a clerk could exist. "It was characteristic of Nathan," says Martin, in his "Stories of Banks and Bankers," that "he never paid his employés a farthing more than was necessary for their bare subsistence — or at least not a farthing more than they could compel him to pay. This meanness towards those who assisted him in building up the edifice of his enormous fortune is a reproach to the character of the man from which even his warmest adulators have not been able to free him." This is a reproach from which we are glad to say the present heads of the firm are free, for their liberality is too well known to require our confirmation.

"One cause of his success," says the author of "The Stock Exchange," "was the secrecy with which he shrouded all his transactions, and the tortuous policy with which he misled those who watched him the keenest. If he possessed news calculated to make the Funds rise, he would commission the broker who acted on his behalf to sell half a million. The shoal of men who usually follow the movements of others sold with him. The news soon passed through Capel Court that Rothschild was bearing the market, and the Funds fell. Men looked doubtingly at one another; a general panic spread; bad news was looked for; and these united agencies sank the price two or three per cent. This was the result expected, and other brokers, not usually employed by him, bought all they could at the reduced rate. By the time this was accomplished, the good news had arrived; the pressure ceased; the Funds rose instantly; and Mr. Rothschild reaped his reward." To tell who was and who was not his agent was well-nigh impossible, for he is known to have made his very enemies his tools to serve his purposes. He was informed one day that a broker had been openly abusing him on the Stock Exchange, and boasting "how thoroughly he detested Rothschild and the whole Jewish race." Nathan listened quietly and unmovably to the statement, merely remarking—

"Thank you; I am much obliged. That man will be useful."

Shortly afterwards this abusive broker sold out on behalf of a third party, acting secretly for Rothschild, £600,000 Consols; "For," said Nathan, "they will never suspect he is bearing the market on my account." It was a common practice with this mighty speculator to have one set of agents selling, and another buying, the same stock, so that there was no ascertaining what in reality was the object of his manœuvres. The probable result was a secret confined to his own breast.

Owing to his enormous power, subtle stratagems, and profound mystery, no one could conjecture, with any certainty, his purposes. A general suspicion and mistrust followed him in all his actions. If business was flat and dull, it was caused by Rothschild, while, if matters improved, the improvement was declared fictitious and only temporary. The whole Stock Exchange became filled with an uncomfortable atmosphere of suspicion and incredulity, which kept the members ever in a fever of apprehension and doubt.

It may not be out of place to mention that Nathan Mayer attributed much of his success to the observance of two maxims: "Another advantage I had. I was an off-hand man; I made a bargain at once." The second maxim shows that he had a grain of superstition in his composition, for he would never, as he said, have anything to do with an unlucky man or an unlucky place. "I have seen many clever men, very clever men, who had not shoes to their feet. I never act with them. Their advice sounds very well, but fate is against them; they cannot get on themselves, and, if they cannot do good to themselves, how can they do good to me?"

His methods of business and his conduct procured him many enemies. The satirists were ever ridiculing his portly figure and slovenly appearance, caricaturing his Jewish accent and his uncouth manners. He was indeed a subject created for caricature, but he was at the same time utterly insensible to the jeers and laughter he occasioned. He pursued his path without paying the least regard to anything that might be done to give him offence.

Undoubtedly he was responsible for much of this satire and ridicule. In his manners and address he seemed to delight in displaying his thorough disregard of all the courtesies and * amenities of civilized life. They were to him superfluities and shams. He appeared to pride himself on his blunt and outspoken style of speech, which he mistook for frankness, but which was usually so violent and uncouth that in any other than a millionaire it would not have been tolerated. He was, like most of his family, a man of unbridled temper, which led him into excesses of passion and language quite unworthy of his position in society. A clever anonymous writer thus describes him as he was seen on "'Change":—

"There is a rigidity and a tension in his features too that would make you fancy, if you did not see that it was not so, that someone was pinching him behind, and that he was either afraid or ashamed to say so. Eyes are usually denominated the windows of the soul; but here you would conclude that the windows are false ones, or that there was no soul to look out of them. There comes not one pencil of light from the interior, neither is there one scintillation of that which comes from without reflected in any direction. The whole puts you in mind of a skin to let, and you wonder why it stands upright without at least something in it. By-and-by another figure comes up to it. It then steps two paces aside, and the most inquisitive glance that you ever saw, and a glance more inquisitive than you would ever have thought of, is drawn out of the erewhile fixed and leaden eye, as if one were drawing a sword from a scabbard. The visiting figure, which has the appearance of coming by accident and not by design, stops but a second or two, in the course of which looks are exchanged which, though you cannot translate, you feel must be of most important meaning. After these the eyes are sheathed up again, and the figure resumes its stony posture. During the morning numbers of visitors come, all of whom meet with a similar reception and vanish in a similar manner; and, last of all, the figure itself vanishes, leaving you utterly at a loss as to what can be its nature and functions." Nathan Mayer must indeed have at once attracted attention as he leaned against his favourite pillar, with his shoulders drawn up to his ears, and his hands plunged deep in his ss. breeches-pockets, motionless, and apparently speculationless

"The name of this gentleman, the entertainments given by him, the charities to which he occasionally subscribed, and the amount of his transactions in the money market were blazoned abroad. Peers and the princes of the blood sat at his table; clergymen and laymen bowed before him; and they who preached loudest against mammon, bent lowest before the mammon-worshipper. Gorgeous plate, fine furniture, an establishment such as many a noble of Norman descent would envy, graced his entertainments. Without social refinement, with manners which, offensive in the million, were but brusque in the millionaire, he collected around him the fastidious members of the most fastidious aristocracy in the world. He saw the representatives of all the States in Europe proud of his friendship. By the democratic envoy of the New World, by the ambassador of the imperial Russ, was his hospitality alike accepted; while the man who warred with slavery in all its forms and phases was himself slave to the golden reputation of the Hebrew. The language which Mr. Rothschild could use when his anger overbalanced his discretion was a licence allowed to his wealth; and he who, when placed in a position which almost compelled him to subscribe to a pressing charity, could exclaim, 'Here! write a cheque; I have made one———fool of myself!' was courted and caressed by the clergy, was feted and flattered by the poor, was treated as an equal by the first minister of the Crown, and more than worshipped by those whose names stood foremost on the roll of the commercial aristocracy. His mode of dictating letters was characteristic of a mind entirely absorbed in money-making; and his ravings when he found a bill unexpectedly protested, were translated into mercantile language ere they were fit to meet a correspondent's eye. It is painful to write thus depreciatingly of a man who possessed so large a development of brain; but the golden gods of England have many idolaters, and the voice of truth rarely penetrates the private room of the English merchant. There was, however, an occasional gleam of humour in him, sternly as his thoughts were devoted to heaping up riches. I am as good as you, said he to the Duc de Montmorenci, when his title was granted, 'you style yourself the first Christian baron, and I am the first Jew baron.'"

This reminds one forcibly of another anecdote. A German Prince, bearing letters of introduction and credit to the great financier, called at New Court, and was shown into the private room where Nathan Mayer was sitting busy with a number of papers before him. On hearing his visitor's name, Rothschild nodded and motioned him to take a seat, whilst he went on steadily with the examination of his papers. This cool treatment was not quite what the Prince expected should have been shown to one of his dignity and rank. After standing a minute or two, he exclaimed: "Did you hear, sir, who I am? I am———," naming his full title. "Very well," said Rothschild, "take two chairs." More often the point of his jokes was due to his imperfect pronunciation of English. When dining at the Mansion House one evening, he was heard to remark to a guest who had declared his preference of mutton to venison: "Ah, I see; you like mutton because it is sheep (cheap); others like venison because it is deer (dear)!"

Fig. X: NATHAN M. ROTHSCHILD ON EXCHANGE —CARICATURE

"A Pillar of the Exchange", caricature of N.M. Rothschild by W. Clarke (1856), British Library

Wealth, whatever luxuries it might command, was unable to secure its possessor happiness or tranquillity of mind.

Rothschild was a prey to empty fears, and the care and anxiety inseparable from the control and safe-keeping of his million effectually prevented him from ever enjoying any peace of mind or relaxation. He had made numerous enemies; he had ruined many a man of business by his stratagems and speculations, so that it is not surprising to learn he was continually haunted by dreams of assassination. Threatening letters poured in upon him by the hundred, and one in particular, sent to him by a secret political tribunal on the Continent, which declared that as he, by his loans, had supported the Governments in their tyrannical oppression of their subjects, his death had been decided upon and the agents appointed to carry out the crime, is said to have caused him special uneasiness. So great a hold did his fears have over him, that for many years before his death he is reported to have slept with loaded pistols at his side. "You must be a happy man," said Sir T. Fowell Buxton, as he surveyed the comforts and luxuries of his splendid mansion, "in such a home as this." "Happy, I happy!" was the bitter reply; "what! happy, when just as you are going to dine a letter is placed in your hand saying: 'If you do not send £500—I will blow your brains out.' Happy, I happy!"

Two tall, dark men, with heavy moustaches and penetrating eyes were once ushered into his room. The financier bowed; the visitors on their side did the same, but-said nothing. They were feeling in an anxious, nervous manner in their pockets, as if to find something they had concealed there. Rothschild's fears at once led him to the conclusion that his assassins were at last before him, bent on carrying out the foul deed. Without a moment's hesitation or thought, he seized a ledger within his reach and hurled it with all his force at the unsuspecting visitors, and shouted for assistance.

When at last an explanation was forthcoming, and Nathan Mayer discovered that the strangers were two bankers bearing letters of introduction, which they in their nervous haste were unable to discover, his mortification was intense, and he was heard to mutter to himself: "Poor unhappy me ! a victim to nervousness and fancied terrors! and all because of my money!"

What little pleasure and happiness Nathan Mayer did enjoy was derived not so much from the possession of unbounded wealth, as from the excitement and intriguing attending the making of it. He revelled in the plotting and tricking, the manipulations and stratagems which his gigantic speculations necessitated and created. "This is the key," said one who knew him well, "to an understanding of Rothschild's character. His ambition tended to the accomplishment of elaborate financial operations —of making money, if you like; but in this phrase the emphasis must be placed on the making; for he did not value either money in itself or the things that could be procured by it. He had no taste or inclination for what every Englishman seeks as soon as he has money enough to buy it— comfort in every respect. His ambition was to arrive at his aim more quickly and more effectually than others, and to steer towards it with all his energy. When his end was reached it had lost all its charm for him, and he turned his never-wearying mind to something else." This view of his character and disposition is confirmed by his own lips, as he declared in answer to the question asked by one of his guests: "I hope that your children are not too fond of money and business to the exclusion of more important things. I am sure you would not wish that?"—"I am *sure* I should wish that," was the outspoken reply; "I wish them to give mind, soul, and heart and body—everything to business. That is the way to be happy. It requires a great deal of boldness, and a great deal of caution, to make a great fortune, and, when you have got it, you require ten times as much wit to keep it." Outside his business Rothschild had few pleasures. Whilst his mansions were crowded with works of art, and the most gorgeous appointments, it was not because he was a patron or admirer of the arts, but because, with his millions, it was expected of him. When Spohr, the famous violinist and composer, called upon Nathan, with a letter of introduction from Nathan's brother in Frankfort, he was told by the banker: "I understand nothing of music. This"—patting his pocket and making his money rattle and jingle—"is my music; we understand that on Change. But you can come and dine with me." "Nevertheless," added Spohr, "the letter of recommendation to Rothschild was not wholly useless, for he took a whole box at my benefit concert." At long and rare intervals Rothschild would be seized with a charitable freak; but that his benevolence was due to nothing better than caprice is proved by his own words: "Sometimes to amuse myself I give a beggar a guinea. He thinks it is a mistake, and for fear I should find it out off he runs as hard as he can. I advise you to give a beggar a guinea sometimes. It is very amusing."

The directions of old Mayer Amschel of Frankfort, that his sons should always remain united, were carried out to their fullest possible extent, by the practice of intermarriage. Thus Baron James, the head of the Paris house, had married one of his nieces; and in 1836 it was decided that Lionel, Nathan Mayer's eldest son, should marry his cousin, the daughter of Anselm Rothschild of Frankfort. Nathan Mayer went to Frankfort to be present at the marriage festivities. He was in bad health at the time, suffering from a carbuncle. On the day of the wedding he was taken seriously ill, but he obstinately maintained that it was but a passing attack. He grew, however, rapidly worse, and, when matters had assumed a threatening and hopeless aspect, his physician was sent for from London. But his services were summoned too late, and the great man, after being delirious for a day or two, gave in to his great enemy. He died on the 28th July, 1836. The first news of his death was conveyed to England by one of his own specially-trained pigeons, which was shot by a sportsman near Brighton. On a slip of paper attached to its leg were the words, *"Il est mort."* His remains were brought over from Frankfort for interment. Sur rounded as he had been during his life by all the luxuries which money could command, he was placed in his last resting-place with a gorgeous pomp and display that seemed hardly appropriate to the solemnity of the occasion. The coffin which contained his remains was described in the press as being "different in shape from those made in this country, and so handsomely carved and decorated with large silver handles at both sides and ends that it appeared more like a cabinet than a receptacle for the dead." A procession of carriages, nearly a mile in length, followed it. Among those who were present in the Jewish East-end Cemetery out of respect to the Deceased, were the Austrian, Russian, Prussian, Neapolitan, and Portuguese ambassadors, besides the Lord Mayor, the sheriffs, aldermen, and a crowd of minor dignitaries.

Much speculation and curiosity was manifested by the public after Nathan Mayer's death as to the amount of the fortune he had left his children, but this was not made known in the will, and has consequently always remained a secret. The directions to his executors were clear and simple. Those gentlemen were expressly bidden to confine themselves to their administrative duties, and not seek to pry into matters which were outside their functions. No statement of the amount of his property, or of the securities in which it was invested, was given in the will, and the main points touched upon were the conduct of the business and the marriage of his daughters. The business was to be conducted by the four sons in co-operation with their uncles abroad. To each of his daughters he left £100,000, which was to be forfeited if they ever married without the consent of their mother and their brothers. Legacies to his employés and dependents, as well as charitable bequests, were conspicuous by their absence—there were none.

CHAPTER VI

BARON LIONEL DE ROTHSCHILD.

THE LONDON FIRM *(continued)*.

NATHAN MAYER ROTHSCHILD left four sons and three daughters to participate in the immense fortune he had won. Of these four sons, one, Nathaniel, chose France as his home, whilst the other three, Lionel Nathan, Mayer, and Anthony, succeeded to the management of the fine business bequeathed them by their father. The control and management were really confided exclusively to Baron Lionel, for his abilities and skill justly entitled him to that proud position, whilst his brothers, having no great inclination for financial matters, were content to concentrate their attention and energies on more congenial pursuits—the encouragement of art and sport in all their forms.

Baron Lionel was only twenty-eight when his father died—an early age at which to be called upon to direct and conduct a business so complicated and so vast as that which he had inherited.

But Baron Lionel proved himself fully equal to the responsibilities of his new position. He possessed great natural abilities, and much of his father's financial skill, which had been cultivated and developed under the careful eye of his father himself. For some years before the latter's death, Baron Lionel had assisted him in the business of the firm, and, owing to a wise rule followed by Nathan Mayer, had acquired a thorough insight into all its various details and perfectly mastered the principles on which it was conducted. Nathan Mayer invariably insisted that all the correspondence and negotiations respecting important trans-actions should be carried on either by himself or his sons; he discussed the details with them, and encouraged them to study every financial proposition in all its bearings, thus making them participators in the wisdom derived from his vast experience, and training them in the best possible way for the charge which must eventually become theirs. Young as he was, Baron Lionel, thanks to the thoroughly sound training he had received, and to the great financial talents he had inherited from his father, soon showed that the fame and reputation of his firm would not diminish whilst the management remained in his hands.

Nathan Mayer had wisely observed that it took a "great deal of boldness and a great deal of caution to make a great fortune, and ten times as much wit to keep it when you have got it," and the justice of this remark was fully appreciated by his son. Baron Lionel, having perhaps little inclination for gigantic speculations, with all the excitement and worry attending them, such as his father had revelled in, concentrated his thoughts exclusively on the consolidation and preservation of the immense fortune and business his predecessor had made with such unparalleled rapidity. Great prudence and unfailing caution invariably marked the enterprises on which Baron Lionel entered. He never mixed himself up with any bubble companies, and carefully avoided purely speculative undertakings. On the Stock Exchange he dealt largely, but he never stooped to avail himself of any of the tricks and stratagems to which his father resorted so successfully. The unrivalled sway and control his father possessed over the stock market Baron Lionel did not aspire to retain in its entirety, as that would have necessitated the employment of those underhand manipulations and expedients which were in his eyes anything but admirable, even if generally adopted by the members of the Stock Exchange. Naturally his influence on the stock market was great, still it was far below that which his father had enjoyed; but what the firm lost in influence they more than gained in the respect and favour of the public.

In the negotiation of foreign loans Baron Lionel was particularly active, as this business, at once lucrative and comparatively free from risk, was one which he preferred before all others. During his lifetime his firm was interested in the issue of no less than eighteen Government loans, amounting in the aggregate to one hundred and sixty million sterling. To enter into the details of these transactions would be to give the financial history of Europe for the last fifty years, and after all no advantage would be gained by our doing so, as the immediate cause of the whole of them was the same—the pressing necessities of the borrowing States. The only difference was the circumstances and conditions under which each loan was issued, and these particulars belong rather to the history of the individual countries than to that of the

Rothschilds. In all these great loan trans-actions the direction was invariably left with Baron Lionel, not only on account of his influence as head of the family, but also on account of his matured judgment. His skill in detecting the moment for buying or selling, his delicacy in feeling the pulse of the market, and his promptness in seizing every opportunity favourable to his purposes, were universally recognized. Among the many loans issued by Baron Lionel we may mention the Irish Famine loan, which he negotiated in 1847 for the English Government, for whom he also in 1854 raised a sum of £16,000,000. During more than twenty years he was the agent for the Russian Government. In the successful funding of the debt of the United States he took a prominent part, and in 1876 he advanced the English Government the sum of four million sterling for the instant purchase of Suez Canal shares from the Khedive. By the latter transaction alone he cleared a profit of nearly £100,000. On the conclusion of the Franco-German war, Baron Lionel, at the head of a group of bankers and financiers, guaranteed to maintain the foreign exchanges, and so facilitated the payment of the French indemnity. The fact of this delicate and important business being confided to his management was a remarkable and flattering tribute paid to his great financial ability and unerring judgment.

Whilst speaking of foreign loans, we may be allowed to recall an anecdote in connection with a Russian loan which Baron Lionel was asked to negotiate. He was a man of action, quick in coming to a decision, and prompt in carrying it out. On this occasion an unusual hesitation and irresolution overpowered him, and led to the loss of the loan. The cause of this unwonted irresolution was that he found himself placed in an awkward predicament in which he must either abandon a

Fig. XI: BARON LIONEL DE ROTHSCHILD
(1808–1879)
HEAD OF THE LONDON BRANCH
SUCCEEDING TO HIS FATHER NATHAN
CHAIRMAN OF THE *N.M. Rothschild and Sons* FIRM.

Painting by Moritz Daniel Oppenheim (died 1882), National Portrait Gallery: NPG 3838.

profitable business, or else damage himself in the eyes of the public. It was at the time when he was posing as the champion of freedom, and of the liberties of the subject; when he was fighting the House of Commons to obtain possession of the seat to which he had been elected. On the other hand, the loan was required by the Russian Government presumably to enable it to carry on its campaign against Poland, then in arms against the despotism and oppression of the great Russian autocrat. Baron Lionel was in a dilemma. If he negotiated the loan, he would be publicly accused of having proved false to his spoken opinions, of having cast aside all his regard for the liberty of the subject a3 soon as his pocket was affected. In place of the public support and favour, he would at once bring down upon himself a shower of sneers and satire.

If he were once to estrange the public from him, if he were once covered with obloquy and contempt, he knew full well that all chance of bringing his struggle with the House of Commons to a successful issue would be gone. But he did not wish to lose the loan. Indeed, he was anxious to secure so profitable a business. The Russian Government, he was aware, had not limited its negotiations to himself, but had communicated with other and rival firms on the subject. Baron Lionel knew that a decision must be made promptly, but he was so assailed by opposing considerations, that he could not decide which to sacrifice: his political popularity, or his profit. When at length he had resolved to undertake the negotiation of the loan, he found that hi3 hesitation had lost him the business, as a more energetic competitor, unembarrassed by any such considerations, had succeeded in coming to an arrangement with the representatives of the Russian Government. This was a lesson the Baron never forgot.

Whilst the business life of Baron Lionel calls for no detailed narrative, it is different with his political career, owing to the remarkable and persistent efforts he made to procure the abolition of the civil and political disabilities with which the Jews were hampered. It is hardly necessary to say that Baron Lionel was never ashamed of the race from which he had sprung. His wealth did not, as in the case of Samson Gideon, lead him to turn apostate to the creed which his fathers and forefathers had professed and followed. In all that concerned the welfare of the Jewish community, of which he was the recognized head and leader, Baron Lionel took an active interest and was always foremost to do all that his influence and money could command to ameliorate the condition of his coreligionists. He was for many years president of the Great Synagogue, and was also, for some time, one of the council of the United Synagogue. In 1869 he laid the foundation stone of the Central Synagogue. At the time of his death, in 1879, he was a member of the Jewish Board of Deputies. In common with all his co-religionists, Baron Lionel was placed under a ban in the eyes of the law, for, great as had been the services rendered by them to the nation in time of need, the Jews were still regarded as an outcast race, not worthy to be ranked on the same level as their Christian fellow citizens. When the law was passed emancipating the Roman Catholics from all the civil and political disadvantages they had suffered, and they were given equal rights with the Protestants, it occurred to some of the leading members of the Jewish community that the moment had arrived for them to make an effort to free themselves from the fetters which restrained their liberty. Conscious of being to the full as orderly and as good citizens as the Roman Catholics, they saw no reason why they likewise should not, in this land of freedom, enjoy the same political and civil privileges as Protestants and Catholics now possessed in common. They little imagined they would meet with a long and protracted opposition to their wishes, still less did they see in their demands any danger to the constitution. All this and much more did the enlightened Christians, professing liberal principles, perceive in the agitation for the removal of the Jewish disabilities. The Christians were undoubtedly influenced and blinded by prejudice, by the stigma which has always been connected with the Jewish race. At the beginning of the present century no Jew could serve as a magistrate or hold office as sheriff in any of the municipalities, owing to the test of the sacrament and other obstacles in his way. Gradually these hindrances as far as regards municipal offices were abolished. In 1837 Sir David Salomons was elected Sheriff of London and Middlesex, but could not fill his office owing to the state of the law. Anxious to propitiate the City by conferring on its citizens a boon which the Ministry valued very lightly, Lord Campbell introduced and carried a bill which enabled Sir David Salomons to accept the shrievalty. But even this did not enable Sir David to serve as alderman, so Lord Lyndhurst was eventually compelled in 1844 to alter the declaration which had barred him from that office. Although all impediments in the way to municipal offices were thus removed, the Jews found themselves still barred from entering upon a parliamentary career, owing to the Oath of Abjuration which every member was bound to take before being allowed to sit and vote in the House. This oath concluded with the words "on the true faith of a Christian," which no Jew could conscientiously repeat. Owing to the powerful majority of the Tory party in both the Lords and the Commons, no move was made to procure the abolition of the Jewish disabilities for some years, as any agitation for that purpose would have been vain, owing to the great repugnance which the Tories displayed to all measures of reform. To have introduced a measure at that juncture would have been to court defeat, seeing that it was certain to be violently opposed and rejected.

When, however, Baron Lionel was elected in 1847 a member for the City of London, with Lord John Russell as his colleague, appearances seemed more favourable to the attempt. Accordingly his Lordship, who was then Premier, took an early opportunity of moving a resolution: "That the House do resolve itself into a committee to consider the propriety of the removal of the civil and political disabilities now affecting Her Majesty's Jewish subjects." In his speech supporting this resolution, the noble lord stated that the question concerned the rights, political and religious, of a community numbering more than forty thousand souls, distinguished by their love of order and their industry, who were neither inclined nor able to instigate a public agitation in support of their rights, nor to threaten the security and peace of the empire if those rights were withheld. He showed that historically the Oath of Abjuration had no reference to the Jews, and pointed out that it was mere prejudice which led the Government of 1753, after passing an Act for their naturalization, to repeal it hurriedly and without due consideration the next session. Having carried the resolution successfully, his lordship announced his intention of introducing at an early date a bill dealing with the subject. The debates on this resolution were remarkable for the support given to the Whigs by Mr. Gladstone, who with Sir Robert Inglis at that time represented the University of Oxford in the Tory interest. His support was all the more noteworthy as his colleague was one of the most bitter and vigorous opponents of the proposed reform. On previous occasions Mr. Gladstone had objected to the removal of the Jewish disabilities, but having once acknowledged the Jews meritorious citizens, worthy to fill magisterial and municipal offices, he confessed it would be illogical and inconsistent to prevent them from entering parliament. Mr. Disraeli, then the Tory member for Buckingham, also supported the resolution, making an earnest appeal to the House to perform a great act of national justice, and to discard the superstitions of the Dark Ages which influenced them in their opposition. The bill embodying this resolution was introduced early the next year, and the debates to which it gave rise remind one forcibly of the Bradlaugh scenes. In both cases the agitation turned upon religion and prejudice. There was, however, one noteworthy difference in these two agitations. The House of Commons recognized the justice of the claims of Baron Lionel and the Jews, whereas they were strongly opposed to the admission of Bradlaugh and his co-irreligionists. The arguments were very similar in both cases. The opponents to the admission of the Jews asserted that the latter sneered at Christianity, and were consequently unfit persons to sit in the House. On the other side, it was argued that, even if this were true, it was notorious that many prominent members of the House had openly sneered at and ridiculed Christians and Christianity. Gibbon, a rank Deist, was admitted to Parliament, and allowed to take the Oath of Abjuration unopposed, although he openly expressed his disbelief in the doctrines it was supposed to involve. No objection either was raised to the admission of Hume, who was certainly far from being a Christian, and whose works were calculated to damage Christianity much more than the voice of any Jew. Moreover, it was argued that the clause "on the true faith of a Christian," to which the believers in the Mosaic dispensation chiefly objected, had been introduced only during the reign of James I, and that another formula had been previously used. In addition to all these arguments, it was urged that, as the Jews already possessed the franchise—a far more important privilege to the community than that one of its members should be chosen a representative of the electors in Parliament—and could "send the makers of Acts of Parliament to Parliament," it was illogical and weak to curtail their right and to debar them from the House. After a lengthy discussion, a division was taken, and it was found that the Bill had been carried by a respectable majority; when, however, it was submitted to the Lords, it was thrown out by thirty-five votes. In consequence of its rejection Baron Rothschild at once resigned his seat. Not that he meant to allow the matter to end so quietly as that; he was of too determined a disposition to abandon a struggle at the first reverse, when he felt that justice was on his side.

He offered himself for re-election, and was once more returned a member for the City by some seven thousand votes. Great indignation and discontent prevailing among the prominent City politicians at their representative's being kept out of his seat, pressure was brought to bear on the Ministry to provide a remedy for the evil. Lord John Russell, as another member for the City, was almost bound to move in the matter owing to the forcible representations made to him by his constituents. He had indeed pledged his word to see the matter brought if possible to a satisfactory conclusion, and a second Bill was accordingly introduced and read for the first time on the 30th May, 1850. The Ministry being apparently very lukewarm in supporting the measure, and not too desirous of pressing it on to the Lords, the citizens summoned a large meeting in the City, at which it was decided that the Baron, who had hitherto studiously avoided asserting his rights in the House, wishing to have his claims recognized peacefully and amicably, should present himself before the Speaker and have some decision as to his right of admission. Accordingly, on the 26th July, 1850, Baron Rothschild walked up to the table of the House of Commons, and demanded to be sworn as one of the members for the City of London. When asked by the clerk whether he wished to take the Protestant or the Catholic oath, he replied: "I desire to be sworn on the Old Testament." The attention of the Speaker being called to the subject, Baron Rothschild was forthwith requested to withdraw, which he did. A fierce discussion, opened by Sir Robert Inglis, at once took place, and was brought to a close by the Attorney-General, who proposed that the Baron, should be heard at the bar of the House, either by himself, or by his counsel or agent, with reference to his claim to sit and vote in the House after having been sworn on the Old Testament. This proposition was violently opposed, and, when the debate had been adjourned several times, it was finally resolved on the 5th August, "That the Baron Lionel de Rothschild is not entitled to sit in this House, or to vote in this House during any debate, until he shall take the Oath of Abjuration in the form appointed by law." This forced the Government to redeem its promise to effect some alteration in the statute, so that Jews should no longer be kept out of their seats. Even if no such promise had been made, some action must have been taken, as matters were fast approaching a crisis. In 1851 Sir David Salomons was returned a member for Greenwich, and, in defiance of the rules of the House, sat and voted without having previously taken the oath. For his contempt of Parliament he was fined five hundred pounds by Baron Aider-son. But this incident, combined with the active agitation conducted by Sir Isaac Lyon Goldsmid and his son, Sir Francis Goldsmid, Q.C., rendered some action on the part of the Government necessary and unavoidable. Early in April, 1851, a new Abjuration Oath (Jews) Bill was submitted to Parliament, and rapidly passed through the Commons, only to be again rejected when it reached the Lords. The complications with Russia and the outbreak of the Crimean war distracted attention from domestic politics for a while, but, although the Jewish question was momentarily shelved, it was by no means forgotten. In 1852, Baron Lionel was once more elected, and, when the question was re-introduced to Parliament in 1853, a fresh Bill was presented and passed by a larger majority than ever. Once again the Lords showed their opposition, but on this occasion the majority against the Bill was much smaller than on previous occasions. Matters had now reached a climax, for, the faithful citizens showing once again in 1857 their firm resolution to see their chosen representative admitted to take his seat, it became clear that a solution of the difficulty must be soon found. A fresh Bill was introduced, but, although Lord John Russell urged that some recognition of the persistency and determination of the electors should be made, the Lords refused to listen to his counsel, and rejected the Bill as they had done all its predecessors. It was, however, their last effort. Day by day it became more evident that the claims of the electors must be recognized, and the Lords at length managed to save their dignity, and yet yield to the pressure brought upon them, by rejecting the Bill presented by the Commons and passing a measure of their own, with practically the same enactments for the removal of the Jewish disabilities. This Bill received the Royal Assent on the 23rd July, 1858. On the 26th of the same month Baron Lionel presented himself to be sworn, and, on being offered the form of oath prescribed in the Bill just passed, declared in the words of the clause intended to meet his case, "Sir, I beg to state that, being a person professing the Jewish religion, I entertain a conscientious objection to take the oath which by an Act passed in the present session has been substituted for the oaths of supremacy, allegiance, and abjuration, in the form therein required." The attention of the Speaker being called to this circumstance, Baron Lionel was requested to withdraw. Lord Russell then moved a resolution that the words: "on the true faith of a Christian," should be omitted from the oath, and, this being carried unanimously, Baron Lionel was re-admitted. He then was sworn on the Old Testament, signed the oath, and at last was allowed after nearly ten years' contest to take his seat. In commemoration of the successful issue of this hard struggle, he endowed the City of London School with its most valuable scholarship, and it was no doubt most gratifying to his feelings to see this scholarship carried off in 1866 by a scholar of the Jewish persuasion. He continued to represent the City almost without a break until 1874, when he suffered in the general Liberal defeat. He had never taken a prominent part in politics; indeed, he is not known to have spoken in the House on a single occasion.

It was not his ambition to shine in the political arena, although in his quiet unobtrusive way he exerted considerable influence on the Ministry. For many years he had been unable to walk owing to the rheumatic gout, from which he suffered severely, and, as this prevented him from making an active canvass, his failure to secure re-election is not surprising. His colleague, Mr. Goschen, declared publicly that Baron Lionel from his desk in New Court exerted far greater influence than a much more active representative could exercise; but this, though true, would not satisfy the City electors. Besides, Baron Lionel himself contributed largely to his defeat by a bold and unpopular proposal he made. He pointed out that Mr. Gladstone's scheme to abolish the income tax would cause a large deficiency in the budget, and he suggested that this deficiency should be met by the creation of fresh taxes. When his audience shouted "No" and "Economy," he replied that economy would not enable us to save four and a half million a year. The great objection against the income tax arose from its inquisitorial character, and Baron Lionel thought that new taxes should be on property. He therefore suggested the introduction of licence duties, such as were paid by commercial men in Austria. This self-denying ordinance was not, however, approved by the City.

The Baron was, as we have said, a great sufferer from rheumatic gout, brought on by exposure in the hunting-field. He was for many years before his death unable to take any exercise whatever; he wheeled himself about his office in a chair made specially for him, and had to be carried to his carriage. The consequences of such a painful infirmity could hardly fail to be prejudicial to the temper of the most passive and resigned of mortals, and its influence on the manners of the Baron was unmistakable. The worry and anxiety attendant upon the management of his vast business were of themselves calculated to affect his nerves and spirits, independently of the painful malady with which he was afflicted, so that if he was peevish and harsh in temper, giving way at times to violent bursts of passion, there was much to be said in excuse of his conduct. However fractious and irritable he may have appeared, it is certain that his natural disposition was really a kind and benevolent one. Those who knew him well will bear us out when we say that under his rough and forbidding exterior there beat a warm heart. He would never withhold from anyone whom he knew to be deserving and honest a helping hand or a kind word. In his paroxysms of pain he could not always control his temper, and none regretted his immoderation more than he himself did afterwards. He had great administrative abilities, and always insisted on superintending personally all the details of his vast business. Nothing irritated him more than to learn that any of his clerks had had the audacity to give an answer on any business or to come to a decision without having first asked his advice. This practice naturally entailed upon him much worry and annoyance which he might well have spared himself, though on the other hand it kept the whole of the machinery in first-class order. To particularize the philanthropic actions of Baron Lionel would be impossible, seeing that they were frequently unknown to his most intimate friends. Many of his donations were given on the strict understanding that they should not be published, and whenever his sons attended a charity festival there were always large anonymous subscriptions, the origin of which it is not difficult to guess, although there is nothing to confirm the justice of the conjecture. Large acknowledged donations were given with munificent liberality to the charities of all creeds and nations, and it is said that, enormous as was the Baron's income, he distributed more than a tithe of it in the relief of suffering and distress. If the distress to be relieved was abroad he was the first to send remittances direct through his agents, besides subscribing after-wards to the funds that were organized. His exertions in organizing the Irish Famine Fund were acknowledged by the "Times" in the following words: "It was in Baron Lionel's own room in New Court, in December, 1846, that the British Relief Association' was organized, Messrs. N. M. Rothschild and Sons subscribing with others the munifi-cent sum of £1,000. This led to the formation of a committee, consisting of the most eminent merchants and bankers of the City of London, of which Mr. Samuel Jones Loyd, afterwards Lord Overstone, was subsequently elected chairman, and the collection of a fund amounting in the aggregate to upwards of £500,000, for the relief of the starving peasantry of the sister kingdom. Throughout the period of extreme pressure Baron Lionel was indefatigable in his exertions."

Bound to his seat as he was by physical suffering which made his manner varying and sometimes harsh, so that his temper grew to be something watched like the weather for its influence on the Stock Exchange, Baron Rothschild found his relaxation in giving, and his eyes glistened when he heard that his alms had been beneficially bestowed. Great, however, as was his charity, he was perhaps outdone in sympathy with the suffering and the distressed by his estimable Wife. This worthy lady devoted the whole of her time to philanthropic deeds; her delight and pleasure seemed to be in works of love. She was indeed the almoner of the family, and was particular in ascertaining that the objects of her sympathy were deserving of it. She would not rely on reports or hearsay evidence, but was in the habit of personally visiting her pensioners, said to number nearly two thousand. Many a struggling artist or student was indebted to her quiet but substantial aid, accompanied by kind words of encouragement, for his subsequent success. This estimable lady died in 1884, leaving by her will to charities in which she was interested donations to the extent of £120,000.

In 1857 society was set agog by the marriage of Baron Lionel's eldest daughter, Leonora, with her cousin Alphonse, the eldest son of Baron James de Rothschild, and now the head of the Paris house. It is needless to say that the wedding was one of the most magnificent of the season, and was attended by the most distinguished and noble members of all ranks of fashion and society. At the banquet after the marriage ceremony, Count Persigny, the French Ambassador, proposed the health of the bride and the bridegroom. He was followed by Mr. Benjamin Disraeli, whose duty it was to propose the health of the bride's parents. His speech on this happy occasion is said to have been one of the best social addresses he ever delivered, which is not strange, for he is known to have been for many years one of the most intimate friends of the family, and of Baron Lionel in particular. In the course of his speech he made a remark worth reproducing:—"Under this roof are the heads of the name and family of Rothschild—a name famous in every capital in Europe and every division of the globe—a family not more regarded for its riches than esteemed for its honour, virtues, integrity, and public spirit." Eight years later another festive gathering brought the family together. On June 7th, 1865, the youngest daughter, Evelina, was married to Baron Ferdinand, the eldest son of Baron Salomon, of Vienna. Unhappily, these joyful festivities were followed by a mournful conclusion, as the bride, who had been at all times so charming for her sweetness of disposition and gracious manners, died the next year in giving birth to her first child. The shock was a severe one to both Baron Lionel and his amiable wife, for both had been fondly and tenderly attached to their daughter. They neither of them ever recovered from the blow, rendered all the more painful by the death of the child, which did not survive its mother. The Evelina Hospital in Southwark was built by Baron Ferdinand in memory of the wife he so fondly loved, and so early lost.

The town residence of Baron Lionel was the well-known mansion adjoining Apsley House, a magnificent building some six storeys high, fitted up with every modern luxury and improvement. It is said that when Baron Lionel determined on building this palatial mansion he was anxious to secure the next house, belonging to Sir Edmund Antrobus, and throw it into his own, but his brother banker, although asked to state his own terms, would not, like Esau, sell his birth-right, and declined all overtures. He was indeed so fired with rivalry, that he even had an additional storey built to his own house to make it overtop that of Baron Lionel—a peculiarity that may be at once noticed. Here it was that Baron Lionel was wont to give his sumptuous dinners—the wonder and the talk of society.

The following graphic description of one of these dinners will convey to the reader a very good idea of the luxury and comfort by which Baron Lionel was surrounded:—

"My daughter and myself left Paris and reached our hotel in time to fulfil an engagement to dine with the Baroness Lionel de Rothschild, to meet Lord and Lady Lyndhurst, for whom the dinner was given. Nothing could exceed the splendour of the banquet. Silver and gold plate shone on the table and buffets; exquisite flowers delighted the eye; while the retinue of servants in full dress, so well trained that not a footfall told of their presence, and the ease and repose that prevailed, the result of perfect training, were forgotten in the distinction of the company. Another still more splendid and prolonged fete in Lord Lyndhurst's honour, to which we were also bidden, was given by the Baroness Mayer Rothschild at her Venetian villa at Mentmore—rather palace than villa, however. The Baroness had sent early in the week to have the house and grounds put in perfect order. Such pictures, such furniture, such park scenery, racehorses and hounds! Such a breakfast and lunch alfresco, afterwards a dinner at Baron Anthony's, as words cannot describe."

Baron Lionel was not by nature a society man, and he was further prevented from participating in fashionable gaieties by his physical infirmities. The true representatives of the family in society were his two brothers Anthony and Mayer, who had little inclination for business, and were far more inclined to pleasure and sport in all their forms. The only relaxation from the worry and trammels of business that Baron Lionel knew was derived from his pictures and flowers. A writer intimately acquainted with the Baron stated that "when, after many hours of absorbing transactions, he left the precincts of his City establishment and entered his home, he found himself at once transferred into an atmosphere of beauty which freed and raised the mind and restored it to its harmony and equipoise. For to him works of art were no mere decorative ornaments. That remarkable soundness of judgment which he displayed in all practical concerns of life guided him no less safely in matters of taste; and the pictures he had acquired comprised examples of the finest works from the brushes of the principal masters. These treasures were not his pride but his joy; they proved to him an unfailing source of regeneration. In such genial surroundings the mind spontaneously opened itself to a simple and healthy cheerfulness, which now took pleasure in the sallies of wit, and now followed with interest some of the graver questions of the present or the past."

That there was a vein of humour running in Baron Lionel's disposition the following anecdote will show. He was dining at a friend's house and chanced to sit next to a lady who had an only son whom she was anxious to bring up in business rather than in a profession. Like most fond mothers she was extremely anxious to do the best for the youth in whom all her hopes were centred. She determined to utilize to the utmost the favourable opportunity she had of consulting a man so well qualified by his vast mercantile experience and sound judgment to advise her on so important a question. Accordingly she plied the Baron with questions, and extracted all the information she could, but, when the vital question was asked: "What he would consider the best business for her son to adopt," she found her neighbour become suddenly reserved and uncommunicative. The truth was the Baron strongly objected to giving advice, to which a certain responsibility was always attached. Again and again the lady returned to the attack, but the Baron was always on the alert, and turned the conversation adroitly to other subjects. At length, finding that she would not be denied, he replied, "Well, madam, in my opinion, selling matches is a very good business, *if there is enough of it.*" A trite and pithy remark, displaying much common sense and wisdom.

Baron Lionel continued to manage and superintend the affairs of his firm up to the very eve of his death, which happened with painful suddenness on the 3rd June, 1879. He had for twenty years been a sufferer from rheumatic gout, but this did not prevent his attending at his office up to the very last. His death occurred quite unexpectedly— without the slightest warning. On Friday the 30th May, 1879, he held his usual business levee at New Court, and those, who from time to time brought him reports of the various markets, or went to him for the purpose of obtaining subscriptions to charities, perceived no indication that they then for the last time saw proof of the well-stored mind, the tenacious memory, and the sound decision which were known throughout Europe. The Baron was in the habit of driving daily to Gunnersbury Park, the favourite residence of the Baroness, the gardens of which are famous in horticulture, and situated in the midst of a wide domain of land belonging to the family. He passed some time there as usual, and returned to Piccadilly on Sunday afternoon. He then complained of feeling unwell and appeared to be forgetful. The symptoms were declared by the doctors to be those of gout, which need give rise to no alarm or anxiety; but on Monday, about noon, he was seized with an attack of an epileptic character from which he never rallied. He died early next morning. His brothers, Baron Mayer, or (as the name was afterwards spelt) Meyer, and Sir Anthony de Rothschild, had both died some years before; Baron Meyer on the 6th February, 1874, and Sir Anthony on the 3rd January, 1876. Both were highly popular in society owing to their amiable dispositions and agreeable manners. The banquets and receptions they gave were of the most brilliant and dazzling description, whilst their mansions were embellished by the choicest works of art which money could procure. They were both patrons of the turf, not so much on account of the excitement attending horse-racing as from a laudable ambition to see the Rothschild colours take the foremost place in sport as in everything else. In chronicling the death of Baron Meyer—to the public the real "Baron Rothschild" owing to his great popularity—the "Times" paid a very flattering but well merited tribute to his memory. It ran as follows:—"Baron Meyer was the youngest surviving son of the distinguished founder of the London house of Rothschild, and his death is in every respect premature. He was only fifty-five, and in the enjoyment of the interests and pursuits to which he had devoted himself. He held a seat in the late Parliament at the time of its dissolution, but it was well understood that he would not stand again. It is not in Parliament, however, that he will be chiefly missed. Like all his house, he was a steady adherent of the Liberal party, but, like them also, he was a silent member. It is the world of Art and Sport which will suffer by his loss, and he will there leave a vacant place that will not easily be filled. His splendid hospitalities at Mentmore, his numberless charities, his munificent patronage of art, his unstinted support of the highest kinds of sport, formed a rare combination which we could have wished to preserve among us for many more years. Rich men are not uncommon in England, and the world is seldom observant enough to notice distinctions in the use generally made of wealth. For such a man to surround himself with everything beautiful and agreeable in houses, estates, pictures, sculptures, and all the pleasures of the field has in it at first sight nothing to attract attention. It may seem, and may be, nothing more than a lavish expenditure of money on not unworthy objects. But men are not apt to suspect nor ready to admit that there may be an opportunity in such a life for the exercise of the finer qualities. It does not seem like the career of a man of business, or a politician, or a financier. But there is a great error in such a hasty estimate, and Baron Rothschild set an example which should tend to correct it. The ancient world had a conception, which we have in great measure lost, of there being a distinct excellence to be aimed at in the expenditure of great wealth. The common idea among ourselves is simply that a great man should do good with his money, but we do not go beyond the moral virtue of benevolence and just management. The ancient conception we think once prevailed in England and perhaps, like most other sentiments connected with the finer tastes, it was trampled out by the Puritans, or corrupted by the Cavaliers. But the Greeks at all events recognized that magnificent expenditure had a virtue of its own, distinct from mere liberality or unselfishness. It was the art of using great wealth appropriately as distinguished from that of using moderate wealth rightly. There are some developments of human genius and civilization which men of great resources can encourage, and which cannot be, or ought not to be, encouraged by anyone else. The highest art in such matters as painting, or sculpture, or in animal culture, would never be pursued for the sake of the demand which men of ordinary means could maintain. Great literary works can be multiplied, and the literary artist can consequently appeal to so wide a circle as to be independent of individual support. But it is otherwise where the product of genius or skill is something of which the charm or excellence ig incapable of indefinite multiplication. Rich men can foster the labours of genius in such matters, and it is one of their functions to do so. It is their function, moreover, to do it well and thoughtfully. It is easy, of course, for a great man to get rid of his superfluous money by lavish orders to architects, painters, sculptors, and musicians. But a man may foster bad as well as good art by such means, and both patron and artist lose in dignity and in the artistic capacity, which is associated with it, by indulging the mere extravagance of luxury. It is possible to be frugal and conscientious in dealing with million not less than to be lavish and thoughtless in dealing with hundreds. It was Baron Rothschild's merit to understand this function and to discharge it thoughtfully. A passion for art of all kinds engrossed his life to the last; but he indulged it under a control and with an orderliness similar to the qualities which in business have made the fortunes of his house. He spared no money for his purposes; but he had a purpose in all his expenditure. It was easy for him to make Mentmore a palace, supplied with every form of modern luxury; but he made it much more. It was a Museum, adorned with all that is beautiful. In such an expenditure of vast wealth there was felt to be nothing inappropriate or out of place, because the sense of waste could never be felt. Great resources had been bestowed to produce a great result, and the result was something which had an aesthetic value of its own.

"Baron Rothschild's career on the turf was marked by similar qualities, and if his example were more generally followed this national sport might yet be saved from the degradation which threatens it. The professed object of racing is to improve the breed of horses, and no doubt if rich men would pursue it with this single object they would do what cannot otherwise be done. To Baron Rothschild, accordingly, a fine racehorse was an animal worth producing for its own sake, and he applied himself systematically to breeding racehorses. He never squandered money in speculative purchases, but kept a stud which he diligently and patiently improved, and it was by the qualities of a thorough man of business that he at length achieved a conspicuous success. When he won, two years ago, the Derby, the Oaks, and the St Leger, all the

Fig. XII: LORD NATHANIEL ROTHSCHILD
(1840–1915)
HEAD OF THE LONDON BRANCH
SUCCEEDING TO HIS FATHER LIONEL
Chairman of the N. M. Rothschild & Sons Bank

Credit photo: ©Jewish Encyclopedia (1901–1906)

reader, and what little relaxation he can snatch from the worry and toil of business he finds either in the company of world felt that a piece of good and useful work had been justly rewarded, and they rejoiced at the evidence thus shown that the Turf was capable of reinvigoration. We cannot afford in these respects to forget his example. This is an age of great fortunes and, though few can be compared with those of a Rothschild, there are many who have similar opportunities, and it cannot be said that these are at present turned to the best account. . . . Baron Rothschild pursued a career that will always have attractions for men of wealth, but he pursued it in a manner which enabled him to render real services to the community. His friends will always bear in mind his kindness and generosity, and he will be personally regretted among a large circle. But the public will also feel that they have lost a man who had a rare capacity for making a really magnificent use of great wealth."

The destinies of the firm, since the death of Baron Lionel, have rested in the hands of his three sons, Sir Nathaniel (Lord Rothschild), Leopold, and Alfred de Rothschild. Sir Nathaniel, who came into the baronetcy on the death of his uncle, Sir Anthony, is in reality the ruler of the fortunes of the London firm. He is heart and soul a man of business. All his thoughts are centred upon the welfare and prosperity of the firm; he allows neither the pleasures of society nor the excitement of the racecourse to withdraw his attention from his duties as the head of the family in England. He is a great his books, or in quiet rambles through the open fields. Conscious of his greater abilities and more thorough devotion to the interests of the firm, his two brothers are content to leave the control and management in his hands. Not that we wish to say that either of the two brothers is in the least indifferent to its interests. Both attend regularly at New Court to participate in the conduct of affairs, but, as they cannot boast of such an intimate acquaintance with the smallest details as Sir Nathaniel possesses, their duties partake largely of a mechanical nature. They are both shrewd, quick-sighted men of business, and, if they were to study the welfare of the firm as closely as does their eldest brother, they would soon rival him in ability and business knowledge. Much, however, of their time is devoted to other objects. Mr. Alfred is as essentially a man of pleasure as Sir Nathaniel is a man of business. The balls and dinner parties given at Seamore Place are the talk of London society. They are arranged in the most sumptuous and luxurious style. Art and wealth are called into requisition to satisfy the most varied and exacting tastes, so that it is scarcely surprising that the elite of society throng together at these receptions. There one may safely reckon on meeting the most distinguished personages in the diplomatic and political world, with the probability of discovering that royalty is likewise represented. But the pleasures of society do not monopolize the whole of Mr. Alfred de Rothschild's attention. He is a munificent patron of the arts. He delights to encourage talent, whether it be found in the ranks of sculptors, painters, or actors. Many a man who has acquired distinction in his profession owes his success to the liberal support and patronage so readily accorded by Mr. Alfred to struggling talent. Different from his brother Alfred, Mr. Leopold de Rothschild is seldom seen in London society. A country life, with its hunting and horse-racing, has irresistible charms for him. When free from New Court, he hastens down either to his stud at Newmarket, or to his hounds at the same place. Racing, or rather the breeding of racehorses, absorbs the greater part of his time. Nothing so disappoints or discourages him as for his horses to prove failures on the turf. Following racing as a hobby, and betting very little, it annoys him greatly to find that his efforts at improving the speed and stamina of the English racer meet with very poor success. The disappointments and disgust which many of his favourite horses cause constitute perhaps the greatest trials in life he has to endure. Individually, Mr. Leopold de Rothschild is good-nature personified. His charity and benevolence are unlimited. He is as pleased and as ready to relieve distress as the recipients of his bounty are glad to receive the welcome and much-wanted aid. He cannot, in fact, refuse aid to a suppliant without doing violence to his inclinations. A playfully ironical, but accurate, description of the three brothers was given in a book recently published, entitled: "Society in London," which attracted much attention. This description we cannot do better than reproduce here:—

"It is, so far as the Rothschilds themselves are concerned, a species of trinity, the first person of which is Sir Nathaniel (now Lord Rothschild), the second Mr. Alfred, and the third Mr. Leopold de Rothschild. The baronet is the supreme head of the establishment, occupying the first place at the family tribunal, receiving visitors, and treated with a marked deference by his two brothers. You will find him, at first, a gentleman of curious manner. He is so pre-occupied by the cares of business, he is so habituated to the exercise of authority, that he can spare little thought for the amenities of life, and he is not so much intolerant of contradiction by others as fond of contradicting others himself. But this is merely one of the superficial idiosyncrasies of the man. A contradiction with him means no more than an interrogation with you. It is only the way in which he puts a question. Instead of asking on what evidence your assertion rests that the day is fine or wet, he considers it the more effectual to meet your statement that it is wet or fine with a point-blank denial. In this fashion he hopes to elicit your reasons, to put you on your mettle, to compel you to retract your declaration, if it is hasty and ill-considered, or to demonstrate that it is based upon testimony entitled to respect. People who make 'Natty's' acquaintance for the first time may be forgiven if they conceive the idea that he is disposed to be imperious, overbearing, and harsh. There could be no greater mistake. He is not any one of these things. He is, on the contrary, when his interest or regard is enlisted, a generous and loyal friend.

"His two brothers discharge, respectively, parts essential to the economy of New Court. The youngest, Leopold, is occupied with the mechanical minutiae of the business. In the City his vocation appears humble, and he himself little more than a drudge. Outside the City he is a person of importance, a man of sport and pleasure, a member of the Jockey Club, an owner of racehorses and of a modest establishment in Buckinghamshire. The second of the three Rothschild brothers has functions, as he has a physiognomy, altogether unlike either of his two brothers. He is light of complexion, while they are dark, with tawny hair and drooping moustache of the same colour and cut known as the Dundreary. He bestows much attention on the graces of manner. His hospitalities in London and in the country are upon an elaborate scale. The Prince of Wales is frequently amongst his visitors, and no opportunity is wanting to enable him to form an accurate idea of the opinion held by the privileged or official classes in English Society. Add to this that the Rothschilds in London have at their disposal a little army of brokers and touts in the City, a choice detachment of politicians and financiers, whether they do or do not belong to the public service, at the West End; bear in mind, too, that they receive early information from their kinsmen and correspondents in every part of the earth of what is happening or is likely to happen, and you will not be surprised to know that New Court is the abode of power."

Last year the Queen was pleased to raise Sir Nathaniel to the peerage under the title of Lord Rothschild. None will dare assert that the honour was unmerited. Few who have gained this coveted distinction can show a better claim than that which Lord Rothschild possesses in the record of the services rendered by his family to the English Government during the last fifty years and more. During that period the nation has on more than one occasion benefited by the counsel and aid tendered by the great financial firm. Lord Rothschild may well be proud of his title which, though tardily conferred, has been won by merit alone, and is no sign of royal favouritism. The honour is the greater as Lord Rothschild is the first avowed Jew who has entered the House of Lords. Samson Gideon founded the family of Eardley, but he, during his lifetime, abandoned the Jewish Creed. In thus raising Lord Rothschild to the peerage, the Queen has done honour to the whole Jewish race, and taken a step which cannot fail to remove the great barrier of distrust and prejudice which has so long separated Jews from Christians.

As they have scarcely emerged from their business teens, since their father died only in 1879, it is as yet too early to form a judgment of the business qualities possessed by the three brothers. Short as the period is they have yet been able, between 1879 and 1885, to undertake and carry out successfully several large loans, such as those for the Hungarian,

Brazilian, and Chilian Governments. The most important business they have transacted has, however, been in connection with the Egyptian Government. While the European Powers were quarrelling about their rights in Egypt, bankruptcy slowly threatened the future of that country. This disaster was happily averted by advances made by the Rothschilds, on their own responsibility, and against security little better than waste paper. Sir M. Hicks-Beach, when Chancellor of the Exchequer, testified in Parliament to the immense services conferred on Egypt by the liberality of the Rothschilds in the following words:—"The late Prime Minister has stated that Egypt was in imminent danger of bankruptcy. In fact it was saved only by monthly advances made by Messrs Rothschild upon no legal security, but simply on the security of a private note from the late Foreign Secretary. The greatest dangers might have occurred if the issue of the loan had been any longer delayed." This proves beyond question that the risks run by the Rothschilds in advancing a million sterling to the Egyptian Government were by no means visionary, as some would assert, but real and serious. Those who envy the Rothschilds the profit accruing from the loan of nine million issued in 1885, should not overlook the sacrifices which they made, and which gave them a good title to all they earned. The success of the loan was remarkable: the scene in St Swithin's Lane on the morning the loan was issued was one not easily to be forgotten. New Court and its approaches were thronged with a huge, eager, struggling crowd, all anxious to obtain allotments. The stream of applicants poured in so fast that the whole loan was subscribed for soon after the doors were opened. The list was closed an hour or two before the appointed time, a proceeding which gave rise to loud expressions of disapproval and disappointment among the many persons who were thereby prevented from obtaining any portion of the loan.

The successful manner in which these loan operations have been conducted demonstrates, beyond dispute, that the present heads of the firm are by no means deficient in financial skill; but still, without any disparagement, we think they cannot claim to inherit the marvellous powers or the shrewd far-seeing judgment of their father. This they would, if questioned, we think, readily acknowledge. Baron Lionel was a man of uncommon ability; his intellect was of the highest order, enabling him to grapple with and master the most difficult questions. To expect his sons to be as highly gifted as he was would be expecting too much, for it is very rare to find equal talent in two generations of the same family; nor, after all, are such extraordinary powers of mind required by the present heads of the firm; their business is established on so firm a basis, and their wealth is already so immense, that their chief solicitude and care must be to discover safe and reliable investments by which their money may accumulate automatically, rather than to increase it by leaps and bounds through speculative and risky enterprises. This, to all appearances, is the opinion they hold, as all their movements are distinguished by great caution and prudence, qualities which can hardly fail to render their career prosperous and worthy the traditions of their family. It is difficult, nay, impossible, to foresee to what extent their fortunes and repute may even yet grow, if the advice of old Mayer Amschel is followed as faithfully in the future as it has been in the past. Of late years the family seems inclined to break through the rule that its different members should seek to tighten still further the bonds of union by intermarriage. Against this innovation we see no objection—indeed, it is, we think, to be approved. Had the Rothschilds, however, adhered strictly to the intermarriage-system, there is no knowing how wealthy they would have become in the course of time, by thus confining their riches within such narrow limits. Under present circumstances, and always excepting carelessness and want of caution, they cannot help growing richer and richer, as the cream of business invariably falls to them. Large and lucrative undertakings are submitted daily to them, and constantly declined, as they very properly refuse to entertain, or embark in any enterprises which do not come within the well-defined and strictly recognized sphere of their business. Many houses would greedily snap at the proposals the Rothschilds unhesitatingly decline. The great requisites in the heads of the firm at the present time are caution and prudence—qualities which they seem determined to foster. If these are diligently cultivated, the firm must eventually become a dynasty, whose widespread power and all puissant influence— though recognized by no constitution—will far exceed those of any ruling family in Europe.

CHAPTER VII

BARON CARL VON ROTHSCHILD.

THE NAPLES FIRM.

ITALY once consisted, like Germany, of a number of separately governed States, which, however, were not as in Germany associated in a general " Bund" or confederation for the protection and support of their common interests. The language was the only link that joined the various Italian States together. In all else they were separated by long-standing hatreds and jealousies, which were the greatest obstacles to the progress and prosperity of the nation. It was these continued feuds and the enmity of Austria that so long barred the way to the formation or development of a united Italy worthy to take a leading part in the affairs of Europe. To establish a branch of their business in the leading State of Naples, when the political condition of the country was so disturbed and uncertain, may at first sight appear to have been a somewhat rash and ill-advised move on the part of the Rothschilds, but a little consideration will show that this step was the result of mature deliberation and shrewd calculation. The very feuds and jealousies so prejudicial to the welfare of the land proved the source of much of the profitable business which the firm afterwards secured. The States were always in need of funds to carry on their wars, and, being well-nigh bankrupt from past campaigns, were forced to seek from other quarters the assistance they required. Besides, the system on which the administration of the finances of most of the States was conducted was so thoroughly rotten that borrowing was perhaps the only way left open to them of meeting the current expenses. The extent of the business transacted by the Naples branch was small compared with that transacted by the houses in Paris and Frankfort, still it was in pro-portion, perhaps, more lucrative. The number of its clients was limited, but these few clients were regular and frequent applicants for assistance. In addition to this, trade and commerce, favoured by the situation of the country so surrounded by the sea, through the extensive bill business they created, proved no unimportant source of profit to the banker, and over this business Rothschild by virtue of his peculiar relations with the Bourse and the State, held undisputed sway.

During the present century a wonderful transformation has been brought about in the political condition of Italy. Formerly, as we have already said, the numerous states and principalities were divided from each other by continual hostilities and old-established family feuds; to look upon themselves as forming one great people never entered their thoughts, for from their birth all the great princes had been taught that it should be their first duty and absorbing ambition to avenge the insults their family had suffered through the instrumentality of their traditional enemies. To shake hands with their hated rivals, and, for the good of the nation, to live in brotherly amity together, would in their opinion have been dishonourable and infamous. With time, however, these bitter feelings have passed away, for the misfortunes which the various States all suffered in common gradually drew them together, and year by year Italians grew more willing to recognize that they all belonged to one great fatherland, and insensibly yielded to the more elevating inspiration that one invisible bond of union linked them all together. At length an ardent longing to see the nation rise from its ashes, and like a giant refreshed open out for itself a new path of honour and fame, took possession of many energetic minds, who strove, and ultimately with success, to create a "United Italy." The story of Mazzini and Garibaldi, and of the association of "Young Italy," hardly belongs to these pages, and is, after all, too well known to require repetition.

The social conditions ruling in Italy offer the student many an agreeable picture, which he in vain seeks elsewhere. The line which marks the distinction between the nobility and the less favoured orders is not so sharply drawn as in other countries. This is indeed clearly shown by the history of many of the noble Italian houses who rose to their rank from having won wealth and fame as energetic and enterprising merchants; and it is undeniable that the commoners were always highly esteemed, and enjoyed an aristocratic importance which no doubt fostered the opinion, so prevalent in Italy, that it was no disgrace, but rather an honour, for a noble to increase his own wealth and the prosperity of his dependents by commercial enterprises. The nobles and the commoners in Italy were not separated from each other by the haughty pride and the overbearing manners which have in other lands kept the two orders so far apart. This, perhaps, is the reason why the nobility of Italy have furnished so many talented writers and poets, for they were not kept by false

Fig. XIII: Kalman "Carl" Mayer von ROTHSCHILD
(1788–1855)
INTERNATIONAL BANKER & FINANCER
Co-FOUNDER & HEAD of the NAPLES BRANCH

Painted in 1850 by Moritz Daniel Oppenheim (1800–1882), Rothschild collection.

pride from the pursuit of knowledge, but displayed a praiseworthy zeal to place themselves on a level with their rivals, of whatever rank, in science or art.

The finances of the Papal State form one of the darkest and most unattractive pages in the history of the country. We shall not carry our review further back than to the period of the first French Revolution. In the year 1790 a small detachment of French troops marched against Rome. Willing or unwilling, the Romans were forced to accept the revolution; the Republic was proclaimed in the Forum, and the French constitution introduced. To the French commander-in-chief at that time the power of a dictator was given. Bills for large amounts were issued upon the richest of the Romans, on whose behalf the French general was kind enough to accept them, and afterwards to compel their payment on penalty of death. Under the extravagant rule of Pius VI the finances of Rome were in the most deplorable confusion, and the paper money fell to an unusually low value.

The French Government entered into a contract with Torlonia, the banker, by which the latter undertook to purchase some millions of such money, which he could issue afterwards at his own risk. The paper was sometimes quoted at ten per cent., often only at five, but the public had taken it up at almost double this price in silver, so that Torlonia was not only able to carry out his engagement, but to make an immense profit by the transaction.

The Roman system of finances was based on the law of the 19th March 1801, and the mode of carrying it out on the principles borrowed from France was so utterly bad, that it can be safely affirmed that the financial administration could not well have been worse. The cost of collecting the taxes was enormous, but the peculation and fraud prevailing were indescribable. The treasuries should have been full to overflowing, nevertheless they were empty; the State expected to obtain money at a low interest, but could with difficulty obtain it even on the most usurious terms. No budget was drawn up, nor were the accounts examined; no one concerned himself with the financial balance sheet.

Under Sextus V, the income of the Papal Chamber was infinitely less than that contributed by the faithful Catholics all over the world to the Roman spiritual tribunal. The taxes, with the exception of the direct taxes, were all increased, as the falling off in the revenue became evident; the price of salt was raised, and the lottery established. Loans were called into requisition, the interest on them being gradually reduced from six to three per cent., and paper money, which had been so extravagantly issued by the unscrupulous Government of Pius VI, was again put into circulation.

When Pius VII ascended the Papal chair, the people had been drained to their last drop of blood, and, as the paper money had become almost worthless and the credit of the State was gone, it was difficult to see any way out of the impending ruin and bankruptcy. When matters were in this most distressing condition, the financial decree of Cardinal Lante of the 19th March, 1801, was issued. By this the land tax was fixed according to the register of 1777, and all the other old taxes abolished. A house-tax was imposed, as was one on all loanable capital: foreigners and travellers were also affected by the new regulations, and a succession duty was made law. In addition there were salt and malt-taxes, whilst the same law decreed the reduction of the interest on all the loans to three per cent., and the realization of all common lands.

After the abolition of the Roman States in 1809, the French system of taxation was introduced, with some necessary modifications, on this side of the Apennines, the Italian system remaining in force in the provinces on the further side; for instance, the meal-tax was retained in place of the *droits réunis*, the land-tax was augmented, and registration adopted. When the Papal Government regained possession of their land in 1814, the earlier system of taxation was restored. The *motu proprio* of the 6th July, 1816, lowered the land-tax about 400,000 scudi, and, after various gradual modifications, the old system was practically restored. The gross receipts were estimated at nine million scudi, though in all probability they did not exceed seven millions.

Previous to the first French Revolution, almost two and a half million Roman florins in Church-dues found their way from the faithful Catholics to the Papal coffers in Rome. To this large sum Spain contributed 640,000 florins, Germany and the Netherlands, 488,800; France, 357,000; Portugal, 260,000; Poland, 180,700; the two Sicilies, 136,170; the other Italian States, 170,000; and Switzerland, 87,000; while about the same amount was received from Northern Europe. These subscriptions in aid of the Head of the Church afterwards showed a great falling off, consequently the financial situation of the State changed gradually for the worse. Since the incorporation of the Papal States by Victor Emmanuel in the kingdom of Italy, they have ceased to have a separate financial system of their own, as the taxes imposed on the rest of the country are enforced in what was formerly the Pope's material dominions.

The expenditure of the Duchy of Parma was estimated, in the year 1854, at two and a half million lire, and its debt at fourteen millions. The latter had been increased in 1827 by a new loan of twelve million lire, which the Duchess arranged through the mediation of the Rothschilds and the firm of Mirabaud and Co., in Milan. In addition to the compulsory loan, issued in 1849, of 2,700,000 lire, Parma was saddled in 1854 with another five per cent. loan, voluntary in this case, of 2,470,000 lire, in obligations of 500 and 1,000 lire each. This last loan was secured upon the State property and the private possessions of the ruling family.

The expenditure of the Grand Duchy of Tuscany with Lucca was estimated at five million florins, the receipts at about the same sum, and the bank-note and paper circulation at two million florins. Their joint debt dated first of all from a loan of thirty million Tuscan lire, which was issued in bonds of 1,000 lire, bearing five per cent, interest. An additional loan of twelve million lire, in bonds of the same amount, and bearing the same interest as the above, was made in the course of the year 1851, through the intervention of the firm of M. A. Bastogi and Son in Leghorn. As security for this loan the iron mines and foundries belonging to the State were hypothecated. The small three per cent, loan, of three millions, concluded towards the end of 1852, in bonds of 2,000 lire, can hardly be reckoned as forming part of the State debt, as it partook more of the nature of a compulsory loan, issued only to meet immediate and pressing wants. We should have passed it over in silence had not the firm of Rothschild taken part in its issue, as they did in both the loans for the Duchy of Lucca in 1836 and 1843, which, after the union of that Duchy to Tuscany, were added to the public debt of the latter State.

Fig. XIV: ADOLPHE CARL VON ROTHSCHILD
(1823 – 1900)
HEAD OF THE HOUSE OF NAPLES (1855 – 1868)

Portrait of Carl von Rothschild of Napoli (1851) by Moritz D. Oppenheim (1800-1882)

The kingdom of Sardinia, with over five million inhabitants, had an old standing debt on which 5,336,393 francs *rente* were annually paid, and this debt was increased in 1848 and 1849 by the addition of 13,771,680 francs *rente*, so that at the commencement of 1850 the total debt amounted to 382 million francs, costing the State annually 19,108,073 in the way of interest at five per cent. In 1850 a loan of 140 million and a premium loan of 18 million were found necessary, and were followed in 1851 by one for 3,600,000 francs, all being required by the share Italy took in the campaign of the Western Powers against Russia. The State expenditure in 1847 amounted to 90 million francs; in 1856 it had risen to 139,157,335 francs.

Between 1848 and 1856 no less than thirteen new loans were brought out, amounting in the aggregate to 553 million, and swallowing up yearly thirty million francs in interest. What comparatively little profit the State derived from the loans is seen by the loan of the 12th July, 1850, for eighty millions, which, however, only brought in sixty-four and a half millions. So great was the drain upon the resources of the kingdom, caused by the cost of the army in the Crimean war, that a further loan of thirty million was found unavoidable and necessary. The Sardinians might well adopt for their motto the well-known saying of the Prussian finance minister, Hansemann: "Freedom costs money," for the debt by which the State was burdened was out of all proportion to its population. Sardinia, however, was self-reliant and patriotic, and always showed itself ready and willing to respond to the calls made upon it by its rulers. In the case of the loans which were brought out the Sardinians displayed extraordinary unanimity in supporting the Government, for they themselves not unfrequently covered these loans several times over, thus rendering any appeal to the assistance of foreign bankers and nations unnecessary. For instance, in 1849 and 1850, besides providing the annual interest on the large debt already existing, the Sardinians subscribed an additional loan of eighteen millions, and in 1851, when a further loan of eighteen million was asked for, more than double the amount required was subscribed in a very short time by the native bankers and capitalists alone.

Of the many loans brought out by the Rothschild house, only that for eighty million in 1850, and a second for rather more than sixty-seven million in 1853, were for the kingdom of Sardinia, whose usual agents for this sort of business were the firms of Barbaroux and Tron, Migone in Turin, C. J. Hambro and Sons in London, and the Gebrüder Bethmann in Frankfort.

The kingdom of Naples, or the Two Sicilies, suffered for a number of years from the evil influence of a bad financial system, combined with the calamities and trials through which it passed. Measures of every sort—from the introduction of new taxes to the sale of the State domains, from the raising of the taxes to compulsory loans—were all tried to effect some alleviation of the State's difficulties after Joachim Murat was deposed and Ferdinand I ascended the throne. In order to pay the interest on the State debt, loans were repeatedly found necessary. In January, 1821, the yearly rente payable on the debt amounted to three million eight hundred and eighty-two thousand Neapolitan ducats. In 1822 the Government contracted a loan of sixteen million ducats with the Rothschilds. This was followed by three successive loans, which Baron Carl von Rothschild, the head of the Naples house, refused positively to undertake, unless his friend the Chevalier Medici, who had been banished to Florence, was recalled and reinstated as Minister of Finance.

On this condition, and this only, would Baron Carl assist the Government, as that would be the sole guarantee he could, he said, possibly accept of their fidelity and good intentions. There being no other person at that time capable of assisting the Government, it is almost superfluous to add that his terms were accepted, though not with a very good grace. Medici was once more restored to the favour of the King, and the three loans were issued. The first of these so-called English loans concluded with the Naples house of the Rothschilds, was that of 1821, amounting to sixteen million ducats capital, bearing eight hundred thousand ducats interest; the second loan, bearing interest at five per cent., was for twenty million ducats, costing yearly one million rente; the third was that known on several of the European markets under the name of "Rothschild's Bonds," and was for two million five hundred pounds sterling.

By a decree of the 26th May, 1821, the King separated the finances of Sicily from those of the kingdom of Naples, and concluded a loan for the benefit of the former for 1,500,000 ounces (4,500,000 ducats), in bonds of 400 ounces to bearer. The interest on this loan was paid through the Rothschilds in Paris.

In 1834 the Papal Government proposed to convert the Papal five per cent, debt into a three per cent, debt, for which the opportunity seemed highly favourable, seeing that the five per cents, were quoted at 102 to 104. To carry out this scheme, Cardinal Tosti, the Papal treasurer, started off to Paris, in order to arrange for a concerted plan of action with several banking firms in that city. At that time the Parisian financial world stood in peculiar relations with the Rothschilds. The notorious omnipotence the latter exercised in all government loan business, not only of France but of other countries, was an intolerable burden to the notabilities of finance, the other bankers, who resolved at length to make an effort to cast it off. Six of the leading houses, namely, J. Hagermann, Andre and Cottier, B. A. Fould and Oppenheim, J. A. Blanc, Colin and Co., Gabr. Odier and Co., and Wells and Co., accordingly combined to form a syndicate to challenge the Rothschilds, enter into spirited competition with them, and if possible shatter the fetters by which the financial world in Paris was bound.

In the first loan, a Sardinian one, arranged on the plan of the Paris State lottery, the syndicate obtained some success, as they managed to wrest this business out of the hands of the Rothschilds. J. Hagermann personally contributed greatly to the success achieved, as, having formerly been established in Genoa, where his firm was acknowledged to be the first and largest, he was on terms of intimacy with the Sardinian minister Caccia, and through him with the firm of Caccia in Paris. The latter, having neither means nor influence enough to carry out the business entrusted to him by his brother, placed it in Hagermann's hands.

The Rothschilds, who were never so forgiving as to allow a rival quietly to outbid them, felt, as might be expected, annoyed and vexed by this unexpected blow, and were not long before they let the weight of their wrath fall upon the presumptuous confederates by ruining what might under other circumstances have been a profitable transaction, and rendering it a costly and expensive one. The second time the syndicate tried to compete with the despots of the money market, they found that they had challenged a rival whose forces were so immeasurably superior that victory a second time was out of the question.

The fall manipulated by the Rothschilds in the value of French securities reacted upon and affected the prices of the Sardinian stocks, which continued to sink steadily until they reached a heavy discount. This was enough to render the six allies somewhat timid and nervous; still Andre and Cottier saw so clear a profit to be derived from the conversion of the five per cents, into three per cents., that they at length, after some consultation with their colleagues, declared themselves prepared to despatch an agent to the Papal exchequer to secure the business and ratify the contract. When the agent was admitted to an interview with the secretary of Monsignor Tosti, one of the first questions put to him was the weighty one—What guarantee will the Papal Government have for the due fulfilment of the contract about to be made? To this the agent replied, "The names of the allied Paris bankers," adding that he was for the moment forbidden to give their names, but that the secret would be divulged after the conclusion of the contract, and in the event of the names not being satisfactory that the contract could be considered null and void.

After the agent had had several conversations with the Cardinal, the matter seemed to be nearing its conclusion. Inviolable secrecy was promised on both sides, but the Papal officials are not remarkable for their discretion or for their fidelity in business matters. Scarcely had the agent quitted Rome than the matter was publicly rumoured about.

Fig. XV: BARON MAYER CARL VON ROTHSCHILD (1820-1886)

Baron Mayer Carl von Rothschild was a German Jewish banker and politician, as well as scion of the Rothschild family. Born in Frankfurt to Adelaide and Carl Mayer von Rothschild, he studied law at the University of Göttingen and the University of Berlin before joining the family banking firm in Frankfurt. Following the deaths of his father and uncle (Amschel Mayer Rothschild), Mayer Carl and his brother Wilhelm Carl von Rothschild became heads of the firm. He married Louise von Rothschild in 1842. The couple had seven daughters: **(1) Adèle** von Rothschild (1843–1922), married to Salomon James de Rothschild **(2) Emma Louise** von Rothschild (1844–1935), married to Nathan Mayer Rothschild **(3) Clementine Henriette** von Rothschild (1845–1865) **(4) Thérèse** von Rothschild (1847–1931), married to James Edouard de Rothschild **(5) Hannah Louise** von Rothschild (1850–1892) **(6) Marguerite** de Rothschild (1855–1905), married to Antoine de Gramont, 11th Duke of Gramont **(7) Bertha Clara** von Rothschild (1862–1903), married to Louis Philippe Berthier, 3rd Prince of Wagram.

Source : Wikipedia

Fig. XVI: BARON WILHEM CARL VON ROTHSCHILD (1828-1901)

Baron Wilhelm Carl von Rothschild (16 May 1828 – 25 January 1901) was a banker and financier of the Frankfurt House of Rothschild, son of Baron Carl Mayer von Rothschild of Naples and Adelheid Hertz. He married his cousin Mathilde Hannah von Rothschild, the second oldest daughter of Anselm von Rothschild, a chief of the Vienna House of Rothschilds in 1849. They had three daughters among whom Adelheid von who married her cousin Edmond James de Rothschild (Paris Branch) and Minna Caroline Rothschild who married Maximilian Goldschmidt, who adopted the name "Goldschmidt-Rothschild" after Wilhelm Carl's death in 1901. In 1855 von Rothschild became joint head with his brother Mayer Karl of the Frankfurt house. When his brother died in 1886, he became sole head. As he and his brother Mayer Carl left no male heirs, the Frankfurt house was discontinued at his death.

Source : Wikipedia

The Rothschilds, too, through the many influential friends they have among the officials of every government, are always sure to hear of such negotiations, so in this case the Naples house got wind of the proposed financial operation, and at once sent one of the younger partners to Rome. No sooner did he learn the exact position of affairs, than he produced the contract entered into by the Papal Government, when the five per cent, loan was undertaken by Rothschild in conjunction with the firm of Torlonia. This contract contained a clause, till then forgotten, by which the Papal chair engaged to enter into no definite treaty for any subsequent loan without giving the Rothschilds previous notice, and also to accord them the preference when their terms were not higher than those offered by other firms.

The earlier loan had been concluded before Tosti had assumed the management of the finance department, consequently he was quite in the dark as to this important condition in the contract. He and the agent accordingly determined to draw up the conditions of the proposed conversion and leave the Rothschilds and the allied bankers to settle the rest. It was of course to be foreseen that, if the business proposed was lucrative, the Rothschilds would never let it slip from them, and whether it was likely to prove a profitable undertaking they were as well qualified to judge as their adversaries. On the other hand, the only chance left the latter was to undertake the business on much less favourable terms, should the Rothschilds see fit to place themselves in their way. Still, the coalition of the Paris bankers was not to be ignored by the Rothschilds, who might have experienced much annoyance and trouble from the opposition they would have called forth if they had made full use of their privileges and influence to secure the business for themselves. Finally matters were settled in an amicable fashion and a common understanding arranged between all parties with reference to the matter in dispute. Rothschild certainly did not lose by his forbearance, whilst the rivals learnt that their strength was still far too weak to damage the sway of the millionaire financier.

It is unnecessary almost to add that Baron Carl von Rothschild, for the many valuable services rendered to the Italian States and Princes, both by loans or by advances of money, was honoured with titles and orders of every description. He died on the 11th March, 1855. The business was for some years continued by his son, Baron Adolphe de Rothschild, who, however, soon tired of the anxiety and responsibility attaching to the management of so large a concern. Being of a nervous disposition, he could not hear without fear and alarm the rumours of the internal troubles which threatened Italy, and like a wise man, blessed with a handsome fortune, he retired from public affairs to enjoy the comforts and repose of private life.

CHAPTER VIII

BARON SALOMON VON ROTHSCHILD.

THE VIENNA FIRM.

THE importance Vienna enjoyed from its being the capital of the Empire and the residence of the Emperor and his Court, as well as from the large commerce carried on there, was no doubt the reason which led to the establishment of a separate house of the Rothschilds in the Austrian dominions.

The Jews for centuries played a very distinguished part in the affairs of Austria, and in Vienna especially were to be found in the highest circles of society, possessing not only large influence, but holding also prominent positions among the leading public men. The great consideration and authority they commanded were due simply to their money, for the finances of the country and the Court had got so dreadfully embarrassed and confused that the money of the Jews was as a consequence eagerly sought for and demanded. In spite of the wealth of the aristocracy, the assistance of the accommodating Israelites was continually found necessary, and borrowing and lending were the order of the day. Even in the time of Ferdinand H. the Jews were on intimate relations with the Imperial Court, although they were at that time subject to a poll-tax, and compelled to wear pointed hats and a yellow patch on their left arm, that they might be at once distinguished from the Christian citizens. They were not even allowed to live where they pleased, but were cut off from the Christians and forced to dwell in a particular part of the city, the Leopoldsvorstadt. None the less they were readily tolerated, for they were extremely useful, not to say indispensable, to the Court. They also enjoyed very considerable privileges, and were under the direct protection of the Government. They knew how to amass fortunes by evil as well as honest means, for in the Frankfort *Relationen* of 1667 it was stated that "Hirschel Mayer had been arrested for having defrauded the Emperor during a period of twenty-three years of no less a sum than two million two hundred thousand guldens, contributions of his coreligionists." He was sentenced to life banishment from Vienna, and to the payment of a penalty of seventy thousand guldens. In 1670 the Jews and the students of Vienna had a collision, which terminated in rioting and other excesses, causing the Jews to be driven out and compelled to quit the Judenstadt, or, as it is now called, the Leopoldstadt, whilst their synagogue was converted into a Catholic church. However, it was not long ere the President of the Chamber, von Sinzendorf, granted them permission to return to their homes. All the financial business with the Court was placed in the hands of the "Court-Factor," Samuel Oppenheimer, a privilege which secured him the deadly hatred of the whole commercial body. This bitter feeling vented itself in 1700, and again in 1706, in a violent tumult, during which his house was attacked and sacked, money and valuables stolen, letters and account-books torn to pieces. The rich Israelite had even some difficulty in escaping alive with his family. Still the lucrative relations he had held with the Court were resumed as before, notwithstanding that his firm became bankrupt in the interval between the two riots. In 1706, however, his affairs were again reviving, as he had secured the contract for supplying the army in Italy during the war of the Spanish succession.

Joseph II, in 1783, astonished, if he did not scandalize, the Christian world, by creating the first Jewish Baron in the person of the banker Joseph Michael Arnstein, whose wife, Fanny Itzig, of Berlin, was a special favourite of the Emperor. During the Congress of Vienna the families of the sovereigns of the money market, Arnstein and Eskeles, were conspicuous above all in the festivals and carnivals which then took place. The wives of both these financiers were natives of Berlin, being daughters of the rich Jewish banker Itzig, a well-known personage during the reign of Frederick the Great. The Austrian Government, not only before, but after the Congress, arranged many important financial operations with these two firms, as well as with several others.

The house of Rothschild, however, after establishing a house of business in Vienna to co-operate with those already existing in Frankfort and London, soon eclipsed all competitors by their enormous wealth and magnificent receptions. With the formation of this new establishment, a fresh page opens in the history of the finances and money market of the Austrian empire, owing to the influence and sway exercised by Baron Salomon von Rothschild.

Fig. XVII: SALOMON MAYER VON ROTHSCHILD
(1774–1855)
INTERNATIONAL BANKER & FINANCER
CO-FOUNDER & HEAD OF THE VIENNA BRANCH

Painted by Moritz D. Oppenheim (1800–1882)

The Austrian empire, consisting as it does of a union of numerous and varied kingdoms and provinces, is one of the greatest confederations of people and nationalities in the world. Under the rule of its distinguished sovereigns Maria Theresa and Joseph II, its importance and power grew in all directions; its revenues and tax-paying capabilities increased and its finances assumed a flourishing aspect. Many of its loans were arranged through the Dutch bankers, Hope and Goll, and through the well-known firm of Bethmann Brothers, in Frankfort. The Austrian funds were in great favour with the public, and generally saleable at par. It was only when the political sky of Austria became over-clouded, and when its financial schemes were exhausted that these foreign banking houses withdrew, and in their places appeared the Vienna firms of Fries and Co., Arnstein and Eskeles, Geymüller and Co., and Steiner and Co. By the agency of these four firms Austria, during the period of the war of the French revolution, and her struggle with Napoleon, contracted a number of loans on terms far less favourable than formerly. So low indeed had the credit of the empire been brought by the misfortunes and the sufferings incidental to its protracted efforts to oppose the ambition of the French, that the syndicate of the four bankers above named would consent to take up the five per cent, loan of 1809 only at a discount of forty per cent., and with the State domains pledged to them as security. After having amassed million by their participation in the various Government loans, as well as through large and lucrative bill business on Augsburg for the Government account, the firm of Steiner and Co. were content to rest on their laurels, and withdrew from the syndicate. Little did Steiner, the head of the firm, a discreet and shrewd man, anticipate that within a few years of his death the million he had bequeathed his heirs would be all lost or squandered away.

The place formerly occupied in the syndicate by Steiner and Co. was now filled by the firm of Rothschild, who brought with them new schemes on which to conduct the Government loans. The scheme adopted was the lottery plan, which at once became popular with the public. The amount produced by the loans was soon exhausted, owing to the yearly drawings which formed the leading feature of the innovation. The consequence was that the loans brought out on this plan were constantly being renewed. This the contractors by no means regretted, seeing that their profits were necessarily multiplied, and Stock Exchange speculation promoted. After the overthrow of Napoleon, the Rothschilds acted on principles directly opposed to those on which they had always hitherto proceeded. Their object was apparently to reverse all that they had previously done, and so, whereas they had formerly striven to depreciate the Government funds, they now did their best to force them up in the market. Steadily and by degrees the prices recovered, so that the five per cent, loan, which we have said was issued at a loss of forty per cent., was eventually redeemed at 106 to 109. The difference between these two prices was not at all a bad profit for the Rothschilds to realize as the result of their operations. Not so fortunate was the firm of Fries and Co. in its association with the Government loans. Although the only son, Count Fries, inherited some six or eight million guldens and through his bill business gained a hundred thousand annually, he was nevertheless forced in 1824 to abandon the Court and Vienna, and fly to Paris, where he soon afterwards died. By this catastrophe the remaining members of the syndicate were reduced to the firms of Geymüller, Arnstein and Eskeles, and

Rothschild. Later on, they admitted into their ranks the Vienna millionaire and banker Baron Simon George Sina, and these four firms continued to undertake the frequent and endless loans which the Government were forced to solicit from its subjects. The two brothers Geymüller, by whom the business was founded, had already retired and were living on the fortunes they had gained. The sole head of the firm after their retirement was their nephew Falkner, who subsequently assumed the name von Geymüller, and whom they had brought up and adopted as a son. He possessed a capital of one million thalers, which, however, he soon ran through, and then made off one night without leaving any clue as to his destination. On the 12th February, 1843, nineteen months after the failure of the firm, a warrant was issued and published for the arrest of the fugitive on a charge of embezzlement. In like manner the brothers Schickh, Steiner's heirs, were advertised, arrested, and brought to trial. At that time nearly all the business firms were imperilled, and shaken to their foundations. The Rothschilds alone met the shock unmoved, deriving additional power and strength from the trials they had so successfully encountered.

Besides this Government business, the Vienna house of the Rothschilds, at the head of which was Baron Salomon von Rothschild, the second son of old Mayer Amschel, was ever ready to embark in enterprise of any sort which promised to prove lucrative. For Prince Esterhazy and many other members of the high Austrian nobility he issued in conjunction with the house in Frankfort many loans, of which we gave particulars in a previous page. He also established a Fire Insurance Company, the shares of which he was able to sell at a handsome premium. In addition to all these enterprises he had his immense bill business, which brought him in a regular and unfailing profit.

In 1836 the firm took over from the Austrian Government the contract for the construction of the railway from Vienna to Bochnia, and before even a sod had been turned or a shovel used the whole of the twelve million shares were sold at a premium of fifteen per cent. The shares in 1841 had already fallen from 115 to 62, and the Government were compelled to assist the undertaking by an advance of five millions, but before the end of the year they took into their own hands the completion of the line.

As in all other countries where the Rothschilds were domiciled, so in Vienna, the money market was completely under the control of the house established there. The prices of the funds and other securities rose or fell according to the pressure or support they received at the hands of Baron Salomon. Every day, from the opening of the Bourse at twelve o'clock to its close at four, he was besieged by brokers and stockjobbers anxious to give him reports of the tendency of the market, and eager to receive and execute his commissions. Speculation in stocks was, however, far from confined to these hours, as long before and long after the Bourse was open the speculators were in the habit of congregating in the well-known caf6 in the Grünangergasse, which establishment was rented by the Stock Exchange folk, and free to the public. Here the dealings and speculations in stocks were carried on without intermission till late at night, for the prices of the funds and shares of every sort were quoted and dealt in as regularly as on the Bourse itself.

The transactions were indeed far larger on this unofficial market than on the privileged and recognized Bourse. Rothschild had in his service a stockjobber at a fixed salary of 12,000 guldens, irrespective of his immense commissions. This person used to wait upon Rothschild early every morning, when together they concerted the plans for the day's operations. The stockjobber had his clients and customers not only on the Bourse but also in the "Panduren-Lager," with whom he concluded his purchases and sales. He kept a number of runners in his employ, whose sole duty it was to run backwards and forwards from him to Rothschild's with reports of all the fluctuations in prices and the disposition of the markets, and to return with orders to be carried out for the purpose of raising or depressing prices as circumstances or convenience dictated. Naturally those speculators and gamblers who were not initiated into his plans fared badly, and were frequently ruined by Rothschild's manipulations. This factotum of Baron Salomon was a poor man when he first became acquainted with the great financier, but it was not long ere he also joined the ranks of the millionaires. So strong were the faith and confidence placed in him, that he was entrusted with the control of affairs and the procuration signature whenever Baron Salomon left Vienna on business or pleasure.

The house of Rothschild played a prominent part in nearly all the great Austrian financial operations. Most of the loans have passed through its hands, and on more than one occasion was the head of the firm consulted with respect to the private fortune of the Imperial family. He was a trusted counsellor with whom family secrets were perfectly safe, and he had always free access to the ministerial Cabinet. Councillor Brentano, of the Finance Department, had indeed formerly been the agent in Trieste of the Frankfort house for its money transactions with the East, but its present agents there are Messrs. Morpurgo and Parente.

The energies and influence of the firm were not by any means confined to purely financial matters, for it was known to have been interested in the success of several mining and industrial adventures. It is no secret that the large quicksilver mines of Almaden in Spain are mortgaged to the Rothschilds. These mines are the only rivals worthy of the name with which the Austrian mines in Idria, producing some 3,000 centners annually, have to contend. To prevent any injurious competition between the Spanish and the Austrian mines, an understanding was effected through the all-powerful influence of the Rothschilds. By this understanding the price of both quicksilver and cinnabar was kept up at a certain figure, which was not to be altered unless both parties consented to the change. The agreement, however, has for some years past been null and ineffective, owing to the discovery of immense quicksilver deposits in America—a discovery which has put an end to a uniform price being maintained for any length of time in Europe.

The city of Vienna derived many direct and indirect benefits from the presence of Baron Salomon, as, independently of his noble beneficence and liberality, its general prosperity must have been increased by the immense business introduced by his firm. A very pleasing recognition of his great services was made him in 1843, when the Mayor of Vienna, accompanied by the Austrian ministers von Kolowrat and Hardegg, handed him as a New Year's gift the diploma or deed stating that he had been elected an honorary freeman of the city, as he was prevented by his nationality and religious persuasion from ever becoming a free citizen. This document stated that he had been elected an honorary freeman not only "on account of his services to the monarchy in general, but more especially in recognition of his great and praiseworthy exertions on behalf of the welfare of the city, by means of his quiet and unobtrusive charity, which had won him universal respect and esteem."

An amusing tale is related of Baron Salomon with reference to a certain Cabby, who it is to be presumed was generally employed by his son,—a great patroniser of cabs, and a very liberal man with his money. It was nothing unusual for him to give the drivers four or five times the amount of their legal fare. On one occasion Baron Salomon after alighting paid the man the legal faro, not a penny more nor less. The Jehu regarded the coin in his open palm with a significant glance, which caused the Baron to inquire whether it was not correct. "Quite correct, and I am much obliged; but your son would have given me three, four, or six times as much." "Indeed, would he? Well, he has a rich father. I have not."

As we have already mentioned, the Vienna house issued, now alone, now in conjunction with other firms, several loans on behalf of the Austrian Government. The first of these loans was that of 1820 for twenty million eight hundred thousand guldens, undertaken by the Rothschilds and David Parisch in Vienna. This was issued in tickets of one hundred guldens each, bearing premiums, and was paid off in the regular course of time by the end of 1840, by means of yearly drawings. The success of this loan was due mainly to the great inducement held out to the public in the shape of the large prizes to be won.

The same two firms contracted for the second loan of 1821, amounting to thirty-seven and a half millions, in bonds of 250 guldens, and redeemed by means of fourteen drawings by the end of 1841.

At the close of 1823, Austria opened a loan of twenty-five million guldens with Rothschild, Baring Brothers and Irving and Co., in London. This loan was required to provide the payment of the subsidies of two and a half million sterling due to England for her defence of Belgium.

Again, on the 1st December, 1829, a loan of twenty-five millions, required to pay off treasury bills, was concluded with Rothschild, Geymüller and Co., Arnstein and Eskeles, and Sina. In 1834 a further loan of twenty-five million was issued by these four allied firms, and was followed in 1839 by one of thirty millions. Both these loans were issued on far more favourable terms to the Government than had been the case on previous occasions, the interest payable on the first being five, and on the second four per cent.

In 1842 Austria was again forced to seek the assistance of Rothschild and his colleagues, the result being a loan of forty million guldens, on which the contracting bankers are estimated to have made four million clear profit.

After the death of Baron Salomon, the business passed into the hands of his son Baron Anselm von Rothschild, who retained the direction until his death in 1879, when his three sons Ferdinand, Nathan, and Salomon Albert, succeeded him. The two first-named have never taken any active share in its control, preferring to leave the helm wholly and solely in the hands of their youngest brother, Salomon Albert.

Fig. XVIII: ANSELM SALOMON VON ROTHSCHILD (1803–1874)

Anselm Salomon (Salomon Mayer's son) has inherited the control of the S. M. Rothschild bank when Salomon passed down in 1855.

Lithography (approx. 1830)

Fig. XIX: FERDINAND ANSELM VON ROTHSCHILD (1839–1898)

Ferdinand was born in Paris in 1839. In 1874 when his father Anselm Salomon passed down Ferdinand has inherited the control of the S. M. Rothschild bank. But he transferred immediately all assets from his bank of Vienna to the Rothschild's headquarter in Frankfort. In 1874, he joined the London branch where he started a British political career. He is celebrated for supervising the construction of the famous Waddesdon Manor between 1874 and 1889.

Photography (1880). Source: antimatrix.org

They were not anxious to face the worry and responsibility attaching to the management of the firm. Quite satisfied with the possession of a handsome fortune, they, like wise men, determined to rest content with what they had and to retire to the enjoyment of the pleasures of society. Baron Ferdinand has long ceased to be an Austrian, having for many years past been an Englishman by the process of naturalization. He married Evelina, the daughter of Baron Lionel do Rothschild, but lost her after one short year of wedded life. Her loss was a severe blow to him, for he was most fondly attached to his young wife. Of late years he has figured prominently as one of the leaders of society. His country house at Waddesdon is the scene, during the summer months, of the most brilliant reunions and garden parties. Scarcely a day passes by without the arrival of parties of distinguished visitors, often including royalty and members of the diplomatic body, who are received and entertained in a truly princely style. Balls, fetes, shooting parties, follow in rapid succession, until the winter season approaches, when Baron Ferdinand returns to his palatial residence in the Rothschild quarter of Mayfair. He now represents the Aylesbury division of Buckinghamshire in Parliament.

CHAPTER IX

BARON JAMES DE ROTHSCHILD.

THE PARIS FIRM.

FRANCE for nearly seventy years possessed no permanent form of government; each successive government was of a temporary and provisional character. After the fall of the monarchy attempts of various kinds were made in the way of forming a representative government, and following one upon the other in rapid succession came the Legislative Assembly with an interim government, the Convention with the Reign of Terror, the Directory, the 18th Brumaire with the Three Consuls, Bonaparte and his Consulate, Napoleon I and the Empire, the first restoration of the Bourbons under Louis XVIII, Napoleon's one hundred days, the second restoration under Charles X, the July dynasty of the Orleans with its immutable ideas, its fall through the revolution of February, the Republic, the Presidency of Louis Napoleon, Napoleon III, Emperor. Such is the list of the many forms of government to which France has been subjected, varying from the most unbridled despotism to the most extreme licentiousness.

In order to realize the condition of France at the beginning of the present century, and to appreciate fully the boldness and sagacity which led Baron James de Rothschild to found his house in Paris, it will be well to give a few particulars regarding the finances of the country at that time. The first budget proclaimed by Napoleon was that of his Consulate, and it amounted to nearly 600 million francs. On the 20th May, 1804, he was elected under the title of Napoleon I Emperor of the French, the succession to the imperial purple being limited to his descendants and those of Joseph and Louis Bonaparte. With the exception of some sixteen marshals, one hundred members of the Senate, and the judges, Napoleon could dispose at pleasure of all other appointments, so that it is not surprising that with the army at his back he should have been able to get the crown voted to him by some three and a half million citizens. In a few years he made himself master of the European continent, thanks to his skill not only in annihilating armies but in overreaching and deceiving cabinets and ministers, thereby preventing any country from arming itself and taking effective measures to resist his progress. When, however, Spain, with Austria and Russia, and at last Prussia and Germany, combined against him, his star of fortune and destiny began to wane. By arbitrary and violent methods he enlarged the limits of the French Empire, denying and destroying the worldly power of the Pope by declaring the Papal States a portion of France, depriving his brother Louis of Brabant, Zealand, and Guelderland, in order to make the valley of the Rhine the frontier line in that direction; then he annexed Holland to France, and finally, on the 10th December, 1810, declared the necessity of extending the empire to the Baltic, and, accordingly, all the sea-coast north of an arbitrary line drawn from the junction of the Lippe with the Rhino to Travemund became French territory. From the Pyrenees to the Baltic, from Texel to Terracina, the great empire reached, while in Spain, Switzerland, Denmark, and Sicily he had vassals and allies who trembled beneath his sway. In Sweden the succession to the throne had been conferred on a French marshal; Prussia was exhausted; Austria appeared fettered by family ties; only two European Powers withstood and defied the power of France—Russia and England.

However greatly the fame and dominion of the empire had grown abroad, the condition of the country itself was of the worst possible description. The imperial subjects were burdened and oppressed by all sorts of tyrannical impositions, by taxes which steadily grew in amount, and by a budget yielding a revenue considerably exceeded by the expenditure. In 1804, when France became an empire, the country was by the decree of the 23rd February called upon to face a budget in which the expenditure amounted to no less than 700 million francs. This was for a war year. For a peace year 79 million would have to be deducted, so that 621 million would still weigh on the country. In addition must be reckoned the Emperor's civil list, which, with the domains left at his disposal, the appanage of his brothers, and the pay of the grand officers of the Crown, amounted to 30 million. Included in this, however, were 7 million for the Emperor's household, so that to the 621 million we have really to add another 23 million, to which we must still add the expenses of the Departments, 79 million; the cost of maintaining the roads, 15; the expense of collecting, 80; the secret police, 5; so that the total expenditure for a peace year may be put down at 823 million francs, or about 376 million more than under the monarchy. Year by year the budget grew, being estimated in 1809 and 1810 at 740 million, whilst in the following year it was reckoned at 954 million. The preparations for the campaign against Russia—the most gigantic military expedition of modern times—swallowed up million after million.

"Napoleon had collected the most powerful army the world ever saw; from all parts of the Continent had he summoned his forces for the struggle; every variety of blood, of complexion, of language, of dress and arms, were to be found in its ranks. The auxiliaries from whole provinces were led through kingdoms that respected his arms; the artillery of entire fortresses ploughed across the fields; cattle from a thousand hills were collected for the support of myriads who spread themselves like a plague across the plains of eastern Europe, where blood flowed in streams, and where the earth became blanched with the men's bodies. But this gigantic expedition, although successful, gained no object, since the enemy was vanquished, but the conqueror in vain tried to secure peace. The ancient capital of the Czars in Moscow was in his power, but the capture was profitless to him, owing to the refusal of the enemy to come to peaceful terms, and the barrenness of the neighbourhood. The burning of Moscow in one night began Napoleon's downfall, which the frost of a second completed. Upon all the pomp and material of numerous warriors, upon their cavalry, their cannons, their magazines, and their baggage fell thickly and steadily the snowflakes of a northern night; the retreat of the armed hordes was cut off, and their destruction as effectually achieved as if it had been on the battle-field. All Napoleon's endeavours to regain his lost power were never able to remedy the effect of that Russian night. The fire of his genius still burned as brightly as ever; in two campaigns his efforts were superhuman; his resources were even more remarkable than before his courage deserved the reward and prize of victory for which he played—but all was in vain. The weapons remained only a short time longer in his hand; his army was scattered to the winds; his opponents no longer bowed beneath his superior nature, for they discovered that he, like themselves, could be conquered, and they in their turn became bold. Such was the great captain, and such the destiny into which he plunged.

"A mighty genius of the first rank; one of the greatest masters in the art of war, he occupies a place among the generals of the highest class. His genius, however, was not confined to war. In the circumstances of government he showed himself equally sharp—as quick in deciding his procedure in politics as in the field. But with all these qualities he was a conqueror, he was a tyrant.

"In order to appease his thirst for power, in order to satisfy his ambition for empire—an ambition no conquest could still—he trod freedom beneath his feet. He enveloped the world in flames, which the blood of million was unable to extinguish. Honesty, truth, pity, and sense of duty were cast aside by him, who pursued a single and selfish policy. Enghien's death, Wright's horrible sufferings, Pichegru's mysterious death, Palm's punishment, Toussaint's martyrdom, are all blots on his fame."

Equally characteristic is the opinion of Lord Brougham concerning him:—"He sacrificed to his ambition three milliards in money as the acknowledged cost of the wars of 1802-1814 to France alone, and five-sixths of three million men, who were called out for active service."

Following upon his memorable campaign against Russia and his disastrous retreat came his dethronement and banishment to Elba, whence he issued to try his fortune once more against the whole of Europe. The sequel to this attempt is too well known to need repetition, leading as it did to his final overthrow, and to the restoration of Bourbon rule in France, with a constitutional government, under Louis XVIII.

When the Chambers met for the first time after the restoration, Montesquieu laid before them a report of the condition of the country, describing in very striking language the evils arising from the imperial form of government. Still gloomier was the picture painted by the Minister of Finance of the State's finances and requirements. The arrears amounted to more than 1,308 million, which, however, were afterwards reduced to 759. The funded debt amounted to only 93 million. To provide means to discharge these liabilities, it was decided to sell the domain forests and common lands. The abnormal and provisional budget of 1814, and the normal budget of 1815, estimating the receipts at 618 million francs, and the expenditure at 547 million, were passed on the 23rd September, 1814; the civil list of 33 million, and an additional vote of 30 million for the debts incurred by the Bourbons abroad since their expulsion, were likewise voted.

Then came Napoleon's sensational return, with his brief enjoyment of power, cut short by the efforts of the allied forces. Nearly a million foreign troops entered the French territory, and demanded an indemnity of 100 million francs at the expiration of the one hundred days. The budget for 1816 estimated the ordinary expenditure at 548 million, and the extraordinary expenditure at 290 million, in addition to that for the Consolidated Fund of 125,500,000 francs. Taken all in all, the expenditure amounted to 1,069,261,826 francs as given in the law of the 25th March, 1817. the indemnity of a milliard francs claimed by the emigrants, and the war indemnity of 700 million claimed by the Allied Powers, were enormous items in the State accounts, in addition to the cost of maintaining the foreign army of occupation for five years.

In the following years both the receipts and the expenditure rose and fell. In 1824 the Chambers put the civil list for the King at 25 million, and that for the Princes at 7 million. The budget grew steadily under the different ministries until the July revolution. Under Martignac in 1828 the expenditure was estimated at 980 million francs, whilst the receipts reached only 986 million. During the reign of the Orleans family the State finances, in spite of the enormous receipts, were far from flourishing. The indirect taxes exceeded a total of 12 milliard francs, whilst the yearly expenditure amounted to from 1,000 to 1,200 million. The chief cause of this lay in the lasting "armed peace." In 1841 a deficit of 1,000 million was declared. The system followed by Louis Philippe had already brought the country to the verge of a financial crisis. The city of Paris was burdened with a debt, now considerably increased, of 12 million, and the State budget with a *rente* of 600,000 francs. The distress among the working classes was fearful; in commercial circles bankruptcy was the order of the day. Under the fraudulent system then generally prevailing persons had carried on business without any capital at their backs, by means of credit, ill-deserved but too readily obtained. The revolution came without any warning to complete the feeling of anxiety and uncertainty prevailing at the time. A provisional government was placed at the head of affairs, and issued decrees one after the other dealing with all subjects, from the abolition of the monarchy down to the assignment of the millions of the civil list to the relief of the working classes. The indebtedness of the State was fearful; the financial disorder unlimited. Even without the revolution a State loan of 600 million would have been absolutely necessary. There were but two means of saving the newly-created republic—a dictatorship, or in other words, exaction, or credit. If the State had displayed the slightest hesitation in meeting its engagements the word bankruptcy would have been on every lip. Goudchaux, the Finance Minister, resigned; he felt himself unequal to the difficulties of the situation. A man of ability, capable of manfully grappling with and mastering the dangers of the impending crisis, was above all things required. Garnier-Pagès succeeded Goudchaux as Finance Minister. One of his first proceedings, after his accession to office, was to sell the forests belonging to the old civil list. He decreed a voluntary loan, but, as the coffers remained empty, he had recourse to the most pitiable of all financial measures: he laid an additional 45 centimes on the four instalments of the direct taxes, a measure which severely hit the already heavily-burdened peasants and the small landowners. The expenditure amounted to 1,700 million francs, and the State debts, which had increased by nearly a million in seven years, to 5 milliard 170 million. The additional tax brought in 150 million, whilst the Bank advanced 230 million upon the State forests. By these means the State was saved from bankruptcy.

Under the Presidency of the Republic, which ere long was converted into the Empire, the indebtedness of the State continued to increase steadily. The war with Russia required one sacrifice after the other. In April, 1856, the State expenditure, the revenues and the State debts were estimated by the Minister of Finance to be as follows:—

"The regular expenditure amounts to 1,598 million francs. The first portion of this consists of the interest on the debt, which takes 342 million for the dividends, and the redemption of the consolidated debt; 10½ million for the interest on the special loan for canals; 33½ million for the interest on the floating debt, the guarantees, and finally 68 million *dette viagère,* together 455 million francs. The supplies are 25 million for the Emperor; 1½ million for the Princes and Princesses of the Imperial house; 6½ million for the Senate; 2½ million for the Legislative Body, and 3½ million for the Legion of Honour; making in all 38½ millions. The collection of the taxes costs 165 million; 4 million francs are set apart for the completion of the Louvre." In a word, taking the population of France at 35 million, the average contribution per head to the State treasury was about 46 francs for the year 1856.

The fortunes amassed by individuals—bankers and financiers, more particularly—resident in Franco, or rather in Paris, cannot be described nor estimated. In June, 1848, when the proposed decree for the conversion of the floating debt into a consolidated debt was brought before the National Assembly, a Paris paper, published under the title of "The Organization of Labour," gave the following details respecting the wealth of the leading houses in Paris: "The firms Laffitte Frères and Delamarre are estimated at 10 million; Baudon at 12; Rougemont and Lafond at 15; Dourand, Delessert, Aquirrevengon and Halphen, each at 20; Hottinger and Pelaprat each at 25; Fould at 30; Hoop at 40; Baron Gressulhe at 100; Rothschild at 600 million francs." The King was put down as worth 800; the Duc d'Aumale and Madame Adelaide each at 70; and the Duc de Montpensier at 20 million. According to this estimate the combined wealth of the above well-known banking-houses amounted only to 362 million, a total which Rothschild exceeded by no less than 238 million. It was by means of this immense capital at their command that the Rothschilds gained that consideration and influence which no other firm has ever yet equalled or approached.

"Involuntarily" wrote the "Augsburger Allge-meine Zeitung," "one is forced to ask the question how it was that the house of Rothschild managed to maintain its distinguished position undisturbed throughout the manifold changes of government in France? The explanation is easy" continued the writer: "the house belonged to no political party; the Rothschilds are the friends of the kingdom, of law and of peace, and as such could maintain their preponderating influence equally as well under the heterogeneous ministries of a Decazes, Villèle, Martignac, or Polignac, as under the government of Louis Philippe."

When we remember the disturbed state of Europe in 1812, and how much the Rothschild family had suffered at the hands of Napoleon, we cannot but wonder what could have been the reasons which induced Baron James de Rothschild to determine opening a branch house in the French capital. That he did so in spite of the unpropitious aspect of affairs speaks volumes for both his boldness and foresight. It may have been that he had already made sure of his prospects by having rendered the Emperor some services, for few had more need of financial assistance than Napoleon I, and Baron

James, we may presume, was not unwilling to secure himself substantial advantages at the expense of the French nation. This is, of course, all surmise on our part, but, when we recollect that the supplies entrusted by the British Government to Nathan Mayer Rothschild for the army in Spain were conveyed to their destination through France, it does not seem altogether improbable that Baron James must by some means or other have obtained a certain degree of influence with the French Government, or he could never have executed the business with such success. Money is proverbially all-powerful, and in this case certainly did not belie its reputation. A more favourable period, as events proved, could hardly have been chosen for establishing the new firm in Paris. It was started in 1812. In 1815 Napoleon was deposed and business at once poured in upon Baron James de Rothschild. Thanks to the influence and warm recommendations of the Elector of Hesse, Baron James de Rothschild was empowered to receive the milliard of francs war expenses claimed by the Allied Powers when they entered Paris. In the same way the two milliards war indemnity passed through his hands, and we may feel sure that the transaction was most profitable. For some years afterwards we do not find him engaged in any great financial operation; indeed until 1823 his name is altogether lost sight of. In that year, however, he took up the whole of the French loan at the price of 89fr. 55cent., and the Gentleman's Magazine" in chronicling the occurrence testifies to the confidence and influence enjoyed by the firm, by stating that the immediate effect on the French Rentes was that they rose to 90 frs. 25 cent.

In 1824, the Marquis de Villèle, the Minister of Finance at that time, projected the conversion of the whole of the French Five per Cent, debt into a Three per Cent. debt.

Those who were so disposed could exchange the old Five per Cent, stock into bonds of the new Three per Cent, stock by accepting the exchange at the rate of 100 francs new stock for every 75 francs of the old. The whole debt amounted to 3,066,783,560 francs, and it was estimated that perhaps only one-third of the stockholders would accept the conversion; consequently, to satisfy the State creditors, no less than 1,055,556,720 francs would have to be paid them in cash. In order to collect this immense sum, the assistance of all the great financiers on the English, Dutch, and French markets was sought. Subscriptions were received in Paris, London, and Amsterdam by the firms of Baring Brothers, J. Laffitte and Co., and N. M. Rothschild and Sons. A committee under the presidency of Alexander Baring, with Baron James de Rothschild and Jacques Laffitte as his colleagues, was then formed to determine the conditions to be made with the Minister, on which they would provide the cash required for the redemption of the old Five per Cent, bonds. Their plan was to sell the new Three per Cent, stock, as soon as created, at the price of eighty. At this price purchasers would receive 3¾ per cent, interest on their money, and if the paid off debt could only be replaced by bonds of the Three per Cent, stock purchased at 80, it necessarily followed that the Five per Cent, stock, before the proposed conversion, would be relatively worth 106.66, in order to yield a corresponding rate of interest.

Operations based on this calculation were accordingly made on the three markets. The capital required in Paris for the conversion was estimated at 1,000 million. The speculators, thinking that the contractors would not put the new Three per Cent, stock into circulation under 80, bought in Amsterdam and Frankfort at 81—83⅓, whilst at the same time immense sales of the French Five per Cent, debt at the relative price of 106.67 to 110 were effected. Higher prices than these could not be obtained.

Villèle's project in order to become law required the sanction of the two Chambers. After a very stormy debate, it passed the Chamber of Deputies by a Ministerial majority of 68. In the Chamber of Peers it encountered a vigorous opposition, secretly promoted by the Viscount de Chateaubriand, who harboured a private grudge against Villèle. By a majority of 12 votes the proposal was rejected. The Five per Cents., which the day before were quoted at 106, fell at once to 98, and an extraordinary excitement ruled on the stock markets. Chateaubriand resigned, and the day following at the opening of the market the Five per Cent. Rentes were dealt in at 104; then they receded again to 98, and remained for some time stationary.

The rejection of the Finance Minister's scheme was a severe blow to speculators, who had operated freely in the anticipation of the conversion being accepted. Those who had bought largely for the settlement were compelled to sell out again at a loss. Baring and Laffitte were severely hit; the Rothschilds, however, emerged from the fray uninjured, owing to their having confined their operations to selling simultaneously largo amounts of the new Three per Cents, and of the old Five per Cents. As the Three per Cent, debt was not to be created, none of this stock could be delivered, whilst the Five per Cent, stock, which they had sold at 104 or more, could be bought in again at 98.

Fig. XX: JACQUES LAFFITTE
FRENCH BANKER & STATESMAN
(1767-1844)

Credit: public domain, painting is at the Musée du Jouet de Poissy, France

In 1830 the well-known banker, P. J. Ouvrard, in Paris, obtained trustworthy information, a week before their publication, of the coming decrees of the Polignac Ministry, decrees, as is well known, resulting in the July revolution and the fall of the Bourbon dynasty. No sooner was Ouvrard certain of his information, than he summoned to his confidence several bankers and bill brokers, and then hastened to London. On reaching that capital he at once began to effect such heavy sales of stock at ever falling prices that the Rothschilds, who, being among the first purchasers, were interested in the maintenance of the prices, became quite alarmed, and immediately despatched a courier to Paris to learn the real reason of the immense sales that had taken place. The Paris house, however, were no better informed than the London house, and were unable to give the key to the enigma. Baron James, who a few months previously had contracted for the last Government loan of Four per Cent. Rente at the price of 102 francs 7 cents., at once betook himself, in a state of violent excitement, to Polignac, and requested the Minister to enlighten him as to the real state of affairs. The possibility of the Ministerial decrees being issued had already become a subject of discussion on the Stock Exchange, but no one could speak with any certainty on the matter. When the Baron returned from his interview with the Prime Minister, he made no secret of the fact that the latter had given him his word of honour that the decrees were nothing but an empty scheme which had never been seriously considered, and which would now remain a dream. The next day it became known that they had been signed by Charles X after mass, and the following day they appeared in print in the columns of the "Moniteur."

The immediate effect of their publication was that the house of Rothschild and its partners in the transactions found themselves saddled with the whole loan of 78,373,750 francs, which fell to a discount of 20 or 30 per cent. For a long time afterwards this stock remained in such bad odour that buyers were difficult to find. The business, however, was far more prejudicial to Rothschild's partners than to Baron James himself, as the bulk of the stock had already been taken off his hands. He was severely reproached at the time for the part he had borne in the business, as it was generally held that he had abandoned his friends and left them helpless; still it must not be forgotten that till the time of the July revolution he had always shared his enormous gains with his partners. That event came quite unawares upon them, and at once changed what had promised to be a most profitable undertaking into a most costly and ruinous one.

Ouvrard had at a stroke won an immense sum, which his broker Amet set down at 2 million francs. As soon as he had carried out his successful combination, he returned from London to Paris and commenced operations. They were all calculated for the fall. As the Rente, even after Casimir Perier joined the Ministry, fell to 52, and in February, 1831, to 48, some slight estimate may be formed of the extraordinary profits Ouvrard must have realized. It was mainly by the influence of the house of Rothschild that the fall of M. Thiers in 1840 was brought about. Whether right or wrong, Thiers thought he was acting as beseemed a Frenchman, whose only object was to uphold the honour of his country. This consideration, however, never troubled the Rothschilds; for they supported no nationality.

Fig. XXI: CASIMIR PERIER
BANKER & FRENCH POLITICIAN
(1777-1832)

Painted in 1827 by Louis Hersent (1777–1860)

They are—although by some the assertion may be opposed—cosmopolitan, or at least European, neither German, French, English, Italian, Turkish, nor Russian, and, as they possess immense influence in diplomatic circles, they help to maintain peace at the expense of all princes. In his opposition to Thiers Rothschild bore himself as king of the Stock Exchange, and Austrian Consul General. Thiers in the columns of the "Constitutional" pointedly asked Rothschild, of what concern was the honour of France to him, seeing that he was a German? Baron James replied, in a letter which he had published in all the papers, that, if he were a German, so must his brother Frenchmen be Germans. However, it was in the interests of Germany that he acted in the matter of the Rhine frontiers, then under discussion. Thiers resigned, and was succeeded by Guizot, whoso proceedings were always of a somewhat cosmopolitan, antinational character, so that it was not altogether inappropriate when his Ministry was nicknamed the *Ministère de l'Étranger*. It was naturally under the monarchy, where power centred in one person, that the influence possessed by the Rothschilds displayed itself most conspicuously and undeniably.

Few were the public men who did not feel and own that influence. The majority of the deputies, we may say, without fear of contradiction, were more or less under obligations to the firm, and ready to assist in promoting its interests and views. Still, although in diplomatic circles Baron James de Rothschild was a personage of such importance that his opinions could never be altogether disregarded, it was upon the Stock Exchange that his rule was most powerfully felt and universally recognized. Nor did he hesitate to use the sovereignty he possessed to further his purposes, as he could raise or depress prices at his pleasure. His sway was indeed despotic, and none were found bold or rash enough to dispute or oppose his arbitrary edicts, as the gigantic nature of his operations effectually prevented anything like systematic opposition being offered, and induced others to lend him their co-operation by following in his steps. It cannot be denied that the Stock Exchange can boast of intellects which in diplomatic skill and artifice would do credit to a Talleyrand, and it is equally certain that for boldness in conceiving and for vigour in carrying out a plan none could excel Baron James, whose operations were the talk and wonder of Europe. Seeing the facility with which at a stroke fortunes may be won on the Stock Exchange, it is not surprising that speculation should have a strange fascination over the public, nor that the Stock Exchange should become a training school for the development of every kind of trickery and deceit, the centre of genuine business, and of endless swindling.

To live we require the necessary means, and it is the fate and calling of everyone to strive after the acquisition of wealth, and, when he has succeeded, to use the utmost care and thought in the preservation of his gains. There are many ways of attaining this object, since it is possible to acquire riches either by labour, industry, or speculation. Naturally everyone, being more or less anxious to become wealthy, prefers the way which leads most directly and with least trouble towards the goal. The outcome of this innate desire to grow rich speedily and without effort was the invention of games of chance, which have been in vogue from the earliest ages; the dice were as familiar to the Greeks and Romans as they are to us in the nineteenth century. It was the desire for gain which led the people of the Middle Ages to place such faith in the black arts, and in the power of the divining rod. The infatuated and ignorant belief that many had in the boasted powers of the alchemists and astrologers was owing to the latter taking advantage of the cupidity of their dupes, who, in the anticipation of becoming suddenly rich, were ready and willing to place implicit reliance in their mysterious advisers. But the philosopher's stone and all such trash are now discarded, and instead of it we have speculation, stock-jobbing, gambling and swindling; all being different modes of attaining the same object, —the acquisition of wealth with the least possible trouble or exertion.

Real gain is that which arises from industry backed up by capital and credit, the latter of which is proportionate to the industry and capital combined. In many countries credit is the basis of all business, which is facilitated and developed by its means. According to the estimate entertained of the credit and character of the individual, the credit of a State is formed; this in earlier times was so slight that oppressive measures had to be resorted to in urgent cases to procure the necessary funds to meet the State's requirements. For the same purpose recourse was often had to the reduction of the interest on the debt, and to the issue of base money. As years rolled on the evils arising from these practices were recognized, and sounder principles of finance and administration were, by degrees, adopted. Thenceforward the public were induced to confide in the Government, and invest their money in the purchase of the Government stocks, which became at once the basis of a speculation similar to that in private shares. The funded debts of a State, especially of one whose credit has decayed, are, in disturbed times, the most prolific source of that species of gambling for the differences in the quotations, which is known in England as stock-jobbing. In every country the Government stocks are used as the means of gambling. The Stock Exchanges of London, Paris, Frankfort and Vienna are crowded with persons who have neither stock to sell, nor money to pay for their purchases, but who yet embark in large speculations for the rise or fall, hoping to pocket, before the settling day, a handsome profit by the difference that takes place between the prices at which they buy and those at which they sell.

The usual mode of conducting speculation on the Stock Exchange is by means of "time-bargains," i.e., bargains which are not settled before a certain day, usually termed the "account," or settling, day. Naturally during the interval between the closing of a bargain and the account day, prices may experience considerable fluctuations, on which speculators greatly rely for the success of their dealings. For instance, a person may sell an amount of stock for the "account," and owing to a fall of prices may be able to buy that amount in again at a considerably lower price, thereby pocketing a handsome profit in the shape of the difference between the two prices. On the other hand it frequently happens that the market disappoints the expectations of speculators, who are consequently unable to settle their transactions by delivering the stock they have sold, or by paying over the cost of their purchases; in such cases the transactions are usually arranged by the defaulters paying the differences between the prices at which the bargains were struck and those ruling on the account day. From this explanation it will be at once seen how speculation is encouraged, since it is possible for persons without capital or stock to embark in speculations for large amounts, and these speculations, if luck attends them, return fabulous and' easily earned profits.

No wonder that this sort of business has its fascinations. It is, indeed, neither more nor less than gambling pure and simple, and is so considered by the law. There can be no doubt that this gigantic system of speculation is prejudicial to the public interests, as it seduces business men from their own legitimate business, which they neglect in the hope of gaining larger profits, with greater ease, on the Stock Exchange. Were this system of buying and selling for future delivery confined to the Stock Exchange there would be less reason to complain; but, unfortunately, it is practised upon all our produce markets, where panics are by its means created with far too great a frequency. The public are the greatest sufferers in such cases, as the prices of commodities which they require, and with which they can ill dispense, such as corn, tea, coffee, etc., are often forced up to an extraordinary height by the efforts of unscrupulous and greedy schemers.

The want of principle and the readiness of speculators to attain their ends at all hazards, is shown by the many artifices they employ to effect a reaction on the market. It often happens that the market, contrary to their sanguine expectations, makes a movement which if maintained is sure to bring about their ruin; consequently they strenuously endeavour to remedy the evil by the fabrication and circulation of false news, by the publication of lying statements in the newspapers, and by any other dis-honest means which appear likely to produce the desired result. These tricks are bad and objectionable enough, but in more than one instance ruined speculators have as a last resource tried to re-establish their shattered fortunes by forgery and other fraudulent means. In 1803, when the greatest anxiety prevailed in London as to the result of the negotiations then pending between the French Republic and the English Government, the whole city became elated and joyous owing to a statement contained in a letter, posted in a prominent position on the Mansion House, to the effect that: "the negotiations were brought to an amicable conclusion." As this letter purported to be written by Lord Hawkesbury, implicit faith was at first placed in its genuineness, especially as it seemed to enjoy the sanction of the Lord Mayor. The Funds rose at once with a bound. Presently, however, when the matter was quietly considered, grave doubts began to be entertained as to the authenticity of the letter. Many (and among them perhaps the authors) boldly declared it fictitious: a reaction forthwith set in, and was intensified when the forgery was exposed. A similar incident occurred only a year or two ago when a letter pretending to be written by Lord Granville's authority, and stating that the settlement of the bondholders' claims against Chili had been satisfactorily arranged, was placed in a prominent position on the Stock Exchange. It is needless to say that this likewise was a hoax, or rather a forgery. Nor is the pernicious practice of fabricating false news by any means confined to the members of the Stock Exchange; all who operate in the Funds and are interested in bringing about a certain movement in the quotations resort to these objectionable devices. Members of Parliament are not above stooping to such meanness; indeed more than one Stock Exchange scandal has originated in the dishonest practices of honourable members. Few trials created greater sensation in England than those of Mr. Walsh, M.P., and Mr. Cochrane Johnstone, M.P., at the beginning of the present century. Impelled by their fatal love of speculation Cabinet Ministers and other persons holding high official rank have been known to take advantage of their position and turn to profitable account the information which has reached them through official channels. Nothing shows more clearly the baneful effects attending the mania for speculation than the deplorable fact that ministers have been led by its influence to abuse the confidence placed in them, and subordinate the public interests to their own. Take for instance the case of the Count de Guisne, the French ambassador in London at the early part of the present century. Profiting by intelligence received in virtue of his office, he speculated in the Funds with great success for a time, but afterwards his good fortune deserted him, and he was unable to meet his engagements. As long as he was lucky he was willing to acknowledge the contracts made with his broker, but when his luck changed he disowned all knowledge of the transactions, refused to pay the balance due, and quitted the country. Apart from the evils directly traceable to speculation, the amount of bribery and corruption it engenders cannot be estimated. In order to obtain the earliest information of all that passes in political circles, speculators spare neither trouble nor expense. By means best known to themselves, but which may be expressed by the conventional term "value received," they manage to obtain from subordinate officials and court attendants early and reliable reports of all that it concerns their interests to know. The famous Duke of Marlborough is indeed said to have so far forgotten his station as to have accepted an annuity from the great speculator Medina, who found the outlay extremely remunerative, as it enabled him to have the exclusive privilege of forwarding from the field of battle reports of those great successes which fired the spirit of the nation with enthusiasm and joy. Formerly the advantage of possessing reliable information of any important event, such as the declaration of war, the resignation of a cabinet, the illness of a sovereign, was very considerable, since, owing to the slowness of communication, the truth or falsehood of the reports promulgated by speculators could not be ascertained until they had affected the market and brought about the movement in prices which inevitably filled the pockets of those who were in the secret. Thanks to the invention of the telegraph, these lying rumours are now exposed almost as soon as circulated, but twenty or forty years ago it would have taken days or weeks to ascertain how true or false they were.

The year 1847 was a most evil year both for commerce and State finance, especially in England and France. So severe, indeed, were the financial pressure and the scarcity of money in England, that during the month of October bills drawn upon and accepted by first-class firms, with only a week to run, were discounted at the rate of 13 per cent, per annum. The banks in Liverpool and New-castle, owing to a run of unprofitable business, were forced to suspend payment, thereby causing ruin and distress in every direction. The pressure arose more from want of confidence than from any other cause. Everyone had more or less caught the speculation fever raging for railways and corn, and had become liable for sums far beyond his ability to pay; consequently, the value of all railway securities fell rapidly, whilst vast amounts were lost in the corn speculations.

During the following months the prices of the Government stocks rose in a strange fashion, despite the well-known scarcity of money prevailing at the time. Chance and an unlooked-for succession of various causes, rather than the powerful manipulation of the Rothschilds, brought about this unusual phenomenon. Extensive dealings had taken place in the Three per Cent. rentes, and it was found on settling-day that those securities were greatly over-sold. A large portion, which remained uncovered, figured in the names of the Rothschilds. Since the latter had endeavoured to force prices to take a certain path, this amount had been considerably augmented, and, according to estimate made, it was thought that the average price would work out about 75 francs 50 cents. From the systematic sales effected by the Rothschilds, it seemed that their principal object was to maintain this quotation, and that their speculations would prove unprofitable were the prices to rise beyond 75.75, which to all appearances was their limit. The great herd of speculators who faithfully followed all the movements of Baron James, whose actions inspired all their operations, were now placed in an awkward position. They had sold very heavily for the account, but when settling-day arrived stock proved exceedingly scarce, and it became an easy matter for the "Bulls" to raise the price to 76 francs 40 cents., as they were assisted in their efforts by the absence of fresh sellers, the scarcity of stock, and the readiness of persons to buy. Shortly afterwards the price rose to 77 francs, apparently quite contrary to the interest of the house of Rothschild and to the desire of all well-wishers of the new project for a State loan of 250 million francs. Then there ensued an un-expected revival of confidence among the public, similar to that which had occurred the year before; the public entered into the speculation, wrested the sceptre of power from the hands of the Rothschilds, and showed them that at times the public is able to set a limit to their rule. In order to counteract the influence brought to bear upon the market, Baron James determined suddenly to unload on it some 450,000 francs Three per Cent. Rente, which he had borrowed from the three great insurance companies, the Compagnie Générale, the Royale, and the Union, against the deposit of 500,000 francs Five per Cent. Rente. Apparently his object was by this sudden delivery for cash to beat down the price to his old limit, but in this calculation he was mistaken, as means were found to relieve the market of all this stock, and so the operation failed. The "Bulls," who had hardly dared to expect the disappearance of so large an amount of stock, took heart of grace, and kept the quotation up almost to 77 francs. Unwittingly they had helped Baron James to win his game. Dealing in the new loan first took place at 76 francs 50, then the price sank 1 franc, or 75 cents., about the price at which Baron James contracted for the loan in November, 1847, namely, 75 francs. Baron James had scored another victory over the whole financial world in Paris. Directly he undertook the loan he issued a circular calling upon all subscribers to pay an immediate instalment of 5 francs upon every 100 allotted to them, failing which their applications would be disregarded. Speculation had been so rife that Baron James may have decided upon this measure from mistrust of the subscribers' ability to fulfil their obligations; or his object may have been to increase the firmness of the new loan on the market.

While Louis Philippe occupied the throne, money was supreme; riches alone ruled in the land which was credited with possessing—thanks to the system of so-called popular representation bestowed upon it—all the blessings and advantages supposed to attend a constitutional monarchy. In the Chamber of Peers the interests and aims of every class had representatives, the second Chamber, elected under a high census, being the reflection of the rich *bourgeoisie*. Such an Assembly of representatives was, however, as regards the people, a fiction. Moreover, Stock Exchange speculation

Fig. XXII: LOUIS-PHILIPPE I – KING OF FRANCE
Duke of Orleans (1773-1850)
KING OF FRANCE from 1830 to 1848

Painting by Pierre Roch Vigneron, ©Paris Musées / Carnavalet Museum formed the chief occupation of the rich *bourgeoisie*, while Louis Philippe and his Prime Minister Thiers led the van in this playing with fortune. The financial situation was for ever growing worse in consequence of the rapid spread of corruption, especially in the practice of buying votes. The demands of those who allowed their votes to be bought kept becoming more and more exorbitant, but, as the means at the command of the corrupting parties did not increase in the same proportion, the court favourites had to make free with the State treasures to supply the deficiencies. Fearful scandals were brought to light, until the feelings and good sense of the nation could suffer the evil no longer. Stronger and stronger waxed the cry of corruption with which the Guizot Ministry was assailed. In spite of all that he had done for them, by degrees even the *bourgeoisie* began to desert Louis Philippe, and united in the demand for a reform of the electoral system. The whole tone and manners of society were affected by the universal corruption, and to what a depth of vice and degradation the public morality had fallen was shown by the revelations that took place. So far had many persons gone that-the Government were forced to disown them and their practices. Like shipwrecked mariners, the Government consulted their own safety by sacrificing their weaker comrades, and prosecuted numbers who had high rank, and were at the same time friends or relations of the King; such persons, for instance, were Teste, formerly in the Ministry, and Cubières, an old Court favourite, both of whom had either made away with the State moneys or had allowed themselves to be bribed; lastly came Praslin, an old friend of the King.

The monopoly of the State loans which the house of Rothschild had in the course of time secured to itself, and which afforded strong evidence of the immense financial power at its command, has, in consequence of the new principles of finance by which the Government has been guided since 1848, come to an end. At one time it would have been thought a piece of madness to oppose or compete with the Rothschilds in their operations, but now, owing to the powerful and active coalitions formed among many of the leading banking and financial houses, the power and influence of the Rothschilds have received a severe check. They are no longer the all-puissant despotic firm they once were; younger and equally energetic rivals have forced them to descend from the platform they once occupied alone, and they now stand on the same footing as other financial houses. Their influence is of course still immense and powerful, but it no longer secures them the precedence they so long held in monied circles. The effect of the new principles of finance upon the privileges and influence of the house of Rothschild was clearly shown in 1855 when the national loan was issued. The Rothschilds were no longer allowed to pocket, by contracting for the whole loan, all the profits attending the issue; they were forced to subscribe on an equal footing with every other citizen for whatever share they wished to obtain. The policy and wisdom of the Government in taking this bold measure cannot be doubted, as it enabled the public to share in the profit attending the issue—a profit which on previous occasions the contractors had exclusively enjoyed. The loan was issued to subscribers at 63 francs 27 cents, but long before the allotments took place it was dealt in on the Exchange at 65 francs 90 cents.

In addition to the Government business, as we may call it, Baron James engaged in many commercial and industrial undertakings. To him France is in a great measure indebted for the construction of most of her principal railroads. He may indeed be called the "Railway King" of France, as Hudson was the "Railway King" of England. To quote the "Augsburger Allgemeine Zeitung" once more:

"When during the last few years the speculative mania turned towards industrial enterprises, and railways became a necessity on the Continent, the Rothschilds took the initiative and placed themselves at the head of the movement. The Versailles Railway on the right bank of the Seine is their creation, and in Austria they gave the first impulse to enterprise of this description by building the magnificent Northern Railway."

The greatest of Baron James's railway undertakings was perhaps the construction of the Northern Railway of France, which was attended by so many scandals and productive of such widespread speculation that some description of it may not be out of place. In order to secure the country all the benefits supposed*to result from unlimited competition, a law had been passed by which it was decreed that the construction of railways in Franco was not to be effected by granting concessions to particular persons, but was to be confided to those companies whose tenders proved most acceptable. In the case of the Northern Railway, these prudent precautions proved unavailing, as Baron James secured beforehand the co-operation of all who might have been his rivals, and, his being the only tender, there was no alternative but to accept it. The capital of the company consisted of 300,000 shares of 500 francs each. Baron James had no sooner got his company fairly started than he inaugurated a wholesale speculation in the said shares. Every trick and artifice known was employed to force them up to a fabulous price they were given away broadcast to the newspapers, in order that the praises of the latter might be won for the undertaking, or their opposition at least silenced. There was scarcely a person of any importance but received a present of a number of shares, in some cases five, in others fifty, and often more. Ministers, deputies, journalists, everyone, in fact, of any note was bribed to lend his support to the new railway. Naturally the shares soon rose to an enormous premium, and the ignorant and infatuated public, gulled by the reports of the enormous sums already won, and still to be won, hastened to participate in the speculation. The premium on the shares was at one time as much as 348 francs, when Baron James thought it time to realize the profit arising from the operation, and accordingly began to sell out the shares he held. By selling heavily he forced the prices down, ruining the ignorant persons who had purchased the shares at a high premium. He was thus enabled to buy in at a price which left him a handsome profit on the shares he had sold.

And so the speculation went on, Baron James, backed up by the immense support he had secured, raising and depressing the market by his manœuvres just as it suited his purpose. His gains were set down by popular estimate at 140 million francs, but that may be an exaggeration. On the 15th June, 1846, the line was opened with great pomp, and amidst universal rejoicings. Amiens on that day presented a grand spectacle, crowded as it was with princes of the royal family, marshals and generals, deputies, peers, members of the bar, and others who had been invited to take part in the opening ceremony. Unhappily the line inaugurated under such brilliant auspices was, a month or two later, the scene of a terrible accident, by which some thirty persons lost their lives, and an equal number were more or less injured.

Fig. XXIII: ÉMILE PEREIRE
(1800-1875)
INTERNATIONAL BANKER, BUSINESSMAN & MEMBER OF THE FRENCH ASSEMBLY

Photography of Émile Pereire (1874)
BY FRANCK (1816-1906) – BIBLIOTHEQUE NATIONALE DE FRANCE

Fig. XXIV: ISAAC PEREIRE
(1806-1880)
BANKER & MEMBER OF THE FRENCH ASSEMBLY

Portrait of Isaac Pereire (1874)

BY LÉON BONNAT (1833-1922), BNF

The great success and immense fortune gained by Baron James could not fail to win for him a large amount of jealousy and envy, which displayed itself in the combinations formed by rival firms, all anxious to deprive him of some portion of the large profits attending his operations. Among the many formidable rivals with whom he had to contend, none perhaps proved himself so capable and dangerous as Émile Pereire, the head of the firm of that name. So bitter was the rivalry between the two that neither lost a chance of damaging or spiting the other; indeed, so far did matters go that Baron James and Pereire allowed their rivalry in business to grow into a personal enmity, which displayed itself on every possible occasion. Neither hesitated stooping to enter into any intrigue or doing any mean trick if he thought he could thereby damage his rival, either in reputation or pocket. As Pereire's means alone would have been insufficient to attain the objects he had in view and compete with the influence and fortune of the Rothschilds, he sought the co-operation of other influential firms, not only in Paris but in other great capitals. So powerful was the coalition thus organized that even the vast influence of the Rothschilds was ineffectual in the attempt to procure its overthrow. Some idea of the strong opposition with which Baron James had to contend may be formed from the credit and capital possessed by the coalition, which included such well-known and wealthy firms as Barings of London, Hope and Co. of Amsterdam, Stieglitz of St Petersburg, and many others. The rivalry between Rothschild and P6-reire was carried on vigorously, and with ever-increasing bitterness and warmth. Rothschild on the one hand was jealous and annoyed by the young upstart Pereire, whilst the latter, conscious of his exceptional energy and abilities, was anxious to force the wealthy and despotic Rothschild to abdicate the lofty position he had gained on the Paris money market. On more than one occasion Baron James exerted himself to the utmost to crush and annihilate his young rival, but Pereire's strong will and financial skill were more than a match for the ability of Rothschild and his millions. In these contests for supremacy it was not always Pereire who had to yield. More than once Baron James found himself out-manœuvred, and compelled to retire from the arena. In 1856, for instance, Pereire, in conjunction with Hottinger Thurneysser in Paris, and Stieglitz in St Petersburg, succeeded, in spite of all the frantic efforts and the immense and varied influence brought into play by Baron James, in gaining a concession for the construction, during a period of eighty-five years, of a network of railways throughout the Russian empire. This enterprise is certainly one of the greatest and most lucrative of the present century.

Having been thus defeated in his endeavours to secure the concession for the Russian railways, Baron James revenged himself by founding the Vienna Credit Bank. The different offers that were laid before the Austrian Ministry of Finance resolved themselves into two groups, at the head of which stood the Rothschilds on the one hand, and Pereire on the other. In the position it held on the European money market each of these two great houses possessed material advantages, which brought out prominently its individual character. The name of Rothschild had about it a sound of historic fame, of well-merited popularity, and of world-wide wealth which carried with it immense weight, whilst, in addition, its interests and business were looked after by the different members of the family residing in all the great capitals of Europe. The house of Pereire, on the other hand, had in its favour the greater energy, the higher administrative ability, and the superior capacity of its chief. Both houses were all powerful on the great European markets, and for the sake of the new institution it was eminently desirable that the rivalry between the two should cease and a fusion of interests take place. This to all appearances was the opinion of the Finance Minister, who wished to give no decision as to the merits of the two proposals until every effort to secure the alliance of the rival firms had been exhausted. There seemed to be some probability of the much-desired union being consummated, but Pereire, in a letter from Paris, declared he would not undertake the establishment of the new bank in conjunction with Rothschild, unless the latter promised to abandon his opposition to the *Crédit Mobilier*, another of Rothschild's powerful rivals. Baron James positively refused to give the promise, and the negotiations fell through, the ultimate result being that the establishment of the now bank was, as we have said, entrusted to the house of Rothschild.

That Baron James was not successful, in spite of his most careful calculations and circumspection, in all his enterprises, the reader knows. Unforeseen circumstances will crop up at times to mar the best-laid plans, and the Baron, like others, was not exempt •from Fortune's freaks. Great as his winnings were, his losses were on a correspondingly large scale whenever his usual luck deserted him; the amounts he lost at a single stroke were indeed so enormous that they can scarcely be credited. One of his heaviest losses was undoubtedly that caused by the frauds of Carpentier, the accountant or cashier of the North of France Railway. The particulars of this gigantic robbery, without a parallel in the history of crime, were published in one of the papers, and were as follows:—

"The mystery surrounding the theft from the Northern Bail way is by degrees being cleared up. The directors try to furnish as few details as possible regarding this event, which does poor credit to their prudence and watchfulness. They at first desired to give no publicity at all to it; the Paris press had been won over, but, as the foreign journals would not allow the occurrence to be buried in silence, the Northern Railway was forced to step forward with its explanation, in which the losses were set down at six million francs. This estimate is, however, far from correct; it speaks only of the theft of shares, whilst the thieves also emptied the safes of all the money they contained. It has not been ascertained what is the exact loss the Railway will have to suffer; indeed it is a matter of some difficulty to discover the extent of the frauds, as the thieves have destroyed nearly all the papers which could help to elucidate the precise nature of their proceedings. The amount stolen is estimated to amount to from 30 to 32 million. The loss will not fall on the Northern Railway alone, as Messrs Rothschild, André, and De Morny will have to bear their share. Carpentier, Grellet, and their accomplices must have been planning the execution of their project for a long time past, for they had already previous to their flight realized large sums, and six months ago purchased a steamer in England for 1,800,000 francs. From papers discovered after their flight it would appear that they have bought a house in New York, which is, perhaps, the reason why they have left England for America. How far back the embezzlements extend is not yet known, although it has been discovered that the fugitives have been selling shares on the money market here for a long time past. In order to be able to produce the proper number of shares when an examination of those left in their care took place, they adopted a very clever artifice. The shares deposited with the administration were kept tied up in packets of 1,000 each, and the thieves with the assistance of some of the subordinate officials, who were all more or less in the swim, abstracted from each of these packets 200 or 300 shares and tied the packets up again. When the examination, which to all appearances was very superficial, took place, the full number of shares was seemingly forthcoming, and the embezzlement remained undetected. In this way the thieves were able to realize a considerable sum before they carried out their grand and final stroke. Carpentier was the first to quit Paris; he had solicited leave of absence for four days from Rothschild, who readily granted the favour. On this occasion Carpentier had a long conversation with Rothschild, with whom it is well known he was a great favourite. Baron James had just done s, fine stroke of business and told Carpentier that his winnings amounted to some five millions. 'If' continued the rich banker, 'my Algerian Railway speculation turns out all right, I hope to add three more million to my five.' 'Will you put them before or after your five million?' asked Carpentier; 'will you pocket thirty-five or fifty-three million? Put them in front, and hand me your five millions, you will still have a nice little sum left for yourself.' Rothschild laughed at the joke, but would not surrender his five millions. 'I cannot give you my five millions, but here, take my chain; it may serve as a friendly souvenir of this day, which has brought me so much pleasure and profit.' The chain was, we need hardly say, of great value, and Carpentier, although he had already provided himself with far greater wealth, did not despise the offer, and sent the chain as a present to his brother before leaving Paris.

Fig. XXV: BARON JAMES DE ROTHSCHILD
(1792–1868)
INTERNATIONAL BANKER & FINANCER
CO-FOUNDER OF THE HOUSE OF PARIS

Painted in 1850 (approx.), artwork in the public domain.

From the above conversation, which Rothschild communicated to his friends, it will be seen that he and Carpentier were on the most confidential terms. It was Rothschild who had obtained Carpentier his appointment as chief cashier in the Northern Railway Company, and his rage and fury on learning how his protégé had misconducted himself were terrible. He tried every possible means to secure the capture of his ungrateful and dishonest favourite, and when, accompanied by detectives, Monsieur T——— of the Northern Railway started off in pursuit of Carpentier, Rothschild opened an unlimited credit in his agent's favour, saying he was to hesitate at neither expense nor means—that he, Rothschild, would readily give ten minions to get Carpentier in his power. From Paris Carpentier proceeded direct to London, and thence to Liverpool, where the steamer he had purchased was lying. He had her got ready at once and gained the high seas. He there waited for his accomplices to join him. During Carpentier's absence Grellet was placed in charge of the cash. On the day the clerks and workmen of the railway were to be paid, he was not at his post. Information was sent to Rothschild that he had not appeared. Rothschild, who had no suspicions of anything wrong, proceeded to the offices of the Company, and by means of the duplicate keys in his possession opened all the safes, in order to give out the sums required for the payment of the workmen. He opened the small safe, only to find it quite empty. His suspicions were at once aroused, and he ordered the manager to observe strict secrecy, as he would bear all responsibility; he then opened the large safe; that was likewise empty. The loss of shares was not discovered till later. Measures were at once taken to procure the arrest of the thieves, but they had got so good a start that Grellet was able to join Carpentier unmolested.

With Grellet and Carpentier, four subordinate officials disappeared; Carpentier likewise took with him his mistress, a Mademoiselle Georgette, who had been living in Paris in a very extravagant style. Carpentier and Grellet are still very young men; the former is fair, looks exceedingly delicate and pale, and appears to be in a consumption. Grellet belongs to a very good family, and has a large private fortune, said to amount to 500,000 francs. The statement that he and Carpentier were driven to their crime by losses on the Stock Exchange and fast living is false; both, on the contrary, led very regular and quiet lives, and, if they lately have been spending money freely, that is only a consequence of their criminal conduct. They were in no way driven to crime; they simply plunged headlong into guilt."

The immense services rendered by Baron James de Rothschild to the State were recognized and rewarded by the Government, who showered upon him titles and decorations of every description. During the reign of Louis XVIII, when the proud aristocracy had its own way in everything, the Baron was not on the friendliest terms with the Government, owing to a slight which he received at their hands. It is said that, as a modest reward for his services, he asked that his wife might be introduced at Court; but, when the haughty Duchesse d'Angoulême was consulted, the favour was refused, as she declared that she was quite scandalized at the suggestion. "It must not be thought of," said she; "you must not forget that the King of France is the most Christian King." However, Baron James punished this narrow-minded prejudice in his own way: during the remainder of the reign he withdrew his support from the King, and quietly declined to aid either financially or by advice a Government swayed by such mean and paltry principles. The revolution of 1830 made amends for the slight he had suffered. He welcomed the new Government, which he supported with all his influence and money, and became on the most intimate and friendly terms with the new Court. He dined regularly every week at the Palais Royal, and the King's sons never failed to be present at the soirees held in the Rue Laffitte. During the reign of Louis Philippe the influence of Baron James was all-powerful; the reign has been called the reign of stock-jobbing and speculation. It was no longer Baron James who had to solicit favours from the aristocracy; it was the aristocracy who sought the patronage and aid of the rich banker. The splendour and luxury of the entertainments given in the Chaussée d'Antin were never equalled by any given by the Court. The banker's house on such occasions was thronged with a crowd of persons distinguished in the diplomatic and financial worlds. To procure an invitation from Baron James was almost more highly thought of and sought for than a presentation at Court. Smarting, perhaps, under the recollection of the snub once given him, Baron James took a delight in humiliating those who now cringed to him. His roughness of manner, and his blunt if not coarse mode of speaking were well known, and many anecdotes of his utter disregard of politeness have been published. The higher the rank of the victim the greater the pleasure Baron James derived from the confusion and pain caused by what he regarded as his blunt and outspoken manners. Sometimes he met his match, and would receive a severe rebuff, but even that only disconcerted him for a moment. Amongst his guests at the Rue Laffitte on one occasion was Prince Paul of Würtemberg, who had honoured him by accepting an invitation for dinner, during which Baron James persisted in disregarding all etiquette and in addressing the Prince in a most annoyingly familiar tone. At first the Prince treated his host's conduct with contemptuous silence, but, as that proved insufficient, he at last rose from the table and left.

A Conservative deputy met Baron James at the Opera, and inquired how he was. "Not so bad." "And the Baroness?" "What concern is that of yours?" replied the Baron, turning his back roughly on the speaker.

Those who suffered most from this objectionable practice of Baron James were artists, journalists, and others, who, being indebted to him for his patronage, hardly felt bold enough to rebuke his unmannerly behaviour. Jadin was painting some frescoes in the dining-room belonging to Baron Salomon de Rothschild, when Baron James entered and caught him accompanying himself in his work by singing and whistling different airs.

"Holloa! you workman with the decoration, come down a bit; I want to speak to you."

Jadin gave no reply, shrugged his shoulders to show his indifference, and continued his singing.

This behaviour naturally created for Baron James many bitter enemies, who lost no opportunity of holding him up to ridicule in the press. No doubt much that was printed to his disadvantage had no better authority than the writer's imagination, but still Baron James's character offered many opportunities of attack to those who wished to irritate and annoy the great banker. There was in Baron James's character a peculiar combination of seemingly opposite and antagonistic qualities. On the one side there was the shrewd man of business, ready to sacrifice thousands, if by so doing he could gain millions; while, on the other, stood his well-known benevolence and charity. True to his keen business instincts, Baron James showed in the most trivial matters an anxiety and a determination always to obtain as cheaply as possible what he bargained for. This niggardly spirit was naturally ridiculed by his calumniators in the press. The story of the gardener Pâquet is not unworthy of reproduction hero.

By a process little known at that time, but common enough now, Pâquet succeeded in obtaining three magnificent peaches in the month of January. All interested in horticulture hastened to inspect such a marvellous proof of his skill, and among the visitors was Baron James. The following conversation then took place between the great gardener and the great millionaire. The story reads so much better in French[2], that we may be excused for printing it in that language:—

"Fraiment, Monsieur le chartinier," dit-il, "vos bêches sont atmiraples. Gombien en voulez-vous?"

"Quinze cents francs, Monsieur le Baron."

"Bar exemble ! "

"C'est tout au juste," dit Paquet. "Je ne voudrais pas vous surfaire."

"Drois bêches, quinze cents vrancs, Mein Gott ! Et drois bêches qui beut-être ne falent rien."

"Oh! pour cela, je vous arrête," dit l'horticulteur. "Vous allez avoir immédiatement la preuve du contraire."

---

[2] James de Rothschild was a German citizen who emigrated in Paris at the age of 19 years old. His French was spoken with a very strong German accent as it is written in the transcript of this very ironic anecdote.

He at once plucked one of the peaches, cut it in two, and offered one half to the Baron, whilst he ate the other himself.

"Qu'en dites-vous, Monsieur le Baron ? Vous êtes connaisseur; je m'en rapporte à la finesse de votre palais."

"Drès ponne! Télicieuse!" dit Rothschild croquant la pêche.

"Oui, c'est de la meilleure espèce. Chair ferme, saveur exquise. En plein air, cette espèce-là ne murit qu'au commencement de Septembre."

"Foyons, Monsieur le chartinier, ce n'est bas fotre ternier brix ?"

"Pardonnez-moi. Quinze cents francs, comme j'ai eu l'honneur de vous le dire."

"Eh," s'écria le juif, "blaisantez-vous ? Il y a une bêche te moins!"

"N'importe, c'est toujours quinze cents francs— pour vous, Monsieur le Baron. Ce sont-là des fruits de millionnaires ; je n'en rabattrai pas un centime."

Rothschild finally bought the peaches, when the meaning of the gardener's conduct became clear to him.

The well-known anecdote of Vernet the painter did not end so pleasantly for the Baron. When he called and inquired how much the painter would charge to execute his portrait, he was told—

"For you, Monsieur le Baron, it will be four thousand francs."

"The devil! It will cost you only two or three hasty strokes from your brush. Come, now, that strikes me as being rather dear."

Fig. XXVI: The “battle of Smala”, by Horace Vernet, is one the biggest fresco painting existing in the world. We reproduce here the part of the fresco where we can see the supposed Jew the author is speaking about (on the right).

"Ah, you deal in the arts, do you?" exclaimed the artist, with a shrug of his shoulders. "Ah, well, it will be four thousand francs, not a centime loss." And, when Rothschild manifested his surprise, the painter continued: "If you add another word it will be three times the sum. Am I to paint it or not?"

Baron James hastened to quit the studio, apparently alarmed at being in company with one who was, he believed, perfectly mad.

"Wait a moment!" cried the artist after him, "I will do your portrait for nothing!"

And he kept his word. In his picture called "*La Smala*" can be seen a hideous-looking Jew, running away with a casket of jewels and money, his face expressive of the most sordid avarice and ill-concealed fright. That portrait is a gross caricature of Baron James de Rothschild.

However illiberal he was in matters of business, Baron James could display bounteous liberality on occasions when his business instincts were not touched. But even his immense and well-known beneficence was misconstrued and attributed to interested motives, owing to the belief that a man could not be so lavish in his gifts who was known to be so close in his every-day conduct. For many years the greatest suspicion and disbelief of the purely disinterested nature of the Baron's charity prevailed among the public, and this opinion was fostered and encouraged by the vile calumnies printed in the press. In 1847, Baron James, foreseeing the distress and want likely to result from the poor harvest of 1846, took energetic measures to provide a remedy for the evil. He bought, in the European and American markets, prodigious quantities of corn, which he afterwards sold at an is bread was not bread at all; that his flour was not flour. It was bran; it was plaster, mixed with arsenic. Others asserted that Baron James had bought large quantities of damaged flour and that he concealed its bad quality by mixing with it sweet almonds, his calumniators quietly ignoring the fact that sweet almonds are far more costly than the best flour.

In addition to the enormous sacrifices made in supplying corn to the distressed population, Baron James, in 1848, subscribed no less than fifty thousand francs in aid of the wounded and the unemployed workmen. This was certainly a display of the most liberal generosity, seeing that he had himself much to fear from the excesses of the excited populace during the outbreak of the revolution. It must have been an anxious time for him as he learnt of the excesses of the mob, every moment expecting it would be his turn to receive a visit from them. But among those having influence and control over them was Marc Caussidière, who was not unmindful of the charitable munificence of Baron James. By his orders guards were stationed not only round the hotel, but also round the suburban villas of Baron James, whose anxiety was relieved by the grateful thoughtfulness of the citizen.

Less than a year after, Baron James proved that he was capable of appreciating the admirable conduct of Caussidière, who, when he reached London, an exile and a beggar, received the following note from Paris:—

"Sir,

"Allow me to place at your disposal the sum of thirty thousand francs. This little capital will enable you to start some business in the hard land of exile. You may return it to me in ten, twenty, or any number of years you please.

It is a feeble testimony of my gratitude for the great services you have rendered the country.

"I am, etc. etc.

"ROTHSCHILD."

Even this display of gratitude was reported to be owing to prudential and selfish motives, for it is asserted the Baron said: "The devil is never conquered; who knows but that he may return?" It is, however, satisfactory to learn that these thirty thousand francs paved the way to Caussidière's fortune, as he started a wine and brandy business, which eventually proved very lucrative.

If all the stories related of him be true, Baron James displayed remarkable skill in being charitable at the expense of others. He was frequently reproached with his disregard of, and want of sympathy with, his co-religionists in misfortune, and it was suggested to him that he might at least give them the benefit of some Stock Exchange operation. The hint was taken: a manœuvre was carried out one fine morning to effect a rise in the market and was followed almost immediately by a fall which enabled the Baron to make a profit of 850,000 francs, which sum he devoted to the construction of the Jewish Home in the Hue Picpus.

On another occasion he granted an interview to Felix S———, a man of considerable talent, who laid before him the plan of a vast undertaking, which as Baron James acknowledged appeared both novel and ingenious as well as possessed of every quality necessary to secure its success. But, although entertaining so favourable an opinion of the scheme, he positively declined to embark any money to float it. He said,

Fig. XXVII: BARON ALPHONSE DE ROTHSCHILD
(1827-1905)
Photography by Nadar, Paris. Bibliothèque Nationale de France.

Fig. XXVIII: The château de Ferrières is the largest château of the 19th century. It is set on a 12 sq mi estate outside Paris. James de Rothschild destroyed the original castle and rebuilt it completely in 1854.

however, "Follow me, and the capital will soon be forthcoming." He then made his visitor enter his carriage and drove to the Bourse, where they walked up and down, arm in arm, together. They had scarcely separated ere several capitalists hastened to surround the man honoured with the friendship of the king of finance, and after an explanation they assured him of their readiness to support him both by their influence and their capital.

Heine, in referring to his friend and patron, thus described Baron James de Rothschild: "He was a remarkable personage, whose financial abilities I do not pretend to analyse, but they must have been considerable, if their results are any criterion to go by. He possessed the peculiar gift or instinct of observation, by which he was enabled to discover the capacities of other people in every sphere of life. Many persons have on this account compared him to Louis XIV, and truly, in contrast to his colleagues who surround themselves with a generality of mediocrity, Baron James was always to be seen on the most intimate footing with the notabilities of every rank and station. He always knew who was the best man in any business, even if that business was a mystery to him. Though he probably possessed little knowledge of music, Rossini was his constant companion; Ary Scheffer was his family painter; Caréme was his cook. He certainly understood not a word of Greek, and yet the Hellenist Latrone was the scholar whom he favoured mostly. His physician was the genial Dupuytren, and the most brotherly affection existed between them.

At an early date he duly appreciated the worth and ability of Crémieux, whom he found to be a trusty advocate. At the very outset he recognized the political abilities of Louis

Philippe, and was always on confidential terms with that great master of the arts of diplomacy.

"Baron James de Rothschild died on the 15th November, 1868.

The present head of the firm in Paris is Baron Alphonse de Rothschild, the eldest son of Baron James. He inherits much of his father's financial talent, and is acknowledged by the rest of his relatives as the shrewdest and most able man of business among them. He is the head of the family not only on account of his ability, but also on account of his seniority, as he is the oldest of Mayer Amschel Rothschild's grandsons. For some years before his father's death he took an active part in the conduct of the firm's business, whence we may infer that he is indebted to the careful training he then received for much of the remarkable skill he has since displayed in operations of the greatest magnitude. All grand international loans, i.e., loans issued on behalf of a particular Government in several countries simultaneously,—are invariably submitted first to Baron Alphonse, as he is known to be the best judge of the time and conditions most conducive to the success of such undertakings.

The number of loans issued under Baron Alphonse's management is large and embraces almost every nationality in Europe. The good fortune attending these financial operations is proved by the numerous decorations and orders which he has received from the hands of monarchs anxious to recognize the obligations they feel they owe to the head of the Rothschild family. The business of the Paris firm is by far the largest and most extensive of all the Rothschild firms; it embraces not only loan operations, but commercial speculations and undertakings of every description. Its banking business is enormous, and in this respect it differs from its colleagues in London, Frankfort, and Vienna, whose business is more purely mercantile, or limited to bill discounting and Stock Exchange operations. The most responsible undertaking of the Paris firm under Baron Alphonse's management was the payment of the indemnities to Germany at the conclusion of the Franco-German War.

This immense operation called into play all the resources and energies of the Rothschild family and its allies. The mere anxiety and mental labour connected with this vast undertaking would have prostrated any man of inferior calibre. For months Baron Alphonse and his clerks worked incessantly day after day, Sundays included, to almost midnight. The strain on the brain and the constitution was fearful; many even now feel the effects of this trying period. Great as was the anxiety connected with this business, Baron Alphonse no doubt considered it nothing in comparison with that which the lawlessness and violence of the Commune inspired. To curry favour with the mob, Baron Alphonse was compelled to serve, as he had done in 1848, as a volunteer on the ramparts. But even that did not render the property of his family secure from the attacks of the petrolists.

More than one of the mansions belonging to members of the family were invaded and despoiled by bands of those wretched fanatics. In one instance the house had been besmeared and sprinkled with petroleum with a view to its being set on fire, but the presence of mind displayed by the butler averted this catastrophe. He hinted to the unwelcome visitors that the cellars contained a large stock of the finest wines; the hint was acted upon at once, and ere long the butler had the satisfaction of seeing the whole of the ruffianly crew in a state of intoxication. He then sent to the military for aid, the result being that the petrolists were all carried off to pay the penalty of their wanton deeds. Baron Alphonse, in common with his fellow citizens, found that much greater harm was to be expected from the enemies of order living within the walls of Paris than they had ever reason to dread from the shells of the invading Germans.

During the siege, the Rothschilds felt no very serious apprehension, seeing that they had secured the safety of the bulk of their property by transferring it to the care of their relatives in London or elsewhere. To them even the privations of the siege were mitigated, as they were able, thanks to their influence with both the German and French staff, to pass convoys of provisions through the lines. It is well known that the utmost care was taken by the Germans that no injury should be done to Baron Alphonse's "Château de Ferrières". This chateau was made the German head-quarters. It was here that Jules Ferry came to arrange the terms of the capitulation with Prince Bismarck and the Prussian generals.

The strictest orders were given respecting the preservation of the building. None of the furniture, nor any of the valuable paintings and sculptures were allowed to be displaced or removed. It was even forbidden to shoot any of the game in the park without special permission. This act of favour gave rise to a certain amount of grumbling and heartburning among the German soldiers. Provisions, especially meat, were none too plentiful in the German lines, and it was not considered just to let the troops want, simply to confer a favour on one whom all regarded as an enemy.

In their advance to Paris the soldiers had been allowed to seize cattle and sheep, but now, with the prospect of a long siege, they were to suffer hunger when plenty was before their mouths. Nothing could demonstrate more clearly the immense influence commanded by the Rothschilds, than this scrupulous regard shown by the Germans in preventing the spoliation of their property. But, however safe his property outside Paris may have been, it was different with that inside, and Baron Alphonse knew little peace of mind as long as the siege and the Commune lasted. So intense was the anxiety he suffered during this trying period, that his hair, from being jet-black, was turned to grey in a single night. Since the war France has been blessed with peace, which has greatly contributed to the re-establishment of her fallen fortunes. How long this will continue we cannot say, as she seems ordained to suffer from internal troubles at certain intervals.

CHAPTER X

ROTHSCHILDIANA.

IN the foregoing pages we have endeavoured to present the reader with a clear insight into the characters of the heads of the different firms by means of a number of anecdotes which are both more effective and more entertaining than mere description. The anecdotes already given we have good reason to consider authentic, but there are many others which are undoubtedly the creation of lively imaginations, and have little foundation in fact. The Rothschilds have so long held a prominent place in public affairs, their sayings and doings have been so closely watched and reported, that it is not surprising to find that innumerable tales have been published about them. A large number of the anecdotes are, as we have stated, quite unreliable, still there are some so highly characteristic, that it is difficult to believe them entirely devoid of truth. This state of things was somewhat embarrassing. We were at first inclined to omit all anecdotes about the authenticity of which we did not feel confident, but, as their perusal is pretty sure to afford some amusement, wo have, on second thoughts, deemed it our duty to bring them together in a separate chapter, without pledging ourselves in any way for their truthfulness. With this reservation we submit the following stories to our readers, who can decide whether we were justified or not in our course of procedure.

Baron Anselm von Rothschild on one occasion lost a ring which he prized very highly, not on account of its intrinsic value, but because it had been given him by the Emperor of Austria in recognition of the valuable services rendered by the family to the imperial monarchy. The Baron offered a reward of three hundred and fifty florins a year to the person who should restore the cherished ring. The daughter of a humble publican proved to be the lucky individual. She presented herself with great humility at the residence of the wealthy financier, who recognized the article with demonstrations of the liveliest pleasure, and caused five hundred florins to be paid the girl in advance, though that was something beyond the amount of the annuity. He also gave instructions for a bond to be drawn up to secure the regular payment of the allowance in future. Having received her recompense, the girl ran home to her parents, in order that they might share in her happiness and good fortune. The old people could scarcely believe that their daughter had received so handsome a reward for the discovery of an article of such little value. After some consideration they concluded that, rather than wait for the annual allowance, it would be more advantageous to obtain a lump sum down, as they might thereby be enabled to purchase the house in which they lived. The girl returned to Rothschild, who received her very affably, and, having learnt her object, was pleased to give her the sum of seven thousand florins in ready money in lieu of the promised annuity.

Fig. XXIX: OTTO VON BISMARCK
GERMAN STATESMAN (1815–1898)

PORTRAIT OF OTTO VON BISMARCK (1894)
BY FRANZ VON LENBACH (1836–1904).

Dr Busch, the biographer of Prince Bismarck, records, in his well-known work "Our Chancellor," an amusing anecdote of Baron Anselm, which deserves reproduction in these pages. He says:— "At dinner, at which were Marshal of the House hold Perponcher, and a Herr von Thadden, who was designated as a member of the administration in Rheims, the Chief told several good anecdotes of Baron Rothschild in Frankfort. On one occasion he had spoken in his presence with a corn merchant about a sale of wheat, when the merchant said to Rothschild, that being so rich a man he would never think it necessary to put the highest price on his wheat. 'What rich man do you mean?' replied the old gentleman; 'is my wheat worth less because I am a rich man?' He used to give dinners sometimes which were quite worthy of his great riches. I remember once when the present King was in Frankfort I invited him to dinner. Later in the day Rothschild also asked His Majesty to dine with him, to which His Majesty replied, that he must settle matters with me; for his own part he did not care with which of us he dined. The Baron now came and proposed that I should cede His Majesty to him, and that I should join them at dinner. I refused this, and he had the naïveté to suggest that his dinner might be sent to my house, although he could not eat with us, as he partook of only strictly Jewish fare. This proposal also I begged leave to decline—naturally, though his dinner, doubtless, was better than mine.—Old Metternich, who, by the way, was very kind to me, told me that once when he had been visiting Rothschild, the Baron gave him some luncheon to eat on the way back to Johannisberg. With the luncheon were packed six bottles of Johannisberg wine. When Johannisberg (Metternich's estate) was reached, these bottles were taken out unopened.

Fig. XXX: KLEMENS VON METTERNICH
(1773–1859)
PRINCE OF METTERNICH-WINNEBURG
GERMAN-AUSTRIAN DIPLOMAT

PORTRAIT OF KLEMENS WENZEL, PRINCE OF METTERNICH (1815)
BY THOMAS LAWRENCE (1769–1830)
KUNSTHISTORICHES MUSEUM OF VIENNA, AUSTRIA.

The Prince then sent for his wine steward and inquired how much that wine cost him a bottle. 'Twelve guldens' was the answer. 'Well, take these bottles, and the next order you get from Baron Rothschild, send them back to him, but charge him fifteen guldens, for they will then be older?'"

Dining on one occasion with Baron James de Rothschild of Paris, Eugene Delacroix kept his eyes turned upon his host in so marked a manner that when the company rose to leave the dining room Baron James could not help asking his guest what it was that so attracted his attention. The painter confessed that for some time past he had vainly sought a head to serve as a model for that of a beggar he intended to hold a prominent position in a painting on which he was then engaged, and that, as he gazed at his host's features, the idea suddenly struck him that the very head he so much desired was there before him. With this explanation, he ventured to ask whether the Baron would do him the favour to sit to him as a beggar. Rothschild, being a great admirer of the art in all its forms, and pleased to be considered one of its chief patrons, readily consented to sit in a character probably never before assumed by a millionaire. The next day found him at the painter's studio. Delacroix placed a tunic round his shoulders, put a stout staff in his hand, and made him pose as if he were resting on the steps of an ancient Roman temple. In this attitude he was discovered by one of the artist's favourite pupils, who alone had free access to the studio at all times. Struck by the life-like excellence of the model, the newcomer congratulated his master at having at last found exactly what he wanted. Naturally concluding the model had only just been brought in from some church porch, and never dreaming the character assumed by him was far from his true one, he seized an opportunity when his master's eyes wore turned to slip a piece of money into the beggar's hand. Rothschild thanked him with a look, and kept the money. The pupil soon quitted the studio.

In answer to inquiries made, Delacroix stated that the young man possessed great talent but no means; that he had, in fact, to earn his livelihood by giving lessons in painting and drawing. Shortly afterwards the young fellow received a letter stating that charity bears interest, and that the accumulated interest on the amount he had so generously given to one whom he supposed to be a beggar was represented by the sum of 10,000 francs, which were lying at his disposal at the office in the Rue Laffitte.

Amongst the endless number of rich and handsome articles Baron James had diligently collected, his guests seldom failed to be struck with admiration by a magnificent porcelain service, of singular beauty and design, and remarkable for the superb paintings which adorned its exterior. The history attached to the acquisition of this service is as sin-gular as its beauty. One day an old man, feeble, decrepit, and to all appearance on the verge of the grave, solicited an interview with the Baron. At the very outset the old man's careworn looks and destitute condition awoke the latter's lively sympathy, and this sympathy was strengthened on learning that his visitor was a co-religionist. The old man produced from a bag a plate of such exquisite design and finish, that Baron James, with the instinctive envy of a virtuoso, felt he must at any cost become the owner of such an artistic treasure. After stating he was in a most destitute condition, the visitor proceeded to say that want had compelled him to part with many articles which he had regarded as heirlooms. The plate, he declared, belonged to a service which he had reserved to the last, hoping against hope that necessity would never compel him to part with it, but alas! the time had come when the claims of his starving family could be stopped only by relinquishing possession of this, the last resource against famine.

> "I come to offer this service to you, M. le Baron, thinking that so beautiful a work of art can find a fitting resting-place only in the midst of your well-known collection. Will you buy it?"
>
> "It is indeed beautiful; what do you ask for it?"
>
> "Look you, sir," said his visitor, "I am now an old man, bowed down with years, and have not long to live. I am poor, but I wish if possible to end the few remaining years of my life as comfortably as I can. Will you, in exchange for this valuable porcelain service, give me an allowance for life of one hundred francs a month? It is a trifle to you, and I am so old!"

The Baron reflected a moment, examined the plate afresh, and at length answered: "Well, be it so; here is the first payment; send me the service, and leave me your name and address, that the money may be sent to you regularly."

The porcelain service was duly delivered. A month later, as the Baron was sitting in his office, a man entered, and claimed payment of the allowance then due. The new-comer was young, stoutly made, of a vigorous constitution, and likely to live for another fifty years.

> "But you are not the man to whom I promised the allowance!" said the Baron.
>
> "Excuse me, I am indeed the man."
>
> "But he was at least eighty years of age."
>
> "You are mistaken, I am but thirty."

"But your aged appearance and careworn looks were certainly unmistakable."

"Thanks to your great generosity, my recovery has been rapid and surprising."

The Baron smiled at the remark, and gave orders for the payment of the money, exclaiming as he did so:—

"Ah! you are an excellent comedian, and have taken me in completely."

"You flatter me; I am probably the first who has done so" answered the Jew, politely bowing to the millionaire.

Strange as were the circumstances and terms on which the service was bought, Baron James had little reason to repent of his bargain.

This reference to objects of art reminds us of another anecdote, of which, if we remember rightly, Baron Alphonse was the subject. On one occasion he started out for a walk, and presently found himself in the district immediately behind the Pantheon. As the neighbourhood was quite strange to him, he soon lost himself. No cabs or omnibus were to be seen anywhere, nor did anyone pass of whom he could inquire his way. At first the situation rendered him somewhat nervous, but presently, when he thought of the strange novelty such a predicament was to him, he became reassured, and laughed in anticipation at the amusement the adventure would afford him. He therefore continued to walk on without troubling himself as to his whereabouts. Presently he passed a shop for the sale of second-hand goods, and his quick eye caught sight among the rubbish of an article which struck him as worth inspection. It proved to be an antique barometer of the time of Louis XVI. It bore no trace of its original gilding, although the carving was still in a perfect state of preservation. Being a good judge of such things, and an ardent collector, the Baron determined to buy it. The price asked was ten francs, and the Baron congratulated himself on having secured so great a bargain. On putting his hand into his pocket, he discovered that in his hurry he had forgotten to bring his purse with him. It was a day of accidents.

"Well, it does not matter; I will take the barometer at all events," he said to the shopkeeper. "Send it up to my hotel; I am Baron Rothschild; you will receive the money when you deliver the barometer."

"I do not know either your name or address, sir, nor do I ever send things out that are not previously paid for."

This was a startling rebuff for Baron Rothschild. It was a perfectly novel experience to meet with anyone ignorant of his great name. Being, however, in a good humour and regarding it as part of the day's adventure, he was only the more amused. He was about to explain who and what he was, when he happened to notice a porter passing on the opposite side of the road. Beckoning to the man, he asked him: "Have you ever heard of Baron Rothschild?"

"Well, that is a queer question! Heard of Baron Rothschild? Of course I have; but why do you inquire?" said the man, somewhat crossly, as if he suspected his interlocutor was jesting.

"Because Madame here has just refused to trust him for ten francs," was the reply.

"Is that really true, Madame Duclos?" said the porter, in great astonishment.

"Yes, to be sure, Monsieur Pierre; one cannot know everybody," answered the shop woman with a shrug, "but I know you, and if you will become guarantee———"

At these words the Baron interrupted the woman with such a hearty burst of laughter that it was some minutes before he could recover himself.

"Well, Monsieur Pierre," he said, still laughing, "if you will kindly become surety for me, will you go and call a cab, and then we can take the barometer home."

The porter required no second bidding; he hastened off and soon returned with the cab. They then drove to the Baron's house, where the porter received a handsome reward for his exertions.

Attempts to ruin the Rothschilds as well as to frustrate and wreck the operations undertaken by them have frequently been made by persons jealous of their extraordinary success. It is needless to say that all such attempts have signally failed. At the outset luck has sometimes favoured these bold but reckless opponents, but it has been owing to the sufferance of the Rothschilds, who, conscious of the enormous power at their command, knew they could crush their upstart rivals at any moment they pleased. Such attempts would be more common were it not known that the only chance of rendering them successful would be to operate on as extensive a scale as that habitually adopted by the great financiers. One of the boldest of these would-be rivals was a Mr. James H———, who bought and sold enormous amounts of stock in a very brief period, and, so far from imitating the secrecy marking Rothschild's operations, deemed it essential to the success of his scheme that all his dealings should be done as publicly as possible. He was the son of a wealthy country banker, and at the time he commenced speculating on 'Change had £50,000 stock inscribed in his name, though the stock was really his father's. The reputation of owning so large an amount of stock was very useful on Change, as it conferred upon him and his transactions an importance which would otherwise have been wanting. After some time had elapsed the stock was transferred back into his father's name. At the outset, and until he had perfectly mastered all the rules and usages of the House, he acted with the greatest prudence and discretion, confining himself to transactions of a very humble nature. Gradually he enlarged his operations, and the "natives," as the members of the House were called, began to look upon the boldness of his dealings with mingled surprise and admiration. Success attending his speculations, he was watched and followed in them by a crowd of persons such as will always hang about a successful man. He became a power on 'Change; bulls and bears alike dreaded him, for he was as independent in his dealings as Rothschild himself.

Consols, at the time of which we are writing, were quoted at about 96. A few months later symptoms of a panic set in, and the unfavourable tendency of the market was aggravated by the fulminations hurled, for reasons best known to himself, by a well-known writer on money matters against the Bank of England. In spite, however, of these adverse circumstances, prices showed a decided unwillingness to fall. Mr. H——— studied the state of the market closely, and, being convinced in his own mind that a leader alone was wanted to carry on a successful war against the Rothschilds, determined that he himself would be that leader. He at once began his attack by selling out £200,000 Consols at 96. This operation concluded, he advertised it well, and made known his willingness to sell £1,000,000 more. Purchasers were found for the whole at prices varying from 94 to 90, at which price Consols closed for the day. The next day he resumed his tactics to depress the market, and so successful were they that Consols closed at about 84. As might have been expected, a run on the Bank of England took place, simultaneously with this sudden and unlooked-for fall in the price of Consols. He then repurchased so largely that when a reaction set in and prices recovered, his gains amounted to more than £100,000. But the rivalry of Mr. H—— did not long continue to trouble Rothschild. Emboldened by the success of his first effort, he tried to repeat his attack two years later, and even on a larger scale. Rothschild, however, had his eyes about him, and, divining his rival's plans, laid a trap into which that rival fell. The result was that Mr. H—— was utterly ruined.

He was declared a defaulter and his name stuck up on the black board of the Stock Exchange. Then, and not till then, was it discovered that the £50,000 stock was not his own, as had been supposed, but his father's.

At a charitable sale, held in 1858, at the Hôtel Lambert in Paris, by the Princess Czartariska, in favour of the distressed Poles, an incident took place between Georges Sand and Baron Rothschild. Madame Dudevant (Georges Sand) had a stall on the occasion, and displayed a number of fancy articles for sale. Baron Rothschild happened to pass, and the fair saleswoman addressed him with the usual request to buy something. "What am I to buy?" said the Baron; "you have nothing at all suitable for me. But stay—an idea strikes me. Give me your autograph. Sell me that "Madame Dudevant took a sheet of paper and wrote upon it as follows:—"Received from Baron Rothschild the sum of one thousand francs, for the benefit of the distressed Poles.—Georges Sand." Baron Rothschild read it, thanked her, and, handing her a note for the amount named, went away highly gratified.

It is well known that the life-long ambition of all true Americans is to *do* Europe before they die, and none can vie with them in the thoroughness with which they do *do* the sights and places of interest they may happen to visit. Their curiosity is insatiable, and is only equalled by their irresistible determination to satisfy it at all costs. No false modesty deters them from questioning strangers. They will accost the first man they meet, if they think he can remove their doubts or add to their knowledge. The following account, written by an American, confirms our statement, and explains itself:—

"When I arrived in England I set myself to work to accomplish the object of my journey—to see all that I could; and in doing so I attracted much attention. I made many acquaintances, and was told by them that I was the best representative of my nation they had ever seen. In curiosity, and a determination to gratify that feeling I think I was. I spared no pains to see all the sights and hear all the gossip that came in my way. This characteristic at last brought me into an awkward predicament, which I purpose to describe in the following anecdote. one morning, while I was in London, I started out for a walk. I had heard a great deal about the famous place which the Rothschilds were building, and I sallied forth on this particular morning for the purpose of seeing it. I soon reached it; and through the kindness of the master builder was shown over it. I had finished my inspection, and was standing on the side walk gazing at it with undisguised admiration, when I noticed a gentleman a few feet from me, watching the building. He was a fat, portly old fellow, with a good-humoured face, in spite of his haughty look, and I thought from his appearance he might be the contractor for the work, so I determined to accost him and gain what information I could.

"'Good morning, sir,' I said, approaching him. He bowed politely, but without speaking.

"'I am a stranger here,' I went on; 'I have been looking over this building, and I would like to ask you for some information concerning it.'

"'I shall be happy to oblige you,' said he, politely. He was very kind in telling me much that was of interest. At last I said, abruptly,

"'I suppose you have seen Rothschild, sir?'

"'Which one?' he asked.

"'The old cock,' I replied.

"'I see the old cock every day,' he answered, giving me a strange glance.

"'By George,' I went on, 'I should like to have a look at him! People say he is a gay old chap, and lives high. I wish I had him in my power— I'd not let him get away until he had shelled out a pile of his money.'

"The old gentleman burst out into a laugh.

"'Baron Rothschild had to work for his money, and deserves to enjoy it,' he said, at length, when he had got over his merriment.

"May be so,' I remarked; but 'I reckon he did a heap of squeezing to get it.'

"The old man's face flushed.

"'I never heard the honesty of the house called in question,' he said, stiffly.

"'Didn't you? Well, to tell you the truth, neither have I. But I wouldn't be surprised if I'm right, after all.' The old man's face grew as black as a thunder-cloud, and he bit his lip without speaking.

"'People tell me,' I continued, not heeding this, for I thought it natural that the old fellow should be annoyed at anything said against his employers, 'people tell me the Rothschilds have made two fortunes. Now, as most people can make only one, I feel somewhat interested to learn the manner in which this was done. Can you tell me, sir?'

"The old man's face brightened instantly, and he replied, smilingly, with more politeness than he had as yet manifested:—

"'Certainly, sir. People do say the house of Rothschilds made one fortune by being careful to mind their own business, and the other by letting that of others alone. Good morning, sir.'

"With an elegant bow he turned and left me staring at him in blank amazement. I began to smell a rat, and I looked for someone of whom to ask the old gentleman's name. He had stopped at the upper end of the building, and was giving some directions to a workman. I saw a handsome man of about thirty standing a short distance off. He, too, was looking at the building. I liked his face and went up to him.

"'Excuse me for troubling you, sir I said, 'but I am a stranger in this country, and would like to ask you a question.'

"'I shall be happy to give you any information in my power,' he said, politely.

"'Then can you tell me the name of that old gentleman,' I asked, pointing to my sarcastic acquaintance.

"'Certainly,' he replied. 'That is Baron Rothschild, the head of the house of that name.'

"'Whew!' I exclaimed in astonishment, 'I've got myself into a scrape then.'

"'What is the matter?' asked my friend, curiously.

"I told him what had occurred between the Baron and myself. He laughed heartily, and remarked pleasantly when I had concluded:

"'That was awkward.'

"'He's a crusty old chap,' I said, considerably vexed; 'he's as cross as a bear.'

"'Oh, that's only his way,' replied my companion. 'He is a good, kind-hearted man, but is rather eccentric.'

"'I should say so,' I replied.

"The gentleman asked me a great many questions concerning America, and seemed interested and amused by my answers.

"'Do you know Baron Rothschild?' I inquired, at length.

"'I have met him several times,' was the reply, and I have an appointment to wait upon him to-day.'

"'Then I wish you'd say to him,' I went on, 'that I did not know to whom I was talking this morning, or I would not have said so much; and that he need not have been so huffish about it.'

"'I will do so,' said my acquaintance, laughing. You must not mind him. He was a little nettled at it, but will be the first to laugh at the adventure when he recovers his good humour. Good morning.'

"With a bow and a pleasant smile he left me. Just then a workman passed by. I stopped him and asked if he could tell me the name of the gentleman who had just left me.

"'That was one of the younger Rothschilds,' he said, 'and———'

"I waited to hear no more, but, pulling my hat down over my eyes, set off at once for my lodgings. I was absolutely afraid to speak to a stranger for a week, for fear he might be a Rothschild."

THE END

Appendices

Appendix № 1

Table of Currencies Conversions

CURRENCY CONVERSION

METALLIC CURRENCIES

GOLD & SILVER

Ancient European currencies converted to the current US dollar *(mean values)*

Currency (Unit) *Equivalency in 2020* →	*EUR* (€)	*USD* ($)	*GBP* (£)
Franc	13,5	16	11
Thaler	49	59	41
Livre sterling	333	400	278
Florin	144	173	120
Ducat	143	172	119
Ounces	575	690	479
Gulden	26	31	22
Lire	12	15	10
Scudi	240	290	200

Note 1: All currencies listed above are gold currencies except the "German Thaler" which is a silver currency.
Note 2: These values are means; the calculation of each one of these currencies equivalence (in 2020 US dollars) is based on their weight in gold or silver. In addition, the reader should consider them as minimum values according that they are not "inflation corrected".

Appendix № 2

The origin of their fortune in two paintings

by Moritz D. Oppenheim,
official painter of the Rothschilds

(1800–1882)

The painting describes a scene where the Elector of Hesse-Cassel, William IX, is entrusting Mayer Amschel Rothschild with his Inventory.

Scene painted by Moritz D. Oppenheim (1800—1882), National Trust Collections.

Few years later, Mayer Amschel died, but his eldest son, Anselm Mayer along with his four brothers returned the Inventory of the Elector of Hesse substantially increased. The Landgrave refused it, preferring to invest in the Rothschilds' banking activities.

Scene painted by Moritz D. Oppenheim (1800–1882), National Trust Collections.

End of the book

You have just finished reading:

THE ROTHSCHILDS

The Financial Rulers of Nations

by John Reeves

Cover by K. Nolan
Artwork FX by Myrtille / Lvlupixel
Edited and published by L'Apache publishing
Publishing ref: 2020-02-THER

THE ROTHSCHILDS

The Financial Rulers of Nations

By John Reeves

Special Edition — Extended with 30 pages

ISBN: 979-8612-3349-72

CPSIA information can be obtained
at www.ICGtesting.com
Printed in the USA
BVHW031442130320
574989BV00001B/19

9 798612 334972